TRAVELS WITH
Maridadi

TRAVELS WITH
Maridadi

Harley-Davidson Adventures in Saudi Arabia

BIZZIE FROST

The Book Guild Ltd

First published in Great Britain in 2023 by
The Book Guild Ltd
Unit E2 Airfield Business Park,
Harrison Road, Market Harborough,
Leicestershire. LE16 7UL
Tel: 0116 2792299
www.bookguild.co.uk
Email: info@bookguild.co.uk
Twitter: @bookguild

This memoir depicts actual events in the life of the author as truthfully as recollection permits and can mostly be verified by contemporaneously written journals, as well as newspaper and magazine features. A few events have been combined but the essence of what happened is unaltered. All persons within the book are actual individuals. There are no composite characters, but the names of some individuals have been changed to respect their privacy or to protect them and their opinions in a country that doesn't permit freedom of speech or religion. Dialogue has been recreated to be consistent with the characters and nature of the person speaking.

Typeset in 11pt Minion Pro

Printed and bound in the UK by TJ Books LTD, Padstow, Cornwall

ISBN 978 1915352 620

British Library Cataloguing in Publication Data.
A catalogue record for this book is available from the British Library.

For Frosty and my family, especially my grandchildren Lorion, Liv, Tiva and Narina, so they will know something about the adventurous lives of their Grandpa and ShoSho.

Contents

ACKNOWLEDGEMENTS

First, I have to thank my husband, Frosty, for his determination to buy a Harley-Davidson. Without his insistence and encouragement, there would have been no Maridadi Road King in the first place. Next, I have to thank Diamond Robyn for being our mentor, teaching Frosty how to ride a big Harley-Davidson and his invitation to join him and Amr Khashoggi on our first epic ride from Jeddah to Muscat.

When it came to writing this book, I would never have started without the encouragement of Frosty, and family and friends who repeatedly said to me, 'You must write a book about your Harley adventures.' Once I got going, our two children, Dusko and Chania, spurred me on every step of the way, as did Dusko's wife, Zoe, and Chania's husband, Tony. I recorded an audio version of my book for Chania to listen to on her morning walks and she gave me valuable feedback. Frosty read through my manuscript numerous times, ensuring that I got facts right about Saudi Arabia and the motorcycles that I talked about. He was sharp to spot repetitions and missing words and was a great copy editor.

Having an additional beta reader who is a writer and who had lived in Jeddah in the 1980s was another bonus for me. Out of the blue, Jenna Orkin from the USA contacted me via my website and offered to beta read for me. Her turn-around time for chapters that I emailed her was almost by return. Her criticism was at times blunt, but spot-on and very helpful.

My first offer to publish came from Jen Hutchinson from Journey to Words Publishers in Melbourne, Australia. Jen was a friend and writer I first met in Jeddah in 1984. She spent three years in Jeddah, as well as several in Lebanon during the Civil War so had a thorough understanding of the Middle East. Jen sent me pages of invaluable writing advice and tutored me on Zoom calls on how to convert from writing like a journalist to writing in the personal style of a memoirist. She went through a detailed polish edit with me and turned my book from an amateur effort into something ready for publication. Unfortunately, the Covid-19 pandemic put an end to any hopes of publishing with JTW and so I turned to The Book Guild in the UK. Thank you, Jen, for your excellent advice, instruction, editing, encouragement and confidence in me. Jen tragically died from an aggressive form of cancer on 4 August 2022. I am so sad that she won't be here to see *Travels with Maridadi* published.

And lastly, The Book Guild publishing team under the Senior Production Controller, Fern Bushnell, has been very supportive, thorough, patient and great to work with. Lauren Stenning is a brilliant copy editor and picked up on details about Saudi Arabia and Arabic phonetic spellings that all of us had missed.

A big thank you to all of you.

Prologue
Saudi Arabia from 2005 to 2015

The events that took place in *Travels with Maridadi* were during these ten years when Saudi Arabia was still a very closed and strict country, so this gives the book a strong historical element.

With the exception of religious tourism for Muslims to come to perform their Hajj or Umrah pilgrimage to Makkah, outsiders were rarely allowed to visit the country. It was even difficult for expatriates working and living there to get visit visas for their parents and adult children. There were strict regulations about Muslim women covering their hair, and all women, including expatriates, were expected to wear the black cloak called an *abaya* when they ventured out of their homes. The religious police known as the *mutawa* were pervasive and imposed the rigorous rules of Wahhabi Sunni Islam on society, patrolling the shopping malls and ensuring that the shops closed during prayer times. There were no cinemas or outside entertainment, no concerts, no international sporting events, and women weren't allowed to attend Saudi football matches. Alcohol was illegal and it was also the only country in the world where women were forbidden to drive.

During his reign from 1 August 2005 to 23 January 2015, King Abdullah bin Abdulaziz Al Saud was a cautious social reformer. Having been forbidden from working in public places, Saudi women were now allowed to work in shops such as lingerie, clothing and cosmetic shops. Until then, they had to buy their underwear, clothes and cosmetics in shops staffed by men. We also began to see Saudi women among the staff at hotel and hospital reception desks. King Abdullah was a great supporter of women's education and also promoted their involvement in politics. He was a popular monarch, and there was an optimistic sense that the country was gradually becoming more liberal.

When Crown Prince Mohammed bin Salman became the de facto ruler of the Kingdom in 2017, he instigated a whirlwind of dramatic change. Now, women no longer have to cover their hair or wear the *abaya*, they are allowed to drive and attend football matches, the *mutawas* have been banished, tourists can get visas on arrival, cinemas have been opened, and big concerts take place. Formula One racing and international golfing tournaments for men and women have become annual events. Saudi Arabia is becoming more like Dubai and Abu Dhabi – except alcohol is still illegal.

We have not had an opportunity to return to this new, liberal version of the Kingdom. Yet despite the restrictions during our years there, we are glad to have experienced that era. There was something special about residing in a country that banned outside tourism. We had earned the right to explore it by working and living there.

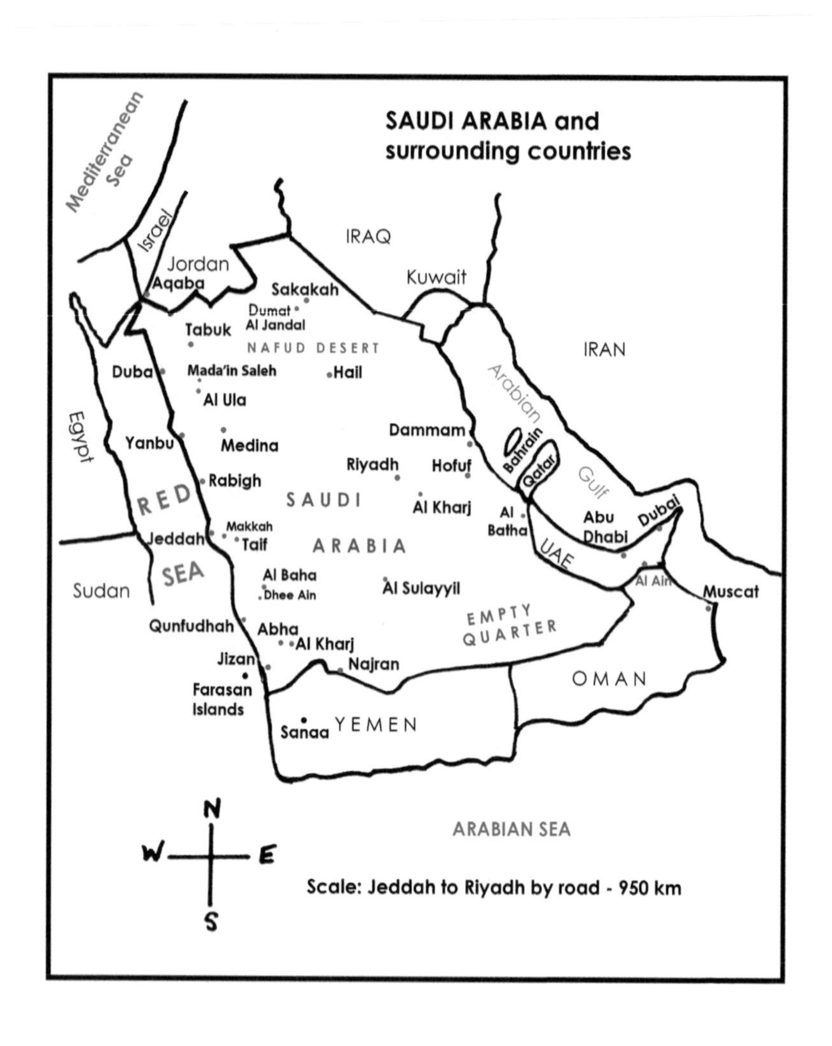
SAUDI ARABIA and
surrounding countries
Mediterranean Sea
Israel
Jordan
Aqaba
IRAQ
Kuwait
Sakakah
Dumat Al Jandal
Tabuk
NAFUD DESERT
IRAN
Duba
Mada'in Saleh
Hail
Al Ula
Arabian Gulf
Egypt
Yanbu
Medina
Dammam
Bahrain
Qatar
Riyadh
Hofuf
Rabigh
RED SEA
SAUDI ARABIA
Al Kharj
Al Batha
Abu Dhabi
Dubai
Makkah
Jeddah
Taif
UAE
Al Ain
Sudan
Al Baha
Dhee Ain
Al Sulayyil
Muscat
EMPTY QUARTER
Qunfudhah
Abha
Al Kharj
Jizan
Najran
OMAN
Farasan Islands
Sanaa
YEMEN
N
W
E
S
ARABIAN SEA
Scale: Jeddah to Riyadh by road - 950 km

1

A CRAZY IDEA

'Why don't we get a Harley-Davidson?' asked my husband.

'No, Frosty, that's a crazy idea,' I replied. 'You'll kill yourself or be killed. And anyway, where will you put your golf clubs?'

It was 2005 and we had been living in Jeddah, Saudi Arabia, for twenty-one years when he came up with this suggestion. He was by this time a Boeing 747 captain with Saudi Arabian Airlines, now called Saudia. We had been married for twenty-seven years and he hadn't once mentioned he would like to have a motorcycle. Both our children had finished university, moved out of home and were earning their own living. I figured it had something to do with his age, then fifty-five, and a yearning to feel young again.

He used his creative logic to rationalise the Harley idea.

'We need something exciting to do here, especially an activity we can do together.'

He was referring to how our lives had changed since my botched spinal operation six years earlier. I'd had a huge herniated disc removed from my thoracic spine, a rare condition. The Saudi surgeon assured us that I would be out of hospital in seven days. In two months, he promised, I would be back on the tennis court.

I woke from surgery in excruciating pain, unable to move my legs. Lying flat on my bed, I stared up at a network of tubes, one of them bright red and feeding someone else's blood into my veins.

Movement came back to my left leg, but unbeknown to me in those early days, my spinal cord and nerves to my right leg had been permanently damaged. I spent my forty-fifth birthday in hospital being told by lying surgeons, 'Not to worry, you'll be able to walk again.'

Two months later, instead of playing tennis, I was still in a spinal injury rehabilitation centre in Jeddah. During the six weeks of residential rehab, my Palestinian doctor said to me, 'You need to look on this as a two-year recovery period.'

Two years. It seemed like a lifetime. Traumatised and full of self-pity, I burst into tears. I could see other people there who were worse off than me, paraplegic or even quadriplegic, but that was little consolation. Crying happened frequently; the smallest gesture of kindness, or someone asking me how I was, triggered tears. My defences were shattered, my life turned upside down.

One morning, after a session with the senior physiotherapist, she sat on the bench beside me, her eyes full of concern. I discovered there is no gentle way for medical professionals to break bad news to their patients. No matter how they deliver it, the effect is a punch in the gut, knocking the air and spirit out of you.

'You know you will never be able to walk again without using a walking stick. And you'll have to buy a wheelchair.'

Determined to prove her wrong, I became obsessive about my exercises, bought a treadmill, went for slow, arduous walks with my crutches in our airline housing compound in Jeddah, swam laps – front crawl, using only my arms – to keep fit and had further physiotherapy in London. The more I tried to walk, the more I realised the complexity of the movements and how far away I was from ever being able to take those steps unaided.

When the two years were up, I had to admit defeat and accept that I could only walk very slowly with a single stick. My disability, discomfort and pain were permanent, a life sentence. An ankle splint was essential on my right foot to stop it from collapsing inwards, which meant my days of wearing stylish high heels, sandals and flip-flops were over.

Frosty and I could no longer play our favourite sports together: tennis, squash and golf. While he joined friends to play these sports, I was left alone at home. When I was out of the Kingdom, I could no longer join in the long weekend walks with my friends or remote trekking holidays I used to love so much. I craved adventure and felt that it had been ripped out of my life. This catastrophic change in our circumstances was gut-wrenching for both of us at the beginning. I fumed at the injustice of it, cried with rage, hating the fact that Frosty could still do all the things I loved doing. The professionals had not warned me of this isolation and the associated grieving process, mourning the loss of my strong, healthy, energetic, sporty, sexy, pain-free body. On his side, Frosty felt guilty for leaving me at home when he went out to play tennis with friends. I knew I shouldn't stop him from taking part in these activities simply because I couldn't do them anymore. My vision of the future had been that I would be strong and fit as I grew older, not a cripple hobbling around with a stick or getting around in a wheelchair.

Several years passed before we accepted this new reality as part of our daily lives. I picked up the threads of my career as a freelance photographer and journalist, and kept fit with more solitary sports like swimming, yoga and going to the gym. But to this day I miss the social inclusion of my previous activities. More than anything, I miss the simple pleasure of walking. Frosty's reasoning about the Harley was almost convincing.

'Think how exciting it would be to explore this country together on a Harley, Bizzie Bee,' he said, turning on his charm and powers of persuasion. 'You know how much you love adventurous travel.'

His only riding experience was on the tracks around the family coffee farm in Kenya where he grew up. With his impetuous character, I feared he and motorbikes were incompatible. It was different when he was flying. The moment he donned his airline uniform, a replacement character emerged: serious, thorough, responsible, predictable, calm, decisive. All the qualities a passenger wants in their captain. But he wouldn't be wearing his uniform on a Harley. I had visions of him riding wild and fast, having a serious or fatal accident. The driving standards in the Kingdom were terrible and most drivers ignored the Highway Code. With me already crippled, the last thing I wanted was another damaged body in the family. Being vulnerable on the pillion seat of a motorbike with a novice rider held no appeal for me either.

'I'll think about it,' I conceded.

But I hadn't bargained for Frosty's colleague, Diamond Robyn. He was also a Boeing 747 captain with Saudia. Diamond was born into the aristocracy of an Indonesian tribe, a dedicated biker who had raced as a young man. After his parents forbade him to continue track racing because of his senior position in the community, he had turned to more sedate Harley-Davidsons. He lived and breathed Harleys, as did his Moroccan wife, Houria, and their three children.

Diamond was a stocky man with a powerful build. With his broad cheekbones, dark-tan skin, jet-black hair and moustache, he looked as though he had stepped out of a Jackie Chan film, not the formal cockpit of an airliner. He even held a black belt in taekwondo. His signature attire was to dress in black from head to toe: black Stetson hat, black shirt and jeans, black leather embroidered cowboy boots. He embellished his look with silver jewellery – rings, bracelets, necklace, belt – all with skull emblems. To the frustration of the airline management, these adornments stayed on with his uniform. Pilots weren't supposed to wear any obvious jewellery. According to the fundamentalist Wahhabi Islam of Saudi Arabia, Muslim men shouldn't wear it at any time, and the airline management didn't like the skulls.

Diamond owned two Harleys in Jeddah, one of them an Electra Glide Ultra Classic, a big, top-of-the-range cruising bike, and the other a 1999 Road King Classic. While I was away in London during the summer of 2005 escaping the desert heat, Diamond took full advantage to teach Frosty how to ride a Harley. During their time off, the two men spent hours together grooming Frosty in the art of riding the Road King. As a starter bike it was huge, with a 1450cc engine and weighing 380 kilogrammes when fuelled up. In the United Kingdom, you had to go through road training on a small motorbike, then pass stringent practical and theory tests before you could advance to training and tests on a big motorcycle.

When he arrived for a few days off in London, Frosty was glowing with excitement.

'I'm really enjoying riding with Diamond. I hope you'll join us when you get back, Bizzie Bee. You used to love riding your motorbike in London, and you were good at it.'

'Yes, but riding pillion is different – I won't have control of the bike, and you're new at it.'

Even if I'd been physically capable of riding a motorbike, in 2005 women in Saudi Arabia weren't allowed to drive cars, let alone ride motorbikes.

'Diamond's a good teacher,' he persisted.

'Okay, okay, I'll think about it,' I conceded again.

Any suggestion that he was too old was useless. Most Harley owners were older, professional men with grey hair. Frosty fitted the profile.

At the end of that summer, our daughter, Chania, was flying back to Jeddah with me. She had graduated from Edinburgh University and now wanted to spend some time at home with us, as well as earn and save money teaching English. Perhaps reminiscing on the long flight back about my London motorcycling days would help me come round to Frosty's new obsession.

2

A TRAIL BIKE CALLED KITU NGINI

I was fourteen years old when I first rode a motorbike. A friend brought one round to our house in the small tea-growing town of Kericho, Kenya. The bike was 125cc, and we all took turns riding it around the garden. Although easy to ride, it didn't leave me wishing I could have one. My few minutes of fun left no clues that motorbikes would end up playing a major role in my life. Or that this would be in Saudi Arabia.

A few months later, in September 1968, my parents sent me to a convent boarding school in Belgium. I wouldn't see them again for ten months as they could only afford to fly me home to Kenya once a year for the summer holidays. The strict atmosphere nourished my independent nature and made me forever wary of religious authority. For the Christmas and Easter breaks, I flew to England to spend the few weeks with relatives and with one or both of my older brothers.

James, the younger of the two, lived in Derbyshire in the heart of the Peak District. His home from home was with an elderly cousin at King Sterndale Hall, a characterful eighteenth-century country house. By the time he was sixteen, he had saved £25 to buy himself a 1950s Vincent 500cc Comet, now a desirable classic bike.

He didn't have a licence to ride on the roads, so I rode pillion with him around the farm lanes.

Two years later, he sold the Vincent and moved to London. By this time, I was at college in Chichester, a small city on the south coast of England. Sometimes at weekends I hitchhiked to London to see him. He now had a full motorcycling licence and had bought himself a Triumph Tiger 650cc. Dressed in his black leathers, he looked the business. The highlight of my weekend was a pillion ride with him, a kid sister in awe of how her big brother rode his motorcycle like a natural. With no backrest, I had to hold on tight with both arms around his waist. There was a sequence of S-bends on the way home to his flat that he loved to lean into, daring each time to tilt a little further. We had both learned to waterski as children, and the fluid cornering on a motorbike reminded me of our graceful slalom turns. As we leaned around these bends, I would visualise my ski turns and the wall of spray curving up behind me.

In 1973 I moved to London to become a student nurse at the Royal Free Hospital. By now the elderly cousin in Derbyshire had died, leaving my brothers and me a few thousand pounds each.

'Biz, now that you've got some money, why don't you buy a motorbike?' suggested James. 'Life will be much easier for you if you have your own transport.'

Very few women rode motorcycles in London – or anywhere else – and I liked the idea of becoming one of these trailblazers. James had already decided what sort of bike would suit me, as one day we climbed onto his Triumph and made for a Yamaha dealer in West London. After a short while in the showroom, I signed a cheque for around £275 and became the owner of a blue Yamaha 125cc trail bike.

With my new crash helmet on, front and rear learner plates in place, but with no road biking experience at all, I was ready for my journey to Belsize Park in North London. As I had a UK driving licence, I was legal to ride any bike up to 250cc, but having to negotiate heavy traffic on two wheels for the first time was daunting. My mind was preoccupied with things that could go wrong. Would I by mistake accelerate instead of brake at a red light? What would I do if I stalled in the middle of a crossroads when the lights turned green for the cross-traffic? Would I remember how to kick-start my bike to get going again? What if I fell over going around a corner?

My heart was thumping as we set off towards Central London. Our ten-kilometre ride took us from the Acton dealer onto the three-lane Westway motorway, with its speedy vehicles, and onwards to the busy Marylebone Road.

When we pulled up at a red light beside a massive truck, the driver looked down and raised his eyebrows when he saw me. He winked, then glared at my brother and said in his Cockney accent, 'You'd better take care of 'er!' We made it to Belsize Park without mishap, my first ride accomplished.

I named my Yamaha *Kitu Ngini*, meaning "something else" in Swahili, the lingua franca of Kenya. With daily riding, my confidence grew, and I revelled in the freedom of having my own wheels. On the way to the main Royal Free Hospital, there was a sequence of S-bends, which reminded me of those I used to love when riding pillion with James. On days when there was little traffic, I could take them without having to slow down. I still recall the poetic sensation of swaying from one side to the other as I slalomed the corners, at one with my machine. Once, at a red light, another motorcyclist caught my eye and nodded.

'You ride your bike with great skill,' he said.

After a few months, I made friends with two other nurses, Vi and Anne. They followed my lead and also bought motorbikes, Honda 125cc road versions.

In the summer of 1974, Vi and I planned our first tour. We got hold of a map of England and chose Cornwall, a county renowned for its coastal beauty. With camping gear strapped to our pillion seats, we kick-started our bikes, clicked them into gear and accelerated away on our 570-kilometre ride to the West Country. What a great feeling, heading off on my first long ride. Bikers – all male – coming the other way always raised a hand to wave, recognition of fellow free spirits.

Once in Cornwall, we took our bikes off-road and followed the footpaths along the tops of the northern cliffs overlooking the Atlantic Ocean. At times, we were only a step away from the edge of a thirty-metre drop to the water below. We rode in jeans and jerseys, without helmets, the wind blowing in our long hair, with the sound of the pounding waves below and the cries of seagulls flying overhead. In the evening, we didn't bother to look for proper campsites, just pulled in at farms and asked permission to camp in their fields. We rode to local pubs for supper and, one night, with no GPS to log where we'd pitched our tent, we had to find our way home along the narrow country lanes through thick fog. A spooky sense of disorientation made me feel light-headed. Where the hell were we? Riding slowly, eyes peeled for the turn-off to our farm, I kept going until our little tent appeared out of the gloom.

By the time we arrived back in London a week later, we had done 1,950 kilometres. Now I felt like a real biker.

Although I loved my independence in London, what I didn't like about motorcycling was the winter cold. I couldn't afford good biking gear so resorted to a trick used by people sleeping rough – I lined the front of my flimsy waterproof jacket with layers of newspaper. This worked, but despite my leather gloves, ice-cold hands were still a problem. The worst time was when I rode ninety kilometres to Oxford for a cousin's twenty-first birthday. When I arrived, I couldn't unfold my fingers from the handlebar grips. I had to slide my hands off sideways, my fingers frozen and curled up. The cold had got through to my bones. I was shivering, my teeth chattering. In the end, the only way I could get warm was to get into a hot bath.

My poor Kitu Ngini also suffered the trauma of being stolen five times in three years. The first time was in 1974, when my precious new bike went missing for five weeks. Had it remained missing for one more week, the insurance would have paid out for a new one. But one day, as I was driving down a road in St. John's Wood with my boyfriend, a flash of blue and chrome caught my eye. I shrieked, 'There's Kitu!' Sure enough, there was my little bike, standing alone in a parking bay. I called the police and Kitu came home, dirty and damaged.

It was my bad luck that 125cc trail bikes were a temptation for young tearaways living in the council flats not far from our nurses' residence near South End Green. On my way out to work, I would find my bike missing, again. There were two young men who ran a small motorbike workshop nearby where Kitu was serviced, so I would turn to them.

'Hi, guys. My bike's gone missing again. Is there anything you can do to help?'

'Leave it to us, luv. We're pretty sure we know where it's gone.'

A few days later, they would call me.

'Hello, luv, we've got good news. We've got your bike back again.'

'That's fantastic. Thank you so much. But do you know who took it?'

They knew, but they didn't let on who the miscreants were. Each time Kitu came back, as well as being covered in dirt, there was more damage done. They'd take my trail bike up to Hampstead Heath and thrash it about on the muddy tracks.

Kitu and I continued our partnership until April 1976 when I qualified as a State Registered Nurse. Leaving my beat-up bike with my flatmates for safekeeping, I took what we now know as a gap year. With a girlfriend from my Chichester College days, I spent two months on the hippie trail, travelling from London to India via Iran and Afghanistan. The idea of doing this overland trip on a motorcycle didn't appeal to me. From the beginning, I wanted to travel on public transport, the way the locals did, mingling with them. Once we reached Delhi, my friend returned to the UK, and I continued with my travels around India alone, trekking in the Himalayas and touring the country.

After two months, I'd had enough of my itinerant life among strangers on crowded second-class trains and in cheap hotels. I wanted to go home to my parents in Kenya. We hadn't seen much of each other over the years, and now I had time to spend with them and see more of the country where I was born.

While there, I met up with Richard Frost who I had known since I was sixteen. I had first fallen for him when I was nineteen and he twenty-three. I don't remember ever calling him Richard – to me he was always Frosty. In those days he had been a bush pilot based in Mombasa, one of a charismatic group of young airmen. With their stories of daring exploits around East Africa, waterskiing boat and capacity to party, they were magnets for the girls. He had flown me from Nairobi to Mombasa, an intimate and romantic night flight in a six-seater aircraft, just the two of us and the bright starlight of the African sky. When we landed an hour later, I was smitten. If there were seats available on his tourist flights, he took me on day trips to game parks and destinations on the Kenyan coast.

A few weeks later, I had left to start my nursing training in London. I hadn't seen him since. Now, he was a first officer flying a Super VC10 aircraft with East African Airways.

When I first saw him again at a sailing club, he was wearing cut-off, fraying, blue denim shorts and a faded blue cotton shirt tucked in, with most of the buttons undone, showing off his hairy chest. He was as good-looking as I remembered. I scanned his suntanned, fit body and sun-bleached hair and felt a renewed sizzle of attraction when our green eyes locked. Over the following months, we met a few more times with mutual friends, sailing and spending laughter-filled days together. Then I left to explore the Kenyan coast and chase a dream to sail from Lamu to Mombasa on an Arab dhow. During my month away, I couldn't stop thinking about him. I had to see him again before returning to London. Maybe, just maybe, he felt the same about me.

On my way back upcountry to my parents, I arrived unannounced at the house he was sharing with two other guys in Nairobi. That evening, he landed from a London flight and had a few days off. He gave me the welcome I had hoped for: a huge hug. Over dinner and dancing in a club that night, followed by a weekend away together, we knew this was the beginning of something special.

In January 1977, I returned to London to my first job as a staff nurse at the Royal Free Hospital. A few days later, East African Airways was unexpectedly dissolved. Frosty was out of work, no longer operating flights to London. The news shattered our expectations that we would see each other once a week on his layovers. Long-distance phone calls were expensive – an hour-long one cost us £65, nearly half my month's salary – so we wrote to each other several times a week, not knowing how long it would be before he was back.

One day, I received a cryptic telegram from him which read: "Arriving London Tuesday. No clothes". He had been at Mombasa Airport after ferrying a light aircraft from Nairobi when he spotted a freighter sitting out on the apron preparing to leave. Wondering where they were going, he wandered over.

'We're going to London,' the captain told him.

'Could you take me with you?'

'Sure, as long as you have your passport.'

By chance, he had the vital document with him. He had decided that he wanted to marry me, so wasn't going to miss the opportunity of a free ride to London. From the airport terminal, he called a friend to send me the telegram. He arrived smelling of the coffee sacks he'd been sitting on most of the way, with no change of clothes. It was midwinter; I had the day off; and my boyfriend had arrived from Kenya. Perfect.

After a few hours, he came to the point of his sudden visit.

'Bizzie Bee, will you marry me?'

I hadn't expected his proposal, so I told him I'd have to think about it. The obstacle was my career plan to study midwifery. My thinking time only took a few minutes. Why spend eighteen miserable months apart? I said to him, 'Can you ask me again?' This time, I accepted.

He stayed on for ten days, ruining my reputation with my Russian landlady who lived below me. She was convinced that I was a girl of the night and not a nurse at all. Every time we came back into my little bedsit, one of many in the big house, we found notes from her shoved under my door, telling me how wicked I was. After he left, I found a flat to share with another nurse.

Kitu Ngini had been waiting for me when I returned to London but was in a sorry state, having been left outside without a cover for ten months. After a service, my bike was back on duty, taking me to and from the hospital. As a nurse I was seen as a responsible member of society, but when it came to Kitu, I behaved like an irresponsible teenager. The lowest insurance premium was way above its value and more than half a month's salary, so I didn't bother to insure. When Frosty returned on another trip, I suggested he ride pillion with me. I was breaking the law again, as I hadn't bothered to take my motorcycling licence and was therefore not qualified to carry pillion riders. So the reckless staff nurse and airline pilot chased around London on a little Yamaha trail bike, in love and defying the law.

Other aspects I didn't like about motorcycling were always having my face covered in grime from traffic fumes and having to wear jeans, along with boots or trainers. I missed wearing my dresses, skirts, high heels and sandals. At the beginning of 1978, when I was packing up to leave for Kenya to be married, I was not sorry to sell Kitu Ngini. The boys at the workshop found a buyer, I guessed one of the lads who used to steal it for a joyride.

I kissed Kitu goodbye, sure that my motorcycling days were over. For good.

I embarked on a new journey of married life, which began in Nairobi on 11 February 1978. By then Frosty was flying for Kenya Airways as a Boeing 707 pilot. I gave up my nursing career and plans to do midwifery. After dabbling with a few other jobs, I became a freelance photographer.

Six years later, we decided it was time to leave Kenya. We now had two children and faced the daunting prospect of expensive school fees. Frosty accepted a job as a Boeing 707 captain with Saudia. We said goodbye to our families and friends, three staff, two dogs and a cat, and our happy cottage with its one-acre garden. With a two-year-old son and an infant daughter, I set off for a country that I knew little about, only that its strict sharia Muslim law forbade women to drive or work.

We moved into a tiny apartment in Saudia City, the expatriate airline compound in Jeddah. This secure, walled-in complex covered a square kilometre, had a selection of villas, townhouses, duplexes, low- and high-rise apartments, and housed several thousand people. It was self-contained with recreation centres, swimming pools, tennis courts, basketball pitches, a baseball diamond, kindergarten schools and a small shopping centre. A concession to women was that we were allowed to ride bicycles in the compound.

But back to the present, twenty-one years on, and I was on the verge of taking on a rather different two-wheeled challenge.

3

FIRST RIDE ON A HARLEY

When Chania and I arrived back in Jeddah after the summer of 2005, I fell into an emotional slump for several days. I felt lethargic, didn't want to do anything, go anywhere or talk to anyone. This was my reaction to leaving England and saying goodbye to my easy-going life there, wearing whatever I wanted, driving my own car and having the freedom to come and go as I pleased. I left with memories of the summer music festivals, vibrant theatre and cinema and life in a democratic, secular atmosphere where men and women had equal rights.

Now I had to reacclimatise to not being allowed to drive, to being dependent on my husband or other men for mobility, to the patriarchal society that treated women like children and to a country that forbade public entertainment and music. Returning to this cradle of strict Wahhabi Islam was claustrophobic. All foreigners required an exit visa to leave the country, but, like a Saudi woman, I couldn't leave the country without my husband's permission. As I wasn't allowed to apply for this exit/re-entry permit myself, my first request on arrival was always for Frosty to arrange for one to be stamped into my passport. I never wanted to be stuck in Jeddah if an emergency arose when he was away on a flight.

The holy month of Ramadan would begin soon, which didn't help. This was when Muslims the world over fasted for a lunar month.

In Saudi Arabia, this meant everyone – Muslims and non-Muslims alike – was forbidden to eat or drink in public during daylight hours. All the cafés and restaurants were closed from sunrise to sunset, and shopping hours were reversed from daytime to night-time. The city came to life after sunset and then vibrated with energy most of the night, with shops open until around 3.00am. Unless friends invited us to join them for Iftar, the first meal after a day's fasting, Frosty refused to go out at night because of the traffic jams.

Chania didn't suffer from the same depression at being back. She was excited to be home. For her, Saudi Arabia represented fun. She grew up in Jeddah and had spent her holidays here during her boarding school years in Kenya and then Bristol in England. She had a wide circle of friends and wasted no time contacting them. Her version of Ramadan would involve teaching English to her students after the final evening prayer at around 9.00pm, then staying out with her friends, living the way the locals did, coming home in the early hours and sleeping most of the day.

After Ramadan, my work as the school photographer for two major international schools would begin, buoying me back to my normal optimistic self.

Chania and I had arrived home before Frosty and settled in. When he returned from his flight, he exploded into the flat, revving like the Harley he couldn't wait to ride again.

'I'll give Diamond a call to see if we can go for a ride.'

'Okay, but I'm not gonna ride with you. I don't think you're ready, and I wouldn't trust you enough.'

'That's no problem. I'm sure Diamond will be happy to take you. And we'll go with a Canadian guy called Steve as well, so Chania can come too.'

The following afternoon, Frosty drove Chania and me over to Diamond's house where the two Harleys lived in an air-conditioned garage. He had parked both bikes on the roadside, ready to go, the Electra Glide Ultra Classic and the Road King.

'Hey, Bizzie,' he greeted me. 'This is great you're coming with us. You can come with me on my Ultra.'

'And this bike,' said Frosty, glowing as he pointed, 'is the one I have been learning to ride. She's a Road King. Isn't she beautiful?'

He had already decided the machine was female, and I could tell by his voice that he was smitten. I had to acknowledge the gorgeous paintwork, in metallic indigo and pearl white with orange flames licking across the fuel tank and mudguards. These were finished off with grimacing painted skulls. He gave me a tour of the details, the most appealing for him being the sensual clutch and front brake levers. They were shiny chrome in the shape of a woman's long legs and naked torso. I noticed how he liked to stroke the curving breasts as he talked.

We heard the growl of a bike approaching us, and Steve Beddoe arrived on his V-Rod Harley. Although he lived in our Saudia compound, he didn't work for the airline. He was a medical technician in a nearby hospital. The men greeted each other, all diverse in their appearance and national origins but connected by their mutual passion for biking. After introducing Chania and me, Frosty asked Steve, 'Would you mind taking Chania with you? I'm not confident enough yet to take a pillion rider.'

'Sure, no problem.'

'Okay, let's hit the road,' said Diamond. 'Frosty, I'll ride first, then you follow. Steve, you come with Chania at the back. Bizzie, this helmet should do for you. If it's a little big, you could put a scarf over your head first. That way you can get a snug fit. Chania, you try this one.'

We donned our helmets, and Diamond helped me adjust the straps. 'How does that feel? Will it be okay?'

'Thanks, Diamond. It's fine.' The helmet had a full-face, dark Perspex visor.

'Now, how can I help get you onto the bike?'

'If I can hold onto you to balance, then Frosty can help me get my leg over.'

I always had a private chuckle when I said this, but that is what I had to do: get my leg over.

While I braced myself on my good left leg and clung onto Diamond, Frosty helped me lift and swing my uncooperative right leg over the high seat. I shifted myself into place on the raised pillion section and, with my hands, helped to manoeuvre my right foot into position on the footrest. Watching Chania, I envied the youthful ease with which she swung her leg across the saddle to get onto Steve's pillion seat.

In Saudi Arabia, it was illegal for a woman to travel with a man who wasn't either her husband or a member of her family. If she was in a car, that was bad enough. But sitting close to a man on a motorbike with her arms around his waist was an offence that could drive the *mutaween* religious police into a frenzy. We ignored rules like this every time we rode in a group. Frosty was with us, so we took the risk that we could blag our way out of a problem if we were stopped. He would say he had given his permission for us to ride with the other men.

Frosty looked torn between giving in to his boyish excitement at going for a motorcycle ride and being a serious airline pilot riding one. I still couldn't believe he had skipped learning to ride a smaller machine and got straight onto this big Road King. The bike was heavy and powerful, and he told me the wide Bikini Beach handlebars made it difficult to steer.

There was no kick-starting a Harley like I had to do with my little Yamaha. At the press of a button, Diamond's engine rumbled into life. What a sound! Something in me also rumbled into life again: biking. I had forgotten that despite the soot on my face and wearing jeans all the time, I had loved it.

An old joke sprung to mind as I sat there, conscious of the delicious vibration coming up through the seat: How do real women start their vibrators? Answer: They kick-start them.

Harley-Davidsons are renowned for their vibration, something most other motorbikes don't have as it's considered a flaw. The company could have stopped it, but due to popular demand, the vibration has stayed, along with their distinctive engine sound. Many bikers also criticised Harleys for their handling, but these American motorcycles have a unique quality the others lacked: charisma.

We set off towards the compound gate leading to King Abdul Aziz Road, a major seven-lane highway with fast traffic. I felt a thrill rush through my stomach as Diamond eased the Harley into the near lane and accelerated. The force pushed me into the comfortable backrest. Like my brother on his various motorbikes, Diamond rode his Harley as though he had been born on it, the machine an extension of himself. Riding pillion on the Ultra Classic, with its cushioned backrest and armrests, was like being on a super-comfortable armchair on two wheels. It came with the bonus of the massage effect from the vibration.

I think I could get to like this, I admitted to myself.

Diamond led our small group to the Corniche Road, a three-lane dual carriageway that meandered for twenty kilometres along the eastern shore of the Red Sea. I never tired of the Corniche, with its adjacent promenade, built some thirty years earlier. We rode past the eclectic mix of artworks, ranging from marble-sculptured urns to huge, wrought-iron outlines of birds in flight, or leaping fish, beautiful when silhouetted against the sunset. Fountains were springing into life, with water shooting out from artworks representing traditional objects: coffee pots and urns.

As the red ball of sun slipped down over the sea, we passed individuals, couples, families with children, who had made their way there to walk, fish, play, ride bicycles, sit on their rugs to talk and sip tea or coffee, have picnics and barbecues, and clamber over the sculptures. When Frosty was away, I sometimes went there in the evening for a "rolling-walk" in my wheelchair.

I had also seen it all countless times from the inside of our Nissan Patrol and compound limousines. But now, on Diamond's pillion seat, I was seeing it as if for the first time. On the motorbike, I became part of where we were, not shut away in a car. I was experiencing the temperature, inhaling the smell of the sea and feeling the wind caressing my face. Whenever I had gone biking with my brother, I had always sensed we were the envy of car-bound people. Here in Jeddah, from the wistful glances from people encased within their vehicles, I discerned the same sentiment – biking knocked the socks off being a passenger in a car. On the bike, I was playing an active part in the journey as my body adjusted in tandem with Diamond as he leaned around the roundabouts and corners.

Over the next two weeks, the five of us rode out together several times, with me still on Diamond's bike. Then, one Friday when we wanted to go for brunch at the Sheraton Beach Resort, Diamond couldn't come. Steve and a Turkish-Canadian flight engineer, Ghilan Alyssa, planned to join us, but I didn't want to ride with either of them as neither of their bikes had backrests.

'Looks like I'll have to risk going with you,' I said to Frosty.

'I reckon he's ready. He's riding really well, Bizzie,' Diamond reassured me. 'You'll be fine.'

The Road King was lower than Diamond's Ultra Classic, so I could mount it without help. It didn't have the large, supportive backrest like the one on the Ultra, but at least it had a token cushioned one against my lower back. I felt more vulnerable sitting there having to hold onto Frosty or grip the chrome bars on either side of the saddle. Again, I wondered if I was mad.

Frosty's confidence was growing, but from where I sat, it was apparent that riding wasn't ingrained in him. I sensed his movements were conscious rather than instinctive. Because he had to concentrate on handling the heavy bike, I picked up that he wasn't anticipating the manoeuvres of other traffic around him. If he'd spotted the red braking lights on the vehicles further ahead, he wouldn't have had to brake so hard when the one in front jammed on its anchors. Turning his head to check traffic coming up alongside us was something he hadn't yet learnt to do. I gave him a dig in the ribs when I sensed danger or shouted a warning loud enough to be heard through his helmet.

We arrived home having achieved a major milestone in Frosty's new passion for motorcycling. We had ridden out together. I had a grudging admiration that he was taking on this challenge, and his angle that biking was an exciting activity we could do as a team was clever. It seduced me onto his side. But I was glad I had my own biking experience – it gave me the clout to be what he called our "safety officer" rather than a back-seat rider.

4

BREAKING THE RAMADAN FAST THE HARLEY WAY

Motorcycling was becoming a feature of our lives and my depression at being back in Jeddah had lifted. Ramadan was underway and one Thursday – our equivalent of Saturday as Friday is the Muslim sacred day, like Sunday for Christians – Diamond called to say that the Harley Owners Group (HOG) Chapter of Jeddah was going on an Iftar ride. Iftar is a social and family event, with large gatherings in homes. Hotels all over town laid on slap-up buffets.

'Why don't we go along?' Diamond suggested. 'We'll be going to a beach somewhere beyond Obhur.'

Ten miles north of Jeddah was a wide creek, cutting several kilometres inland from the coast. Beyond it were numerous private beach compounds. Some belonged to upmarket city hotels; others had beach chalets or apartments available for families to rent. A select few were for Western expatriates only. In those places, we could be normal on the beach – men and women could mingle, and women could wear bikinis or swimsuits without fear of offending anyone. A wealthy Saudi owned the compound we were going to on the Harleys.

'We'll ride over to the dealership and meet the rest of the group there,' Diamond said, 'and then we'll ride out with them. There'll be about forty bikes.'

With Diamond and Houria in the lead as usual, and Chania once again with Steve, we rode towards our compound gate that fed onto King Abdul Aziz Road and headed for the Harley-Davidson dealership. We arrived to find the car park packed with other Harleys and their owners. Most wore black jeans; a few were in blue denim ones; and there was a variety of Harley T-shirts. Many of them sported leather waistcoats, or vests as they are sometimes called, complete with an array of metal badges. A large, embroidered badge with the Harley eagle was on each back with the words "Jeddah Chapter Saudi Arabia" above.

I noted that none of them wore protective clothing, apart from their helmets. Later, I found out that only a few were Saudis. The rest were Arab expatriates from Egypt, Jordan, Lebanon and Syria. We didn't see any other Western expatriates. I saw one other woman riding pillion, but several vehicles with family drivers were there, taking riders' wives and children. Arab women rarely accompanied their husbands on motorcycles in Saudi Arabia, and Saudi women never. It wasn't banned, but I presumed their husbands, or Saudis in general, frowned on this behaviour.

A bellow rang out from a man in charge of the group.

'*Hey guys, listen up!*'

The men stopped chattering and gathered around the speaker for the briefing.

'We're gonna ride out in staggered formation along Andalus, then make our way to King Abdul Aziz Road to go towards Obhur. We'll be in two groups, and we'll stick to the centre lane. I'll be road captain of the first group, Emad for the second. Suleiman and Ehab will be the sweepers. Please stay in your positions, no overtaking. *Let's go.*'

Riders dispersed towards the lines of machines. Crash helmets donned; legs swung across saddles; leaning bikes pulled upright; and stands kicked into place. Pillion passengers usually mount after the rider is on and has the bike in an upright position. In our case, I had to climb on board first. We were still sorting ourselves out when the forty or so Harleys revved into action.

An involuntary flutter of excitement rushed through me. Once settled, Frosty braced himself for my extra weight as he heaved the bike upright and booted the stand away. And then our Road King's engine joined the orchestra of thrumming Harleys. *Potato, potato, potato, potato*. Frosty told me this was the rhythmic sound of a Harley-Davidson V-twin engine, the sound that the company had attempted to patent.

'Stick with me,' Diamond called out.

He eased into position in the crowd of bikes in the first group, followed by Steve and Chania, then us. Our road captain led our convoy onto the busy three-lane Andalus highway. As we carved our way through the traffic, I wondered how this mob of motorcycles, with helmeted men dressed in black, was allowed in the strict environment of Saudi Arabia. Gatherings of people weren't permitted without permission because they might be construed as political or subversive. Permission had to be sought for innocuous social events like weddings and art gallery openings. Yet here was this threatening-looking group, akin to a band of Hells Angels with their noisy machines, riding like they owned the city. They were wealthy businessmen who could afford Harleys, not a horde of rebels, but sitting on the pillion seat, I felt as if I *was* a rebel. Daring to challenge local convention rekindled the flame of my flagging free spirit. Men could do this kind of thing in Saudi Arabia. It was another privilege of their gender. But women couldn't. Chania, Houria and I were part of a tiny minority of women who dared to ride along with these men.

As we passed cars, all driven by men, I caught the eye of the female passengers inside. They couldn't help but look out as we went by because of the noise: twenty growling bikes, some with noisy exhausts. When they realised that one of their gender was on the back of a motorbike, I saw instant recognition. In the cult motorcycling film *Easy Rider*, the character played by Jack Nicholson says, 'What you represent to them is freedom.' Riding behind my husband on a Harley in Saudi Arabia, I also represented freedom.

So many women in the Kingdom wanted freedom – not necessarily to ride on the back of a Harley-Davidson but to govern their own lives. Women waved, smiled, gave me the thumbs-up sign, took photos with their mobile phones. *Go, girl, go*, was the silent message I read in their eyes and gestures. I saw this every time we ventured out, and not only from women. Men also tooted their horns in short, friendly bursts and children leant out of the windows to see the bikes go by.

When we reached the familiar Globe Roundabout with its massive orb of the world sitting in the middle, our sweeper, Suleiman, blocked the traffic allowing us to ride through as a group without having to give way. He was an enormous man, built like a prize bull. A tin helmet, reminiscent of German soldiers in World War II, was perched on his head. It was shiny chrome and looked too small to provide any protection if he came off his bike.

Suleiman rode a black Ultra Classic and transmitted a tough demeanour until I caught his eye. Then his smile gave him away. Behind the bravado of the black leather vest and huge machine, I sensed he was quite a softie.

Our ride took us along the southern shore of the creek with a view of the variegated colours of clear water: light turquoise close to the shore, deepening into a darker blue and, beyond that, the deep water looked almost black. We passed dozens of cars parked along the road with families setting out their Iftar picnics on rugs on the pavement. Children played on the beach, kicking footballs and scrambling on the playground equipment. I saw a few young men wading in the sea, all wearing the standard knee-length black swim shorts that seemed obligatory for Saudis. Women never swam on the public beaches – each was shrouded in her black abaya, a cloak-like garment, topped by a black headscarf, the hijab. Some wore the full niqab face veil.

On the far side of the creek, we turned north along the straight stretch that ran behind the beach compounds. After several kilometres, the road captain slowed and stopped at a large, steel gate. It slid open and the guard allowed us into the expanse of three acres of empty prime beach property. There were no buildings, so we rode straight across seventy-five metres of soft sand to where it hardened right in front of the open sea.

Harley bikers park their machines in neat rows, side by side, the front wheels lined up. The kickstand is always on the left, so they all leaned that way. With every front wheel also turned towards the left, the bikes created an eye-catching pattern.

Once I was off and had removed my helmet, I could hear the tinkling and clicking sounds made by the various cooling metals.

I had just finished taking a few photos of us with the bikes when I heard the chorus of more growling engines coming our way. By now, the sun had set. In the twilight, I turned to see the headlights of the other twenty bikers coming towards us across the sand. They were staggered four or five abreast, like a scene from a film. Again, I felt those butterflies in my stomach and the hair on my arms stand up. I felt embarrassed by my childish delight as excitement took hold of me. I was now one of them, albeit a pillion rider.

Unsteady on my legs and hands shaking, I raised my camera and snapped, hoping to catch something of the emotion those headlights stirred in me as they came towards us, the engines revving as they came to a standstill close to where I stood.

With no on-site electricity, the organisers had brought a generator. Cables with electric light bulbs were strung between posts around the tables and seating area. Iftar dinners are among the most sumptuous of Saudi meals and an array of mezze dishes was laid out on the tables. The word stems from the Turkish for snack or flavour, and this spread of starters is common in all the countries that were part of the Ottoman Empire (1299–1922).

That evening, our feast included black and green olives, hummus made from chickpeas, *muhammara* from red peppers and walnuts, baba ganoush from aubergine, and labneh, a creamy yoghurt cheese. Among the salads and vegetables were *tabouleh*, which is a mix of chopped parsley, tomatoes, onions and cracked wheat; fattoush, a mixed green salad topped with toasted chips of flatbread; falafel from chickpeas and fava beans; plus, courgettes and vine leaves stuffed with a rice mix. The meat dishes were kibbeh – meatballs with pine nuts – and skewers of marinaded, barbecued chicken. There was also a large platter of *maneesh*, a flatbread spread with either cream cheese or zaatar, a savoury herbal mix of thyme, sesame seeds and ground sumac. Water or soft drinks completed the generous offerings.

Greeting other bikers with 'Ramadan kareem' – 'Have a generous Ramadan' – we loaded our plates and sat on rugs spread out on the sand, with rectangular cushions to lean on. This was a typical Saudi way of arranging outdoor seating. Evenings by the Red Sea were always characterised by this convivial atmosphere when people came out to socialise after the heat of the sun had gone, replaced by a soft evening breeze. The setting sun had left an orange glow along the horizon.

Saudis rarely took their time over meals. These men were no different. They ate fast without conversation, then stood up, ready to go back to Jeddah.

The return ride was different, and we split into small groups. Chania went ahead with Steve, Diamond and Houria, while we teamed up with Ghilan because we needed to refuel. On our way towards the gate, Frosty had to manoeuvre the Road King up a small bank of loose sand. He lost his footing and the bike toppled over. My bum slipped off the saddle and I was dumped onto the soft ground. Big Harleys are heavy to lift when they fall, and everyone knew it. Nearby bikers stopped and rushed over to help.

'Bizzie, are you okay?' It was Diamond, looking concerned.

'Yes, I'm fine – we were going slowly, and I didn't fall far.'

'Will you be okay to carry on?'

'Absolutely. I'm not hurt, and I sensed it was going to happen, so I was ready.'

The men helped Frosty get the Road King upright and he rode it to a more stable patch of ground. Without my walking stick, I needed Diamond to hold onto as I dusted myself down, then hobbled to catch up and climb back into the saddle. My fall had been gentle and not enough to put me off.

While we were in the petrol station refuelling, I noticed a police car with an officer inside giving us furtive glances. Bikes filled up, we set off again. The police car followed. Fifty metres out of the station, the officer forced us to pull over. After two decades in the Kingdom, Frosty was well-practised in how to deal with anyone in authority. He turned off the bike's engine, booted the kickstand into position and removed his crash helmet. As the officer approached, he extended his right hand and greeted him in Arabic.

'*Assalamu 'alaikum*.' Peace be upon you.

'*Wa'alaikum assalam*.' Peace be upon you also, the officer responded, shaking his hand. 'Please, *iqama*.'

The *iqama* was the ID card issued to working expatriates. In those days, wives didn't have their own so, along with any children, we were included on our husband's card. Frosty was relieved he wasn't asked for his driving licence because as yet, he didn't have one for motorcycling and had no insurance either. Also, the bike was in Diamond's name and Frosty didn't have the ownership papers with him. He was being even more irresponsible than I'd been in London with Kitu Ngini.

When the policeman saw the *iqama*, his tone turned respectful. Frosty's photo showed him in his pilot's uniform, complete with his gold-braided cap and Saudia emblem. Saudis showed respect to someone in uniform.

'Sorry, but please, Captain Richard,' he said, rolling his "r"s, 'must see face of lady.'

I was still using Diamond's helmet with the dark, full-face visor. Had Frosty been Saudi, the officer wouldn't have dared ask to see the face of the woman on the back. Many Arab women wore the full-face veil to hide their faces from men who weren't either their husbands or relatives.

I couldn't resist playing the officer at their own game. '*La*,' I said. '*Haram*.' No. Forbidden.

It was worth this cheeky jest to see the bewildered look on the policeman's face. He hadn't expected this response. He thought for a while and turned back to Frosty.

'Please, must see lady's face.'

'Biz, you'd better let him see you – we don't want to upset him.'

I pulled up the visor and looked the officer in the eye.

'There you are,' I said, and snapped it down again.

He picked up his radio and, after making a call, turned back to us.

'Everything okay. We worry, lady's hair showing. No want *shebab* chase you and make problem.'

I hadn't realised my long hair, tied in a ponytail, was flowing out of the helmet. *Shebab* referred to young men who cruised the streets of Jeddah in their cars, looking for fun.

'Okay, thank you. My wife will cover her hair.'

We doubted any *shebabs* would bother us, but it was a way for the officer to save face.

'*Shukran*.' Thank you. '*Ma'assalama*,' he said, and went back to his car.

After tucking my hair into my jacket, we continued to Jeddah. It was lucky Chania and Steve weren't with us. Steve wasn't married so there was no wife on his *iqama*.

We arrived back at Diamond's with no other mishaps, another successful ride together that was gradually cementing my support for Frosty's obsession with motorcycling. I had no idea I was soon to become hooked on it myself.

5

A ROAD KING CALLED MARIDADI

A week later, when we arrived back at Diamond's after another Thursday Iftar ride, he said, 'There's a Harley rally in Muscat in December. I'm thinking of riding there from Jeddah. How about you guys join us?'

'Is anyone else going with you?' Frosty asked.

'Amr Khashoggi – he's done that ride before. Houria isn't sure at the moment if she'll come or not.'

'How far is it?' I wanted to know.

'I think it's around 2,500 kilometres.'

I didn't know what was going on in Frosty's mind, but Diamond's invitation had ignited mine in a way it hadn't been for six years. I loved long road trips. Doing this one on a motorbike was as insane as it was thrilling. It was just the drug I needed, a big dose of adrenalin-fuelled adventure.

'It sounds like an amazing ride. What do you think, Bizzie Bee?' Frosty asked.

'I would love to go!' I said, restraining my urge to jump up and down like a kid.

On the drive home, we were both fizzing with enthusiasm.

'It'll be an awesome trip, but we can't borrow Diamond's bike for such a long ride,' I said.

'Well, he's already told me he wants to sell it,' Frosty replied.

I didn't hesitate. 'Let's buy it.'

He and Diamond agreed on a price of 60,000 riyals, the equivalent of US$16,000. This was higher than usual for a used, six-year-old Road King, but Diamond had spent a small fortune on after-market details. To begin with, there was the customised paintwork and those sensual, chromed, naked lady clutch and brake levers. The original front forks and other metal components had been replaced with chrome ones. Electric wiring had been tidied up by running it through the replacement Bikini Beach handlebars. In addition, true to his character, Diamond had replaced every visible bolt for one topped with a chromed skull. Some had been custom cast in Indonesia. Even the battery ignition had a skull switch; the chrome fuel tank cap was embossed with a skull; and the rear night lights had skull-patterned chrome covers. With these exceptional and expensive alterations, the bike was one of a kind.

There is a Swahili word that describes this kind of stylish ornamentation: *maridadi*. From the day Diamond's Road King became ours, we called her Maridadi.

Along with Diamond, we were among the first to sign up at the dealership for the Muscat rally. When Houria heard I wanted to do the trip, she also decided to join us. Other HOGs from Jeddah were planning to truck their bikes to Dubai, then take a short 460-kilometre ride to Muscat, the capital of Oman. It amused me that in these Muslim countries, the Harley owners didn't mind being called "HOGs" – pigs and pork products are forbidden in Islam.

Someone told me that "buying a Harley is just a down payment". I soon understood why. Despite Maridadi's exotic extras, for her to be a suitable touring bike for us we had to spend a lot more before we left for Muscat. The first thing was to fit a tour pack with the supportive back and armrests like the one on Diamond's Ultra Classic. Frosty tracked one down in the dealership in Riyadh, but it was bright yellow. Diamond came to the rescue. Now that Frosty had joined the Harley family, he went out of his way to help us prepare everything. He took the tour pack to Jakarta and delivered it to the artist who had airbrushed Maridadi's fuel tank, mudguards and fibreglass side panniers. Everything had to match.

Our next mission was to find a comfortable saddle. A consequence of my spinal operation was that I suffered from constant burning pins and needles coursing through my left leg. Four-hourly neurological drugs – the kind prescribed for epileptics – combined with a mild antidepressant, reduced the pain to a bearable level. They altered how my brain perceived the distorted stimuli coming from the damaged nerves. Swimming, and mentally absorbing activities like listening to live string instrument music, writing, taking photos or manipulating them on my computer, or having a fun time with friends, also worked their magic in altering my brain waves so that I forgot about the pain. But the pins and needles were always there in the background, tingling away. Sometimes I found sitting in certain chairs aggravated the pain until it became a relentless burning. My left leg and buttock would feel as though they had been hollowed out and filled with hot, burning coals or bee stings. Riding all the way to Oman was going to be a gamble, and we hoped the Harley wouldn't exacerbate this torment.

Diamond had removed his own Mustang saddle from Maridadi and had reinstalled the factory-fitted one. Harley-Davidson sold their bikes with cheap editions that most people replaced soon after purchase. After hours of researching saddles in biker magazines, I ordered a hi-tech leather Road Sofa from California. Another pilot colleague who flew the New York route agreed to bring it back for us.

Joining the HOG was the next step. Diamond took us to the dealership where he proposed we become "Life Members" of this worldwide motorcycling community and join the Jeddah Chapter. From the selection of Harley clothing, we chose a leather waistcoat each and then parted with even more money to buy branded T-shirts and a variety of metal and embroidered badges. Diamond persuaded us these were essential to complete the true Harley biker look.

'I feel as though we're getting ready for a fancy-dress party,' I said.

'The trick is to wear it as though you dress like this every day,' replied Diamond.

I contacted the editor of the *Arab News* to see if he would like the story of our long ride to Muscat for his paper. Until this point I had been writing for the opposition paper, the *Saudi Gazette,* but had become disenchanted with the reduced rates of pay offered to their freelance journalists. The *Arab News* promised to pay more, was the senior of the two national English newspapers, and I had always wanted to write for its highly regarded editor, Khaled Al Maeena. He asked me to write the story in three parts: the preparation for the trip, the journey and a report on the rally.

Travel writing was a major aspect of my freelance work and gave every trip, both inside and outside the Kingdom, an added focus. Making mental notes and taking pictures would give me something to do as we sped thousands of kilometres across Arabia.

When Diamond discovered I was a journalist and photographer, he said, 'Bizzie, our chapter hasn't had any newsletters for a couple of years now. Why don't you become our chapter editor? We also need someone to represent the Ladies of Harley. If you like, I'll recommend to the committee that you take on these officer roles.'

Since my back operation and retreating from our social life as an active sports player, I sometimes felt that I was seen as Frosty's crippled wife tagging along, not as an individual in my own right. To be accepted among the Jeddah HOGs as an active part of their committee meant I was there as *me*, not simply as Frosty's pillion-riding wife. I would be a lone female in an all-male, all-Arab group, but this didn't bother me.

This novel role boosted my morale and confidence, and I thrived on the involvement. My leather vest became adorned with even more embroidered badges, those of Editor, Photographer, Lady of Harley. When I donned my mint-condition kit I felt like a new, reinvented me.

Frosty's experience and confidence were growing too, with our regular rides with Diamond, Steve and Ghilan and his short trips riding alone. His flying, my work as a school photographer and our family life continued in the background of our new Harley craze, together with our active social life in the expatriate community. Hundreds of children's portraits and class photos had to be taken, processed and delivered to the schools before we left for Muscat. After working as my assistant during the taking of these photos, Chania left for London to prepare for a ski season job in the resort of Val d'Isère. Christmas wasn't far away, so I was having weekly rehearsals with two musicians for the annual Christmas carols we held in our flat every year in mid-December. Saudi Arabia forbade the public worship of all religions except for Islam, giving private events like this more significance than they might have had in secular countries.

We also booked a ten-day trip back to London in mid-November because our son, Dusko, had been offered a place as a flight officer in the Royal Air Force. We wanted to be there to drive him to RAF College Cranwell, if he took up the offer.

But Dusko was stalling. He was distraught about leaving his girlfriend, Zoë, afraid that his absence and his new career would split them up. He would need our support while he struggled with this emotional decision.

During one of our many phone calls I asked him, 'Dusko, what would you decide if you weren't with Zoë?'

'I'd go,' he replied.

'Then that's what you must do, or you'll always regret it. Zoë will be able to cope.'

He was in tears. 'But what about me, Mum?'

I hadn't thought about this. In my world, men thrived on the exciting jobs that took them away from home while women were left behind missing them, often lonely and coping with everyday family life. Dusko's distress made me realise how much he loved Zoë.

'Darling, you and Zoë survived a long-distance relationship through three years of university. Then you had another six months apart when you did your ski season. You will manage this too.'

The morning before he was due at the college, Dusko was still in a quandary. On the point of giving up hope of him joining the RAF and feeling disappointed and despondent, Frosty went for a drive and I went in search of photography equipment.

At midday my phone rang. It was Frosty, his enthusiasm audible. 'Early this morning Zoë told Dusko to go for a long walk to make up his mind. He's joining the RAF.'

I felt myself light up and a surge of energy rushed through me.

My next call was from Dusko.

'Mum, could you do some shopping for me?' There was a new confidence in his voice.

We continued as though there hadn't been any crisis. I scribbled his long list of items required by RAF officer cadets and got on with several hours of panic buying that I'd wanted to get done days ago.

The next morning dawned cold and misty. Full of the kind of pride that only parents can feel, we drove to Dusko's flat in North London. When he came out to greet us, I barely recognised my son. The shaggy, bleach-haired look I loved was gone. He had military-style short back and sides. This symbol of the radical change in his lifestyle took me by surprise. It hadn't occurred to me he'd have to cut his hair.

Zoë had left early to visit friends, too upset to see Dusko off.

Car loaded up with an ironing board and everything else in shoeboxes and black bin bags – no suitcases were allowed – we set off on the three-hour drive to Lincolnshire. The mist gave way to glorious sunshine. While I sewed name tapes onto his clothes, Dusko sat in the back with his laptop, wondering aloud how to word his resignation letter to IBM where he'd been working in the interim.

It was a surreal moment when we arrived at the grand, black grill gates of Royal Air Force College, Cranwell. The large RAF insignia with a gilded eagle, its wings spread wide, adorned each gate. We drove through towards the impressive neoclassical College Hall, bathed in autumn sunlight. The building, with its domed clock tower, was more beautiful and less austere than I'd imagined.

'Well, Frosty,' I teased my husband, 'your dream has come true.'

Dusko checked in, and we offloaded his bags and lugged them to his room in the barracks. I was relieved he was sharing with an older, married man who had ten years' army experience. He had a reassuring air about him.

At last, we could relax. Dusko was on his way. When I hugged him goodbye, he was a civilian in jeans and a jersey. We'd see him in nine months at his graduation. He'd be a flight officer in full RAF uniform, marching with his peers at their passing out parade.

On the way home, we bought champagne and stopped off to see Zoë. Her flatmate Mae was with her, and Chania had also joined them. Relieved that Dusko's uncertainty was resolved, we celebrated the new direction their lives were taking.

During our ten days in London, Frosty and I spent hours in Warr's Harley-Davidson off King's Road in Chelsea, making the most of their sale to buy leather jackets. Even at the reduced price of £275, it was the most expensive jacket I have ever bought for myself.

'Go for it, Biz – it looks great on you!'

That was Frosty's advice. It was made from soft, pliable black leather with a pleat at the shoulder to allow free movement of my arms. On the back, Harley-Davidson was embroidered in a flamboyant script in burgundy thread, with flames chasing out on all sides.

We visited another bike shop on the King's Road to buy our crash helmets and Draggin Jeans. These black denims have a layer of Kevlar inside to prevent grazing if you come off your bike and skid across the asphalt. Once home in Jeddah, Frosty found a

Filipino artist who specialised in airbrushing designs on the wave runners that had become popular with young Saudis. He painted our helmets to match Maridadi's design.

My must-have treat for our trip was the latest Nikon D2X. Digital photography was still new, and I'd been disappointed with the first range of Nikon cameras which produced dull, flat images.

We left London the day after dropping Dusko at Cranwell. Exhausted from the emotion, but fulfilled that Dusko was settled, I slept the whole way to Jeddah.

For a change, I was excited to be back. Soon after we arrived, we met Amr Khashoggi, the Saudi who was to ride with us to Muscat. He spoke fluent English, like all the wealthy, well-educated Saudis we met. We both liked him straight away, with his quiet, self-effacing manner and the way he welcomed us to join in on this ride that he and Diamond had planned.

Over lunch in a restaurant overlooking the Red Sea, he told us about his other motorcycle journeys. Like Maridadi, his Road King had been personalised with a variety of after-market adornments and was full of character. Scuffs, stone chips and sand-scarred paintwork told the stories of epic rides across Saudi Arabia, including one through a raging sandstorm on the road traversing the eastern edge of the Empty Quarter desert. That was the rugged look I liked, but here Frosty and I differed. He liked his motor vehicles to be unblemished, whether 4x4s, classic cars or motorbikes. He pampered and polished them as though they were valuable racehorses.

Amr usually did these trips alone. Not many Saudi or expatriate bikers had either the time or inclination to tackle such long distances. Like Diamond and Houria, when group riding, he liked to go with the Riyadh Chapter. Amr was from Riyadh and preferred their more predictable and professional approach to their riding.

When he saw Maridadi he said, 'You'll have to change your wheels and get tubeless tyres. If you get a puncture on the road with those, you can't fix it as you have to take the wheel off. There would be nothing you could do until the bike is back in the dealership.'

Maridadi had distinctive wheels with beautiful, laced spokes, which couldn't take tubeless tyres. They had to be exchanged for nine-spoke cast wheels. This new hobby was proving to be expensive.

Amr was also enthusiastic about Houria and me riding with them to Muscat and the plan for my articles to appear in the press.

'I think it will give our ride great publicity and will encourage more women in Saudi Arabia to get involved in the motorcycling world. Right now, there aren't any Saudi women taking part.'

Essam Istanbouli, another experienced Saudi rider who worked for the airline, gave us a second valuable tip. 'If you get caught in a sandstorm, your chrome and paintwork will get sandblasted. You can protect it by smearing Vaseline over it, so take a pot with you. It's difficult to wash off afterwards, but it's better than having to pay for a new paint job and chrome work.'

Of course, we talked a lot about our trip with our friends. One of them was on the staff of the British Consulate. 'I wish I could come with you,' she said. 'We'll give you an official letter in Arabic to ask for whatever help you may need on the way. Why not leave from the consulate so that we can give you a proper send-off?'

The day of our departure was closing in. *Arab News* had published the first part of my story, giving it a whole page. Frosty checked Maridadi into the dealership for a full service, and we now had to pack for the journey. Our family always travelled overloaded, as though we were moving house. My allowance for the Muscat trip was a small, black-zipped Harley bag, designed to fit into the fibreglass side pannier. Frosty had the same. I made my list of essential items, the most important one being my drugs. It was liberating to know I didn't have to spend hours going through my wardrobe several times over, trying to decide what to take. Everything about this trip was Harley: one pair of jeans to ride in, two spares; one T-shirt to ride in, three spares; two or three sets of undies and socks; one pair of boots would have to do for riding and social events; a jersey to wear under my jacket once we got to Riyadh, which was much colder in December than Jeddah; my fancy new leather waistcoat with showy badges; and a *shammagh*, the red and white headscarf worn by Saudi men. These large squares of cloth are made from soft cotton and double up as almost anything, including a warm neck scarf. I added my wash bag, gloves, sunglasses, sun cream, journal, a couple of pens, cameras, spare batteries, charger, snacks, first aid kit, make-up and perfume. A Chanel representative at a women's coffee morning had quoted Coco Chanel, 'A woman without lipstick has no energy, and a woman without perfume has no future.' I needed both.

Houria agreed. She had been a flight attendant with Saudia and was an attractive, stylish woman, with long, dark hair and was always well turned-out and made-up. During her years of attending rallies in different countries with Diamond, she had bought herself a new Harley leather or suede jacket at each one. She had an enviable collection. When they were in Indonesia, she rode her own Harley.

My camera and journal would just fit into the tour pack, which was filling up with Frosty's stuff: spanners, aerosol cans of puncture repair fluid, spare light bulbs, torches and manuals. We were a travelling workshop. Because we were going through Riyadh, the country's conservative Wahhabi capital, I bought myself a cheap abaya, a garment I didn't wear in Jeddah. I hoped I wouldn't need it since I disliked being enveloped in this black cloak. We had bought two leather water bottle holders which were fitted on either side of Maridadi, behind the pillion footrests. One of these was perfect for my folding walking stick.

Bearing in mind my physical problems, Diamond and Amr agreed to leave a day earlier, taking a night stop in Taïf before tackling the 790-kilometre ride to Riyadh. Diamond also suggested a two-night layover there, to rest and have the bikes serviced if necessary. From the capital we would join the Riyadh Chapter, riding two stretches of around 650 kilometres to Muscat.

In Saudi Arabia, knowing someone with *wasta*, meaning influence, was invaluable. Amr was engaged to the daughter of a Saudi five-star general who was head of the National Guard Intelligence. This man knew about our trip and had read my article in the *Arab News*. He sent us his congratulations and promised he would speak to the traffic police requesting them to pass the message along to assist us.

With three days to go before we left for Muscat, I was in a state of constant butterflies. I couldn't remember when I'd last felt so excited.

6

GOING NOWHERE WITHOUT WASTA: JEDDAH TO TAÏF

News of our trip circulated at the Wednesday pub night at the British Consulate, and friends had read my article in the *Arab News*. Enthusiastic phone calls and messages came in, wishing us a safe journey.

Our Road Sofa saddle had arrived in New York and was due in Jeddah on the eve of our departure. Diamond's flight had been delayed in Dhaka due to suicide bombings, demonstrations and strikes, and he'd get home about the same time as our saddle. Houria had her share of responsibilities to arrange for their three children.

Amr had his backup van coming with us, driven by his Lebanese cousin, Mohammed. It had a track of spotlights on the roof and a rotating blue beacon to ward off aggressive traffic. The custom-built interior was kitted out with tools and spares, jerry cans carrying extra fuel, a fridge and camping gear. There was a winch too, for loading heavy bikes. Amr's Road King would be hauled in because he'd chosen to ride his Honda Gold Wing instead, another large touring bike.

The morning of our departure – 3 December 2005 – dawned and Diamond called.

'I've been signin' on for the ride,' he said, 'which means I hardly slept at all. It happens to a lot of us before a long ride – we're too excited to sleep!'

I was exasperated by how unprepared he was for the trip, with no visas arranged for the United Arab Emirates (UAE). He had also decided to alter the look of his Ultra Glide. The repainted parts had just arrived from Jakarta and only now was he reassembling his bike.

Our plan was to leave the British Consulate at 1.00pm, giving us enough time to do the three-hour ride to Taïf in daylight. During the last hour, we'd be negotiating the steep Al Hada escarpment road with its numerous hairpin bends. That would be a challenge for Frosty. I felt sick with suspense. By the time Frosty drove over to Amr's to drop off our excess stuff for the van, including my wheelchair, it was already 12.35pm.

I called the consulate and the *Arab News* journalist reporting our departure, warning them of our delays. We arrived at the security gates two hours late. The guards were expecting us, and the huge grills slid open. All eyes looked our way as the three loaded bikes growled their way into the compound. A thrill rushed through me to be embarking on this exotic adventure that no other expatriates had done in Saudi Arabia. The two Harleys and Amr on his Honda Gold Wing lined up at the main entrance, an eclectic mix of bikers on the same mission: Frosty, a white Kenyan; me, British; Diamond, Indonesian; Houria, Moroccan; Amr, Saudi; and Mohammed, Lebanese.

A farewell group gathered around the bikes to inspect them, ask questions and take photos. The Deputy Consul General gave me the promised letter and wished us luck.

Our warm send-off meant a lot to me. This was much more than the initiation of our touring on Maridadi. It was the launch of an exciting new phase in our lives.

At 3.00pm, with the rev of engines, and everyone waving and shouting, 'Good luck!' we were on our way.

My patience was tested again ten minutes later when we pulled into a petrol station. Diamond's battery wasn't charging; our front tyre pressure was low; and Diamond, Amr and Mohammed wanted to pray. Muslims are supposed to pray five times a day, and this was the *Asr* mid-afternoon prayer. No one was around. They were all in the mosque. We couldn't top up because the pumps were closed during prayer time. I was itching to be out on the open road, away from the city, but we seemed to have a steady stream of delays. Most of our ride to Taïf would now be in darkness, including the tricky Al Hada escarpment. Night closed in at around 5.30pm in December.

Diamond, Amr and Mohammed emerged from the mosque and came over to us.

'Huddle up everyone, we'll say the Muslim prayer for travellers,' said Diamond.

We stood in a circle, arms stretched across each other's shoulders, heads bowed, while Diamond chanted the Arabic prayer. I hadn't heard a traveller's prayer since my school days in the Belgian convent where every time we got onto a coach or train, one of the nuns would pray to the Guardian Angel of Travellers to protect us. I am not pious, but I liked this.

At last, at 4.00pm, we headed out of Jeddah on the three-lane highway towards Makkah, the holiest city in Islam and birthplace of the Prophet Muhammad (peace be upon him). Elsewhere, it is spelt "Mecca", but the Saudis had changed the spelling to disassociate their holy city from the Mecca gambling houses. Diamond and Houria were in front, then Frosty and me, followed by Amr and Mohammed in the van. What Frosty hadn't told me was that he had changed Maridadi's original exhaust pipes. Up front, he was unaware of the deafening noise the new ones made. From my pillion position, I got the full blast of those decibels. As we picked up speed, so did the racket from the exhausts, battering like a jackhammer inside my helmet.

The sun was setting when we arrived at the junction for Makkah. A large sign spanning the three-lane highway was divided into three sections. The one on the left read, "Muslims Only". In the centre was the word, "Makkah". A warning red sign on the right said, "For Non-Muslims". I snapped a photo with Diamond and Houria riding towards the sign.

We peeled off to the right as instructed, taking the alternative route to Taïf. We knew it as the Christian Bypass. Frosty and I had been along this road many times before in our Nissan Patrol. It was from this point that I relaxed as a sense of freedom washed over me. The cluttered residential compound we lived in, with its constricting walls, was gone. We were now surrounded by the liberating space and emptiness of the desert. The last rays of the sun accentuated the ripples and small dunes in a sandy panorama that stretched away on either side of us to a fringe of dark hills on the horizon. Tufts of greenery sprouted through, despite the lack of rain, or any groundwater. In the distance ahead was the high, jagged silhouette of the Hejaz Mountains, rising to over 2,300 metres.

We had picked up speed to 120 kilometres per hour when Amr slowed down. He had a rear-wheel puncture. With the bikes lined up on the side of the road in the soft evening gloom, the van's row of spotlights gave the light for Mohammed to pump the tyre full of aerosol foam repair. We got going again but had to stop once more at the next fuel station to get the puncture properly fixed.

Whenever we stopped to refuel, I also used the opportunity to dump fuel myself to make sure that my bladder didn't get overfull. The spinal cord damage had affected it, and the risk of wetting myself was a constant anxiety. Frosty would drop me off as close as possible to the nearby mosque – there was always one at a fuel station – or wherever the attendants said there was a toilet. Wherever we went – shopping centres, hotels, restaurants, friends' homes – my first question was always, 'Where is the nearest loo?'

Darkness had fallen by the time we reached the base of the Al Hada escarpment. Now we rode behind the van, making the most of its spotlights blazing ahead. Amr was in front of us this time, with Diamond and Houria behind us. We faced ninety-three hairpin bends on our steep, twenty-one-kilometre climb up the mountain. I was gripping the sidebars on either side of my seat. The dual carriageway snaked its way along the contours, doubling back every 225 metres.

Twice on the ascent, large signs stating "Check Point" warned us to pull up at the roadside concrete kiosks, which had police vehicles parked alongside. Mohammed and Amr presented the letter from the consulate and had a brief chat with the officers. They waved us on.

Everything was going well until halfway up. A police car overtook our convoy and forced us to pull over just as we were preparing for a tight left-hand turn. As Frosty slowed and steered the bike off the asphalt to the sloped, gravelled hard shoulder, I steeled myself for what was going to happen. As he put his right foot down to brace the weight of the bike, his boot slid on the loose surface. Maridadi fell, dumping me onto the unforgiving ground. My right hand bore the brunt as I tried to break my fall.

Shit! I swore to myself. *Why the hell did that stupid policeman make us stop right on the corner?*

Maridadi had chrome crash guards which protected my leg from being crushed. The bike ended up at a thirty-five-degree angle to the ground. Diamond was with us in seconds, helping Frosty to lift Maridadi, then me.

'Don't worry, I'm fine,' I reassured him.

The officer had no idea there were women on the pillion seats. It was dark; we were dressed in black, helmeted and didn't look any different to the men. He had stopped us because he had decided that motorbikes weren't allowed on the mountain road. Instead, he wanted us to use another one known as the truck route. This would mean returning via Jeddah, although if we'd all been Muslims we could have taken the shortcut through Makkah. We were already halfway up the mountain, but he was firm.

Meanwhile, Mohammed was pestering me to ride in the van with Houria. He felt that we, as women, were the problem. I refused. I was set on travelling the whole way on a Harley unless physically unable to do so.

No reasoning with the officer worked, and he ignored the consulate letter.

Amr decided to call his prospective father-in-law, the general, who spoke to the police officer.

Problem solved.

From where Maridadi stood on the sloping gravel, it was going to be a tricky start. With her loaded up and both of us on board, she weighed around 545 kilogrammes. Sensing that Frosty's confidence was shaken, I suggested I ride with Amr to the hotel.

The policeman was now our ally and escorted us to the top of the mountain.

My ride on the Gold Wing was a treat after Maridadi. The seat wasn't any more comfortable, but the earbashing from Maridadi's exhausts was replaced by pipes so quiet I could hardly hear them, and music flowed from the two loudspeakers.

By the time we reached the top of the escarpment, the temperature had dropped ten degrees. An official waved us through another checkpoint on the way into Taïf, and from there we had a hair-raising ride through the town, avoiding speeding vehicles zigzagging through the traffic. Every junction was a life-threatening hazard – would the driver stop or drive straight out across our path? When we pulled up in front of the Intercontinental Hotel at 8.45pm, I experienced a sense of relief that was to become familiar.

Phew. We made it. Words I said to myself without thinking as the knot of butterflies in my stomach settled down.

Once our helmets were off, I looked at Frosty.

'Why are Maridadi's exhaust pipes so damn noisy?'

'Because I put Thunderheader ones on.'

'But why?'

'I saw them advertised in a magazine in Diamond's garage. They are the kind that some Hells Angels use, and I thought they would be…well, I liked the idea of being like that.'

'How can you be so crazy? They're a nightmare.'

'I know – Diamond warned me they would be noisy.'

'So what can we do about them?'

'Nothing, until we get to Riyadh.'

'But that's nearly eight hundred kilometres away.'

There was no more to be said, so I took out my notebook and recorded our time and distance. It had taken us six hours to ride 214 kilometres. Amr, feeling guilty that he had delayed us with his puncture, treated us all to dinner.

By the time we got to bed, it was midnight. We would have a short night, as our planned departure was 6.00am for the 790-kilometre ride across the Central Arabian Desert to Riyadh.

We were both awake at 4.00am, too excited to sleep, and chatted until the 5.00am alarm.

Our room phone rang. Amr was on the line. At first, we thought he was calling to say that the police had banned our ride, but he had other bad news. He had been throwing up from eating smoked salmon for last night's supper. After letting Diamond and Houria know, we all dressed and trooped over to Amr's room to offer home remedies for dealing with an upset stomach. He looked terrible.

'Amr, whenever this happens to us, we take this antacid powder,' I told him. 'You dissolve a teaspoonful in a glass of water, drink it down in one and then force yourself to vomit again. It clears all the nasty stuff out of your stomach. It should make you feel a lot better.'

We left him in peace. Half an hour later, Diamond rang.

'Amr has followed your suggestion and is going to try to sleep. He'll call us when he feels well enough to leave.'

While Frosty, Houria and Diamond also tried to get more sleep, I headed for the hotel's business centre. I felt too wired and excited, so I wrote a few emails and had a look through the hotel brochure. It stated that the facilities were open to *all* guests – except the swimming pool and gym were for men only.

By midday, Amr felt well enough to leave. A group of staff gathered around the bikes, eager to be photographed with us. They had seen my article in the *Arab News* and the report of our departure from Jeddah in the morning paper. After half an hour of chatting and taking pictures, the muezzin's voice boomed from the minaret, '*Allah hu Akbar!*', the call to the *Dhuhr* midday prayer. Amr, Diamond and Mohammed once again disappeared into the mosque for fifteen minutes to pray.

When the men returned from the mosque, we huddled up again for the traveller's prayer and were set to go. It was 1.00pm. The smiling staff, sharing in the spirit of our adventure, wished us well and waved us on our way.

After an uneventful fuel stop, we continued through the town under a clear sky and glorious sunshine.

Amr's Gold Wing was destined to give him trouble because forty-five minutes out of Taïf, he had another puncture in the rear tyre. We were now well into the Central Arabian Desert, surrounded by sandy, stony wilderness. The three-lane highway, straight and flat, disappeared into the distance, with camel protection fencing on either side and down the central reservation. We pulled up on the side of the road again, and this time Amr exchanged the Gold Wing for his Road King. This is what Diamond had wanted all along, three Harleys riding together.

As the men were sorting this out, a police car on the other side of the highway stopped. Mohammed walked over to it and chatted to the officer across the camel fence. He wanted to know what was wrong and why there were women with the motorcycles. After reading the letter from the consulate, the officer said, 'No problem, you can continue.'

But life was seldom that simple in Saudi Arabia. We were about to move on when another police car showed up, this time on our side of the highway.

7

STARLIGHT RIDE ACROSS THE CENTRAL ARABIAN DESERT

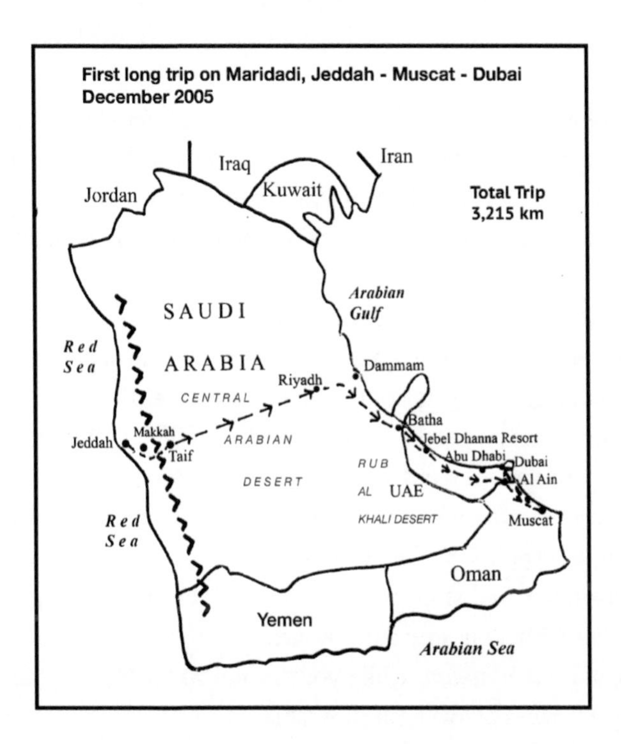

A short, skinny Bedouin policeman, wearing a khaki uniform, got out of his car. His head came to Frosty's shoulder. What he lacked in height he made up for in power. My letter from the consulate didn't help, and he was adamant that we couldn't continue. I asked Amr what he was saying.

'He wants us to call the British Consulate to order a truck to take us and the bikes back to Jeddah.'

When Amr told him that we were not going to do this, the man called his superior. A backup officer arrived in another police car. They were determined we go no further.

While Amr tried to reason with them, Mohammed turned on Houria and me.

'Take your lipstick off! Cover your face! Why are you wearing your crash helmet? They'll think you were on the bike.' He ranted on as though he was a religious policeman. I began to think his dramatics might be making things worse when dealing with the police.

'Mohammed, back off and leave us alone. I'm not going to wipe my lipstick off or cover my face. There is no law that women aren't allowed on the back of their husband's motorbike. The issue is that the police don't want motorbikes on the road at all, women or no women.'

There was nothing Houria, Diamond, Frosty or I could do to help, so we sat leaning against Amr's van and made ourselves a picnic. At least it was cool in the Taïf area at this time of year. Occasional heavy trucks and tankers thundered past, buffeting us with wind as they did so. Company appeared, this time out of the desert in a Toyota Land Cruiser. A middle-aged bearded man wearing the traditional *thobe* – an ankle-length white shirt – and a baseball cap, had stopped to have a look at the motorcycles. He called out with a big smile and wave.

'*Assalamu 'alaikum*. I like your motorbikes. My son, he has a Harley. He rides all over Saudi Arabia.'

Amr and Diamond went over to chat to him while one of the policemen examined the bikes. The other officer was still on his mission to stop us from continuing and persisted in trying to find a rescue truck to take us all home.

Meanwhile, Amr was trying to call his fiancée, but she wasn't picking up. At this time of the day, he guessed she might be sleeping. He was reluctant to bother the general again unless it was our last resort. In the end, he decided he had to. Our only way out was to call on *wasta* once more. Phone calls buzzed back and forth, and Amr was told to organise a group photo of us wearing our full safety gear, including helmets. Everyone's IDs also had to be photographed. Smartphones were still rare in 2005, but Amr had one. While he was forwarding the images to the Traffic Police Headquarters, a low-loader truck arrived to take the bikes to Jeddah. It was 3.30pm.

We had all lived in Saudi Arabia long enough to know that patience is essential. We went back to sitting on the road, leaning against the van, whose shade had lengthened as the sun sank towards the horizon. After another hour, an officer gave Amr good news.

'They say we can carry on,' Amr told us. 'All the checkpoints and police stops on the way to Riyadh have been informed, so hopefully we can travel in peace. The message has gone all the way up to Prince Mohammad bin Naïf, the Minister of the Interior.'

It turned out that our letter from the consulate had worked against us. Instead of wanting to help us, the authorities were concerned about our safety and hence wanted us to return to Jeddah.

At 5.00pm, with the sun low, we were on our way again. We'd been delayed three and a half hours and had to ride the remaining seven hundred kilometres to Riyadh through the night. An hour later, we pulled in for a fuel stop just as the muezzin was calling out the *Maghrib* sunset prayer. We had gone through a police checkpoint and, as promised, the guards waved us through, calling out, '*Ahlan*.' Welcome.

So far, a huge relief for both Frosty and me was that my usual pain had not been aggravated by the riding, or by any of the waiting and hanging around. The vibration from the bike transmitted through the saddle and backrest was like a soothing massage. The seat's design was ergonomically perfect, supporting my back and making me sit straight, with legs in an ideal position. However, Frosty had a problem with our new Road Sofa. Although comfortable when on the move, the neck of the seat was so wide that when we stopped, he couldn't place his feet flat onto the ground. This had been part of the problem when we fell over on Al Hada escarpment the night before. We would have to change it – *and* the Thunderheader exhaust pipes.

Off again into the darkness of the Central Arabian Desert, three Harleys and a van. There was no light pollution apart from our headlights. On that moonless night, stars flooded the sky, and I had uninterrupted time to stargaze. We were heading north-east, in a direct line from Jeddah to Riyadh. The few constellations I knew were easy to spot. I kept my eye on the dim, twinkling cluster of Pleiades, better known as the Seven Sisters, as they rose from forty degrees above the horizon to sixty degrees. Orion came into view to our right, and I saw the Big Dipper high up in the sky, right overhead. The Southern Cross, tilted a little sideways, was low in the sky behind us.

Diamond had suggested I keep Frosty awake by massaging his shoulders and back from time to time. I found his shoulders tense and hunched from concentration and gripping the handlebars. With some massage, the tension fell away and his shoulders dropped to their normal position. By the time I gave him another massage, his shoulders were tight again. Now and then I hugged him to let him know I was okay and happy to have joined him on his motorcycling fixation.

The temperature was dropping, and I could feel the cold seeping through my jacket. When I wasn't stargazing, or massaging Frosty's shoulders, I was mesmerised by the reflective broken white lines in the middle of the road strobing past and the continuous orange stripe marking the edges of the road. Specks of light from any truck coming towards us grew into big bright lights, then flashed past, leaving blackness again. Dots of red rear lights, and sometimes strips of multicoloured lights, denoted trucks ahead of us. We roared past them, onwards into the darkness.

After another fuel stop and police checkpoint, it was our turn to have a puncture. Thanks to Amr's advice about Maridadi's wheels, we dealt with the problem on the spot. Mohammed took control of the roadside repairs, pumping two cans of liquid rubber into the tyre. We rode slowly to the next fuel station to have it fixed, passing yet another checkpoint. Although they waved us through, a couple of officers followed us to the garage in their police vehicle. When we stopped, Amr came and told us what they wanted.

'They are insisting we have dinner with them.'

We all sat together in a rudimentary restaurant where truck drivers stop, tucking into a tasty lamb stew with rice. It was as well they had insisted because otherwise we would have continued through the night without a proper break. After the meal they followed us back to the bikes, becoming the first in a chain of vehicles to escort us the rest of the way to Riyadh. After every fifty kilometres another car took over, sometimes in a seamless relay, while others involved a brief wait until the takeover vehicle arrived.

When we stopped at 2.00am for fuel, Amr's eyes were drooping with fatigue.

'I'm too tired to ride. I feel as though I am going to fall asleep on the bike,' he said. 'I'd like to take a rest and let Mohammed ride the bike for a while, if that's okay with you.'

Mohammed was dying for a chance to ride and wasted no time in asking one of the police officers to drive the van. Amr settled himself in the back of the police car, and we continued on our way. I kept my vigil, tracking the stars. The Seven Sisters were now high in the sky over my left shoulder, the Big Dipper still visible in the eastern sky but, by 3.00am, both Orion and the Southern Cross had disappeared over the horizon. I saw three shooting stars blazing their white-hot trail until their fire burnt out, leaving no trace of where they had come from or where they ended. I don't know anyone who isn't thrilled by the glimpse of a shooting star streaking across the sky. Superstition imbues them with all sorts of magic. Some cultures claim they bring good luck, others that you should make a wish when you see one. Still others believe they represent souls who have been relieved from torment and are on their way to peace, or even the soul of a new baby coming to earth.

When we planned this trip, I had envisioned crossing this expanse of desert in daylight, with only flat, yellowish-brown wilderness on either side to look at. What I was experiencing now was what bikers tended to avoid: lengthy night rides. The rider can't afford to take his eyes off the road, but as a pillion rider, I had that privilege. Despite the constant hammering of the Thunderheaders, I was basking in the romantic adventure of charging through the Arabian night on a Harley-Davidson.

After our next fuel stop and police relay swap, our ride changed. The night had grown cold and misty, and the temperature had dropped to ten Celsius. We had been riding as a tight group, maintaining a speed of 110 kilometres per hour. Now, without any warning, the van, driven by a policeman, raced ahead with Mohammed and Diamond following. Their red tail lights grew dimmer as we struggled to keep up with their 140 kilometres per hour. Maridadi's engine wasn't powerful enough, her headlight ineffective in the fog. Riding at this speed through the night in poor visibility created a knot of fear in my stomach.

Neither Diamond nor Mohammed had told us that they wanted to have a late-night burn. After a while, we saw them ahead, waiting on the side of the road, but they didn't stay long enough for us to catch up. They raced on ahead again.

'Please slow down, Frosty. I don't feel safe trying to catch up with them. It's too dangerous. Let's go at our own pace,' I pleaded.

The police car with the sleeping Amr inside was lagging behind us. I felt anger bubbling inside me that the protocol of sticking together had been broken, as well as the speed we had agreed on. The gap got wider still until we lost sight of them. As the van with its powerful spotlights was ahead of their bikes, Mohammed must have instructed the policeman driver to go that fast.

By the time we caught up with them, the van and bikes were parked on the side of the road. Mohammed, Diamond and Houria were already off their machines, relaxed and waiting for us. As soon as we had Maridadi on her stand, I was off, hobbling as fast as I could towards them, my outrage fuelling me on.

'What the hell were you guys doing racing off like that? We couldn't keep up with you, and there's no way in that mist it was safe for us to ride at that speed!'

Diamond looked surprised.

'You didn't have to go as fast as us. You had the police car with you. We just felt like speeding up for a while.'

'But you didn't tell us that was your plan. I thought we were supposed to stick together,' I replied.

Frosty arrived beside me, equally furious.

'We were all fine until he' (pointing at Mohammed) 'started riding. With Amr, we were all in tune and stuck together. I'm not riding any further with Mohammed.'

Hearing the raised voices, Amr emerged from the back of the police car.

'Amr, I'm not going any further with Mohammed on your bike,' Frosty said, his voice hard with anger. 'Please could you take over your bike again.'

This was the last thing we had expected to happen, a row in the cold, early morning darkness, towards the end of our journey to Riyadh. All of us, except for the policemen and Amr, were offended for different reasons. Diamond couldn't see why we were mad at him or that he had done anything wrong. Houria was upset with how we'd spoken to Diamond. I don't think Mohammed cared we were upset; he was more miffed he had to revert to driving the van. Amr was resigned. For the sake of peace, he had to get back onto his Road King and catch up with his sleep once in Riyadh.

The atmosphere of the night ruined, we continued towards Riyadh in our previous configuration and speed. As we approached the capital city, the flashing crimson and blue beacons of six police saloon cars were waiting to escort us to our hotel. Our sixth and final relay vehicle peeled away, and we sped through the quiet streets surrounded by our cortège, bathed in an eerie glow of street lighting diffused by the mist. Additional police vehicles blocked the cross-traffic at every junction. As we approached red traffic lights, a horn squawked and a siren wailed a warning, and we cruised through without slowing down.

I revelled in the surreal sensation of this triumphal escort into the capital, treatment normally reserved for heads of state and VIPs. It was like watching ourselves in a film. A mixture of fatigue, adrenalin and drama of the night-long ride added to the dreamlike quality of our cavalcade. Having tried to send us home twice, the authorities cosseted us until we reached our destination. They delivered us to the Sheraton Hotel at 5.00am, relieved, exhausted and emotionally drained.

8

MINISKIRTS AND A COLD BEER: DANAT JEBEL DHANNA RESORT

I woke up to find Frosty already dressed and ready to go out. Today was supposed to have been a day of rest in Riyadh, a chance for some sightseeing, but our all-night ride had killed that option. Our disagreement with Diamond and Mohammed had also left both of us feeling queasy.

'I'm going with Diamond to take the bikes for a quick check,' he said. 'Our headlight needs a new bulb as it's too dim for night riding. I'll see you later.'

'Okay. I'm going to try to catch up on some more sleep.'

He picked me up later to return to the dealership for a briefing for the ride to Muscat the following day.

This Harley-Davidson showroom was more impressive than the smaller Jeddah branch. We walked through the array of new Harleys towards a short, stout man with dark hair and a goatee standing at the counter. Frosty introduced me to Marwan AlMutlaq, one of the owners. His brother, Monther, owned the branches in Jeddah and Bahrain.

'Ah, I'm pleased to meet you. I read your article in the *Arab News*, and I have something for you.' Marwan reached for a couple of small boxes on the shelf behind him. He handed them to me with a beaming smile. 'I thought you might like these as you wrote that you would miss your daily cappuccino on the journey.'

I was amused and touched that he had taken the trouble to buy me two packets of cappuccino sachets.

'Tomorrow I will be one of the road captains,' he said. Turning towards a man standing near him he added, 'And this is Amer AlKhaldi, our other road captain. Now let's go to the briefing.'

Like Marwan, Amer exuded warmth, and we also liked him at first meeting.

Only a few of us were there for the thorough audiovisual instruction given by these two men on the etiquette of group riding. We were to ride in two groups of ten bikes, each led by its own road captain with a sweeper, a rider at the back who makes sure everyone is okay and looks after anyone who breaks down.

'Most of the time, we'll ride in two lines of staggered formation,' Marwan told us, 'so each bike is about five metres behind the one in front. Please don't get out of line – stick in your position and no overtaking.'

With the aid of projected images, he demonstrated the hand signals used in group riding.

'When the road captain makes a hand signal, the rider behind must copy it, and the rider behind him, until it reaches the sweeper. Everyone needs to know what is going on – when we plan to turn, when we have to ride in single file, hazards on the road, and so on. There will be no stopping for anything but an accident. If anyone has a breakdown, the sweeper will take care of you. We have the backup van and a mechanic with us. We'll build up to a speed of 120, and if you're all happy we'll go to a max of 130. Fuel stops will be after every 160 kilometres.'

At the end of the briefing, we were given an article and a leaflet to remind us of the rules of the road, tips on group riding and the hand signals. The Riyadh Chapter seemed crisp and professional, with an emphasis on safety. We both felt a little nervous about riding with them and didn't want to mess up.

As we left the briefing area we bumped into Diamond and Houria. Although Frosty had been trying to patch things up with Diamond, the atmosphere between them and me crackled with unease.

'When you do more riding, you'll find this happens in groups,' said Diamond. 'People take off and go faster if they want to.'

'Well maybe they do, but last night you should have told us what you were planning to do. That is what upset us – you just took off,' I replied.

'If it makes you feel better, I'll say sorry.'

What I felt like snapping back at him was, 'Fuck you, Diamond.' But I bit my tongue. We stared at each other for a few moments, and I am sure he could read from the anger in my eyes what I thought of his spurious apology. But there was no point in me carrying on with the argument. I liked Diamond, and I didn't want our friendship damaged. Without him we wouldn't be here at all.

Mohammed had left on an early flight back to Jeddah without saying goodbye. The van was no longer needed and was staying in Riyadh with Amr's family. Caught in the middle, Amr was unhappy with the whole saga. He was a quiet man anyway, but he told me he would try to smooth things out between me and Houria. She was not looking me in the eye or greeting me. I hoped that by the time we reached Muscat, the atmosphere would have settled down.

I felt disappointed in Diamond. I had looked up to him and how he had taken care of Frosty, and then me, with his instruction and support. As an airline captain, he had been trained in the importance of communication. Riding off into the misty darkness after hours of night riding together, leaving us behind, seemed out of character. I couldn't figure out why he couldn't understand that.

We were up early the following morning to meet with the others riding to Muscat. The temperature was five Celsius so we had both layered up with a jersey and leather waistcoat under our leather jackets. There were twenty-two bikes, with Houria and me the only pillion riders. Nine of the men were Western or Arab expatriates, but what added to this amazing adventure for me was that we were sharing it with Saudi nationals. They accepted it as normal that expatriate women rode pillion with their husbands, but not one of them had brought a wife along, not even in a separate vehicle with a driver.

By 7.40am, we were rolling away from the Riyadh dealership behind Marwan on his cherry-red Ultra Glide. Because we were the most inexperienced in the group, he wanted us right behind him. Diamond and Houria came after us, and Amr came further back. At least we were still together.

I soon became aware that the Thunderheaders were still there. 'Frosty, I thought you were going to change the Thunderheaders in Riyadh?' I yelled at him over the noise.

'I'm sorry, I forgot,' he yelled back. 'We'll have to change them in Muscat.'

Muscat was 1,500 kilometres away. I guessed he had forgotten because of the stressful situation with Diamond.

As the day progressed, the temperature rose, and at each fuel stop, we removed another layer. Amr added another dent to his Road King when it slipped from under him on an oil spill as he cornered out of a fuel station onto the highway. He and the bike skidded across the road in opposite directions, leaving him shaken but not injured. It made us forever wary of anything that looked like oil on the road.

Our ride took us on a three-lane dual carriageway towards the east coast of Saudi Arabia. The desolate desert landscape was flat, with tufts of grass dotted about and small sand dunes here and there. Apart from a few trucks, there was little traffic. After we peeled off towards Al Ahsa, the largest date palm oasis in the world, we had miles of two-lane highway stretching ahead of us, skirting the edge of the vast Empty Quarter desert. In Saudi Arabia, the roads were excellent; we didn't have to worry about potholes. Long stretches had no camel fences, and a few times we came across these ungainly beasts grazing beside the road. They looked up when they heard us approaching, but we never knew what they might do. Some stood still; others ran away towards the desert; and one group careered across the road in front of us.

I entertained myself by making mental notes of what I saw to jot down in my journal later, taking photos and copying whatever hand signals came from Marwan. My right foot was still a background worry as it had a habit of slipping off its footrest, but I didn't feel it. I would see Frosty reach down to lift it back on, giving my leg a reassuring pat as he did so.

If the group was getting too spread out, I would hear the snarl of the sweeper's bike as he came up the line, urging us to keep up. Because Marwan had taken the precaution of warning the police that a big group of Harleys would be riding this route, we had no trouble at the three checkpoints.

Eight hours after leaving Riyadh we arrived at Batha, the coastal border town to the United Arab Emirates (UAE). At Jeddah airport, the immigration authorities can be surly and unwelcoming, so it was a surprise to be greeted by cheerful, pro-British border officials here.

'*Ahlan*.' Welcome. 'Brittania good!'

Anytime we mentioned British, we got the thumbs-up sign and big smiles.

Our entry into the UAE was efficient but still took a couple of hours because we were a large group, and everyone had to buy motorcycle insurance. By the time we were through, the light was fading, and we faced another few hours of night riding. UAE time was an hour ahead of Saudi, making it 6.20pm when we set off towards the Danat Jebel Dhanna Resort. Despite the setting sun, none of the Muslims mentioned prayers – they hadn't done all day, and huddling up for the traveller's prayer didn't happen again after Taïf.

The moment we had entered the more liberal Emirates, everyone relaxed. We no longer had to worry about police checkpoints, motorcycles not being allowed on the road, women riding pillion or religious police harassing us. Petrol stations, shops, cafés and restaurants didn't close for prayer times. We were also looking forward to a legal, cold beer or a glass of wine.

We rode along a three-lane highway with street lighting the entire way, and Marwan led us at a steady 110 kilometres per hour. By now, the hammering of the Thunderheader exhaust pipes sounded as though it was coming from speakers inside my head. I was surprised I didn't have a throbbing migraine and couldn't wait to have them changed in Muscat. We stopped once at a petrol station and what a huge difference to the grubby ones in Saudi. Everything was clean, rubbish-free, with a café and small supermarket included. But best of all, I walked into a clean washroom with sit-on toilets. I used to dread using the dirty squat-down ones in the Saudi stops, with nowhere to wash or dry my hands. The UAE economy depended to a great extent on Western tourism, so the country met their expectations, whereas Saudi Arabia catered to their local traffic, predominantly truck drivers from developing countries. Western expatriates who bothered to explore the country had to put up with these basic facilities.

The fuel stations on both sides of the border had one thing in common. The Asian pump attendants always asked Frosty the same question: 'How much money your bike?' I thought they would ask how fast it went, but they were only interested in the price.

It was 8.00pm when we pulled into the Danat Jebel Dhanna Resort car park after a 780-kilometre journey. The riders reversed their Harleys into place in the usual neat line, the front wheels all facing towards the left. At last, Maridadi's engine went quiet. I lifted my helmet off and blurted out, 'Thank God for that. We have to get rid of those bloody exhaust pipes.'

As before, I got a kick out of listening to the tinkling, clinking, pinging, ticking and other metallic sounds that made up the symphony of a group of hot motorcycles cooling down.

Danat Jebel Dhanna was a five-star resort hotel, the like of which didn't exist in the Kingdom. Miniskirted Russian hostesses greeted us, smiling and proffering trays with welcome drinks. No longer did I have to worry about my shirt sleeves being too short or whether I'd be in trouble for not wearing an abaya. I could be normal. And so could everyone else. Unlike in Saudi Arabia where alcohol was illegal, no one was going to arrest us here for drinking. After checking into our rooms, we headed for the bar, and it wasn't only the expatriates quaffing cold beers. A few Saudis were enjoying them too. This ride was providing an opportunity to socialise on an equal footing. A burden was lifted from us all.

I always think you can tell the true quality of a hotel by the bedding, and Danat Jebel Dhanna Resort knew how to look after its guests. Our tired bodies sank into the most luxurious bed I have ever slept in. Super king sized with high thread count, silky cotton sheets and a lightweight, goose down duvet and two soft, down pillows. Pure heaven.

The lamentable aspect of this opulence was that we couldn't indulge in it for long enough. Our wake-up call came at 5.30am for a 7.00am departure. By the time we had dressed, packed and had breakfast, there wasn't a moment left to explore the other luxuries of the resort. We had to move on to Muscat.

9

ONWARDS TO MUSCAT

When we headed for the car park, the sun was still below the horizon, the air crisp and chilly. The line-up of parked Harleys appeared in the gloom, and men greeted each other as they packed overnight kit into panniers and buffed up chrome and paintwork. Each pulled on his jacket, shrugged shoulders into place and zipped up. Next the helmets wriggled over their ears, then shifted back and forth into a comfortable position and secured under the chin. Engines growled into life, and Marwan signalled it was time to leave.

We set off down the dual carriageway, the rising sun shining through the morning mist, reflecting off the road and suffusing everything in a golden light.

Without any warning, Marwan and the bikes ahead of us came to a sudden stop. Frosty braked hard and Maridadi skidded in a patch of sand. Once again, my behind lost its place on the saddle, this time thumping down onto the hard road.

'Bugger,' I muttered, suppressing an urge to cry. It wasn't the pain so much as the shock and indignity.

Men were off their bikes, rushing to give Frosty a hand to heave Maridadi upright and help me up. We were getting good at this. No harm done, we settled back into the ride.

'I am very sorry; that was my fault,' said Marwan later. 'I missed the turning.'

The UAE was renowned for its superb racehorses and kept its roads in the same well-groomed condition. They were smooth, with marked lanes and yellow lines along the edges and no sign of litter anywhere. Golden dunes rolled away from us on either side.

As we entered Al Ain, a large road sign read "Peace Be With You". It resonated with me because of the conflicts that plague the Middle East, with two or more countries at war almost all the time. When they make peace, others find something to fight about. Some hostilities extend into lengthy civil wars.

Al Ain in the Emirate of Abu Dhabi is known as the Garden City, and it was easy to see why. Trees, hedges and flower beds flourished on either side of us and along the central reservation. After the chaotic driving in Saudi Arabia, it was a pleasure to be amongst other road users who followed the Highway Code.

After Al Ain, we were back in the desert heading towards the brown, rocky hills of Oman. At the border, everyone had to buy insurance for their motorcycles again.

The Omani immigration building was the most modern and imposing we'd seen so far. For the first time in my decades in the Middle East, I saw a "Disabled Parking" sign, a wheelchair ramp, and a disabled toilet facility inside.

While Frosty was dealing with the formalities, I went back outside to the parked Harleys to take photos. They stood in their uniform, neat row, each one a symbol of the personality of its owner. Sun glinted off the polished chrome and paintwork. I wandered along the line, taking shots of various details: glossy flames licking over fuel tanks and mudguards; footrests, foot pegs and gear levers all in matching bespoke designs; big headlights whose curved chrome gave a fisheye reflection of me against the blue sky. Diamond's Ultra Classic and Maridadi stood out, with their elaborate paint schemes and Diamond's trademark skull embellishments.

Two hours later, we were on our way to Muscat, led by a police escort. The day had heated up, and we rode under a deep blue sky along an immaculate dual carriageway. Clipped hedges ran alongside us, and every roundabout was decorated with a fancy monument surrounded by lawns and colourful flower beds. Outside Sohar, an enormous courtyard of double archways spanned the road, heralding the gateway to this historical port and the mythical birthplace of Sinbad the Sailor.

Like the UAE, there was no sign of the litter that plagued the roadsides and landscapes of Saudi Arabia. Where there was no pavement, the sandy roadside was swept and tidy.

If these nations care about their surroundings, I mused, *why can't Saudi?*

As the light faded, the street lights came on, illuminating the highway all the way to the capital. We arrived on the outskirts of Muscat in time to merge with the evening rush hour. I hadn't expected the city to be so large or for there to be so much traffic. It moved fast and we were thankful that Marwan and the police escort were ahead to show us the way.

When we parked Maridadi at the Intercontinental Hotel at 7.00pm, we had ridden 2,500 kilometres. The tension with Houria and Diamond had evaporated, and we could celebrate our achievement. For them and Amr, this was simply the end of another long journey. It represented so much more for Frosty and me. We had embarked on a new personal journey, and were sharing the biggest adventure we'd had for years. I had also discovered the euphoria of fear, making me feel alive again.

When we walked into the lofty lobby of the hotel, there were no miniskirted Russian girls. Instead, we were greeted by a ceiling-high, decorated Christmas tree. We had grown used to Saudi Arabia's refusal to acknowledge any religion but Islam, so to see Oman celebrating the Christian festival was an unexpected welcome. The country was among the Arab nations that had a reputation for peace and tolerance.

That evening we could again chug cold beers and sip other alcoholic drinks as we had done in the UAE. On returning to Saudi Arabia, we would be like flowers that close when the sun goes down – we would all shrivel back into our restricted lives.

Some two hundred Harleys had shown up for the rally. In the morning, Frosty and I joined thirty of them for a fun ride through the mountains which formed a dramatic backdrop to the city. This was our chance to see Muscat in daylight. Al Ain had impressed me, but here someone had done an outstanding job of landscaping this desert city's streets. On either side, and in the central reservations and roundabouts, were flower beds with red, yellow and pink blooms. I could even smell them as we rode past. In the centre of the roundabouts, and any large open spaces, was neat, mown lawn. Trimmed hedges and trees flourished behind the roadside flower beds. There wasn't a scrap of litter anywhere, yet unlike in Jeddah, I didn't see any street cleaners or gardeners.

Dubai and Abu Dhabi are known for their impressive skyscrapers, but Muscat was a low-rise city with all the buildings painted white. Ministerial properties were contemporary versions of traditional forts: big, solid buildings combining ancient features with clean, modern designs. It was strange not to see any shops or people in the streets but, unlike European cities, modern Middle Eastern ones aren't designed with pedestrians in mind. Somewhere hidden in the old section was a characterful *souq*. Like the Old Town of Jeddah, it would be teeming with pedestrians, but it wasn't on our sightseeing list.

Our first stop was at the city's largest fuel station, a set-up that could easily handle refuelling thirty Harleys, but Frosty and I didn't get beyond filling up. As the forecourt resonated with the revving of bikes, Maridadi refused to turn over. Instead of roaring through the countryside with the others, we took a taxi to the Harley dealership. Once we'd bought ourselves souvenir Muscat Harley T-shirts, we were driven back by two mechanics who were standing by all weekend for breakdowns.

While the mechanics fixed the ignition fuse, a character riding an Ultra Glide pulled in beside us to refuel. Seeing us with our Harley, he introduced himself.

'Steve Betz, Director of the Dammam group, and Coordinator of the rally,' he said in an American drawl. 'What's up?'

While Frosty explained the problem, I figured out the two men were about the same age. Steve's silver-grey hair was cropped short, and his long jawline sported a day or two's stubble. His rugged good looks were complemented by an aquiline nose and hazel-green eyes. He wore faded blue jeans, patched in several places and ripped at the knees. His sleeveless T-shirt and well-worn leather Harley vest emphasised the tattoos on his muscled arms, and his raspy voice sounded as though his larynx needed new exhaust pipes. I watched him light up a cigarette, then start up to ride away.

Amused by his maverick persona, I said, 'I can't believe you can ride a motorbike and smoke at the same time.'

He gave me a sideways look and winked, then reached down to the left of his handlebars and produced a small object.

'I even have a cigarette lighter on my bike.'

With Maridadi running again, we took off on our first long ride without the reassuring company of Diamond, Amr or any other bikes. For a few minutes, I smiled at the memory of sexy Steve with a cigarette lighter on his motorbike.

We took the same route as the group, through the mountains to Quriyat, a small fishing village on the Gulf of Oman eighty kilometres away. After the stress of keeping up with a pack, it felt good to be able to cruise at our own pace. The excellent two-way road wound its way up through craggy mountains, then descended to Quriyat. As we made our way through the narrow streets towards the seafront, a boy of about eight stood in the middle of the road, arms outstretched, forcing Frosty to stop. Another boy of similar age then threw a stone at us. It ricocheted off Frosty's helmet. Not quite the welcome we had expected.

Further on, when we stopped by the harbour, a group of young boys dressed in bright red, yellow, blue and green football shirts rushed over to Maridadi. No stones this time. These boys were laughing and excited, their hands reaching out to grasp Frosty's throttle hand, forcing it to twist. They wanted to hear the Harley revs. Unlike me, they loved the roar of our noisy Thunderheader exhaust pipes. When they'd had their fun, we turned around to ride back – there were no waterside cafés in Quriyat to linger in.

On our return trip through the mountains, we came across Marwan and stopped. He was sitting cross-legged like a Buddha on some rocks by the roadside, in the shade of a small acacia tree. Its spindly, leafless branches gave enough shade for one. After the long ride and responsibilities of a road captain, he was hanging out with Arab friends. They stood around chatting, their only refreshment being water from plastic bottles. All were dressed in black biking gear. A few – like Marwan – wore black bandanas knotted on their heads. With the bikes parked haphazardly in a bleak landscape of brown rocks, it looked like a scene from *Mad Max 2*. After a brief chat with Marwan, we continued on our way.

Maridadi got us back to Muscat where her electrics packed up again. By now, I was relieved that these breakdowns hadn't happened on the remote desert roads from Jeddah or on our solo ride to Quriyat. Instead of taking part in the fun and games of the rider obstacle course and entering Maridadi in the Harley concours, we had to order a rescue truck. Maridadi was taken to the dealership for more repairs and to change the Thunderheader exhaust pipes for something quieter. We went back to our hotel, where the rally activities were going on.

While I was admiring some of the Harleys, I got talking to another biker who looked in his mid-fifties, like Frosty. We were noting the average age of the participants.

'We're known as BAMBIES,' he said. 'Born-Again Middle-Aged Bikers. That's why Harleys suit us. They're not speed bikes and aren't the most exciting to ride. We like them because we buy into a lifestyle. Once you're a HOG member, you become part of a worldwide club.'

That evening, as we donned clean black jeans and boots, new Harley T-shirts and our medal-adorned leather waistcoats for the Bikers Ball, I said to Frosty, 'This reminds me of that scene in *Cat Ballou* when Lee Marvin gets spruced up in his black, gunfighter finery to have a dual. We're just missing the spurs and pistols.'

Although I felt a little self-conscious in my new fancy dress, we blended well with the rest of the HOG crowd.

Steve Betz was on the stage, a different man, clean-shaven and wearing beige slacks and a pale striped shirt. He had morphed into a business role to thank the rally's sponsors and helpers. The Harley biking get-up represented an alter ego for these professionals with their serious day jobs. In their offices and at board meetings, or in their airline cockpits, no one would have guessed that this was how they relaxed and dressed at weekends. From the emblem on the back of each vest, we could see to which chapter people belonged. Most were from Middle Eastern countries, but I noticed ones from Norway and Argentina.

A lot of Harley men liked to smoke cigars, so while the rest of the Western expatriate men and women were up dancing, they puffed away and drank beer.

'I don't see many biker chicks here,' the DJ called out between tracks.

None of the Arab men had brought their wives or girlfriends with them, but that didn't stop them from shaking their tail feathers. All-male dancing was part of their culture. Gathered around in a circle, they clapped and cheered each other on, taking turns to perform in the middle. Having never seen our Saudis in a social context like this in their home country, it was a revelation to see their fun, crazy side.

Behind this testosterone-fuelled event was a tall, blonde, buxom Texan, Lisa Schlensker. She was the manager for HOG

Middle East, based in Bahrain, and one of the few Middle Eastern Ladies of Harley who owned and rode her own motorbike. She was the only woman I ever saw greet a Saudi man in the public space of the Jeddah dealership with a kiss on both cheeks. Now she was on the stage with Steve Betz and the AlMutlaq brothers, making announcements, handing out prizes and thanking everyone involved in the event. She squeezed in recognition of our long ride, the bikers who'd ridden the furthest to get here.

During the evening, Marwan introduced me to Lisa and his brother, Monther, who owned the Bahrain and Jeddah dealerships. They had both seen my article in the *Arab News*. It was the first time a story had appeared in the Saudi press about Harley riding in the region.

'Thanks for the article,' Lisa said. 'That was great publicity for us.'

'That was the first in the series,' I told them. 'Two others will follow, so look out for them. I hope *HOG Tales* will also publish my story.'

The following day was the Thunder Roll when all the bikes rode through the town together. We had hoped to have Maridadi back, but when the mechanics took her for a test run, smoke belched out from behind her headlight. They had to replace all the wiring.

Not wanting to miss my first ride with over two hundred Harleys, I asked Amr if he could take me, while Frosty went with another biker. I had imagined it would be a dignified procession through the city because it had been scheduled to last for three hours. Instead, the road captain led the long, double line of motorbikes at a cracking pace. Huge flags fluttered on poles held by pillion riders, displaying which chapter they were from. On the way, by pointing my lens backwards and resting the camera on my shoulder, I captured shots of the snake of bikes coming up a long hill behind us. We continued past impressive roundabout monuments, the arch of the Muscat Gate Museum marking the entrance to the old city, a castle perched on top of a rocky headland and the palm-fringed Corniche Road overlooking the aquamarine sea. Here, the stream of bikes doubled back and smiling riders and pillions waved at each other as they went by. A fizzy thrill rushed through me to be among them. My traumatic years of rehab and litigation dimmed into the past.

Our departure the following morning to Dubai was under an overcast sky with a chill in the air. Maridadi now purred along the highway through her new exhaust pipes. Now that the Thunderheader racket had gone, I could relax into the final 460 kilometres of our adventure. These daily distances now felt normal. With Marwan in the lead again, we rode with Diamond, Houria, Amr and the Riyadh Chapter. Our Harleys were to be left at the dealership in Dubai and later trucked back to Riyadh or Jeddah while we flew home.

As we neared the city of Dubai, the downtown cluster of skyscrapers loomed in the dusty haze. Their jagged outline made me feel as though I was riding towards Manhattan, not another Middle Eastern metropolis. We rode through the heart of Dubai, along its main artery, with glass structures soaring up on either side. Its modern materialism couldn't have contrasted more to Muscat's rich history as the capital of the maritime Omani Empire and the most important trading port in the Indian Ocean.

We parked our Harleys at the dealership and made for the airport.

I'd resisted getting Maridadi, but now I wished we could ride all the way back to Jeddah. Our next long ride wouldn't be for a few months.

10

AL HARIDHAH FESTIVAL

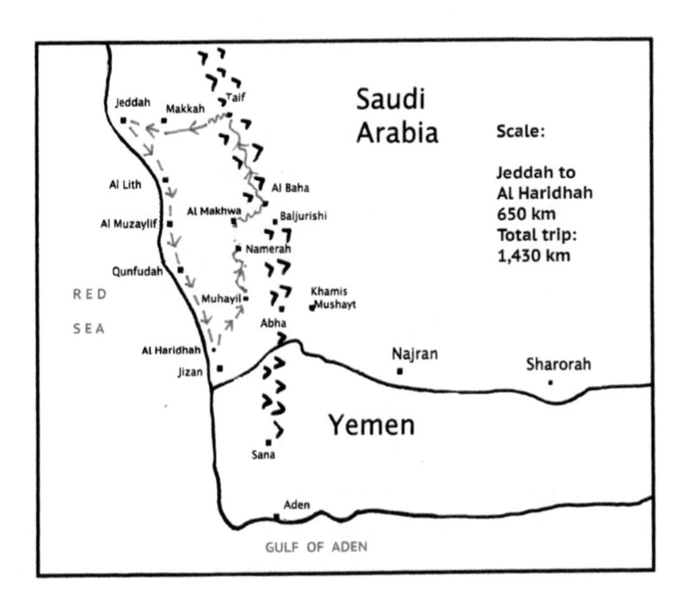

When returning to the Kingdom at the end of any long holiday, I felt like I did as a child when it was time to return to boarding school. My stomach churned during the days leading up to it. In January 2006, when we flew back to Jeddah from our Christmas break in Kenya, Frosty admitted to having the same nausea that had also affected him when it was time to go back to school. Then and now we faced an environment of strict rules, except the consequences of breaking them were more serious in the Kingdom. His fear of losing his job if he made an error with his flying, or caused unintended offence by something he said or did, was constant. And yet ironically, we both thought of Jeddah as "home".

Our gloominess was swept away within days of arriving back. The Harley-Davidson dealership called to announce that Prince Khalid Al Faisal bin Abdul Aziz, Governor of the Asir Region, had invited the Jeddah HOGs to attend the annual Al Haridhah festival. This small town on the Red Sea was six hundred kilometres south of Jeddah. A brochure of Al Haridhah was circulated, showing sailing boats in full sail, people windsurfing and riding wave runners, scuba diving, horse riding, playing beach volleyball and hang-gliding. Apart from images of Saudi men doing their traditional sword dance, and a clown entertaining a group of children, we knew the rest of it was a lot of tosh. Jeddah was the most cosmopolitan and sophisticated seaside city in the Kingdom, so if our city fell short of these activities there was no way that the small, provincial town of Al Haridhah would provide them. No resort from Egypt southwards to Kenya offered anything like the fun promised in the brochure.

From our years of travelling around the Kingdom we knew this. The Saudis, most of whom had done little travelling around their own country, swallowed the hype. Sixty bikers registered.

A few days before we left, a new couple around our age arrived in town on their Electra Glide Classic. Peter and Kay Forward were Australian, set on travelling through every country in the world on the same bike with the same engine. Having failed once to get into Saudi Arabia, they had spent three weeks in Bahrain trying again. There, they got to know the AlMutlaq brothers who helped to arrange their visas, and they rode from Bahrain to Jeddah.

Stickers from sponsors and countries they had visited covered their Electra Glide. They travelled self-contained with motorcycle maintenance tools, camping and cooking gear, so the bike was fully loaded. If they were too far from civilisation they camped by the roadside. En route to Jeddah, they had spent a night in one of the cheap hotels on the Saudi highway, part of the cluster of shops and restaurants around a fuel station.

Before the ride to Al Haridhah, we got to know Peter and Kay over dinner in our home, as well as during an evening out at a local restaurant organised by the Jeddah HOG Chapter. I also interviewed them for the *Arab News*.

We were to learn a good riding policy from Peter, a man used to biking alone or with Kay. He always went at his own pace of a hundred kilometres per hour, never allowing himself to be pressured to go faster.

'No matter who we are with, it's still my ride,' he told us.

This was to become our motorcycling mantra. "It's our ride". At stake on any biking trip was our safety.

It was still dark when we gathered at the dealership for the long journey to Al Haridhah. Peter and Kay were riding with us, but only twenty-five of the sixty bikers registered showed up. Eight police vehicles, plus an unmarked police car and an ambulance, had been assigned to take care of us. We were a mix of Saudis, including our friend Amr Khashoggi, some expatriate Arabs, our Canadian friend Steve and some Europeans. One of the Saudis was accompanied by his wife and three children in their family people mover with a driver. He had attached a trailer for his bike in case he tired of riding. His children had wanted to stay in Jeddah for the weekend, but he had persuaded them they were going to a wonderful beach resort.

We left Jeddah before dawn under an indigo sky scattered with pink clouds, the best time to leave on a long ride. By the time the golden orb of the sun appeared over the Hejaz Mountains, we were well on our way. The two-way road was flat, straight and free of traffic. Empty desert stretched to the horizon on either side of us.

'Thank you, Maridadi,' I whispered as a thrill of freedom chased away my Jeddah blues, 'you've come to my rescue.'

About an hour out of Jeddah, I looked to my right at the massive desalination plant at Schwayba, with its four tall chimneys belching smoke. We had one in Jeddah and gauged the weather by checking the smoke. If it was blowing southwards, we knew our weather was steady. Northwards meant a weather change. Sometimes the south wind brought a rare thunderstorm, but more often it meant a sandstorm was brewing.

That morning, a strong southerly wind was blowing the smoke northwards, flat and parallel to the horizon, leaving a murky mist beneath it. Trouble was on the way.

Compared to our disciplined ride with the Riyadh Chapter, this was at times chaotic. But it wasn't the bikers; it was our police escort. Each time we pulled into a fuel station, police cars barged ahead, their sirens blaring and horns squawking, demanding the other travellers make way. On the two-way highway they were aggressive, overtaking the line of Harleys and driving head-on into the oncoming traffic, forcing vehicles off the road.

At one point a new metre-wide central reservation separated the lanes under construction on the other side. Looking over Frosty's shoulder, I saw an oncoming van mount it to get out of the way, almost flipping onto the bikes ahead of us. It set my heart racing. It would have caused a multiple pile-up, with us involved. The van straddled the reservation, sparks flying as the metal underside scraped against the concrete until it ground to a standstill. At our lunch stop, someone told us one of the police cars had pulled over to deal with the situation. They discovered the van was full of illegal immigrants being smuggled up from the Yemen.

The Forwards kept themselves well out of this nonsense, holding back at a steady one hundred kilometres per hour. Most of the time we cruised at 130 kilometres per hour.

Riding in front of us was a young Saudi who had a chopper bike. These iconic machines, with their extended front forks and high ape-hanger handlebars, were made after World War II when enthusiasts wanted bikes stripped of all the fuss and weight to improve their performance. They chopped them up and rebuilt them, customising new motorcycles to suit personal tastes. The 1969 film *Easy Rider* had given them cult status.

In conservative Saudi Arabia, the police had no idea that the chopper was a symbol of rebellion. The two cruised alongside each other, the chopper and the law, a bizarre juxtaposition.

I kept myself entertained monitoring and taking pictures of our home-grown Easy Rider fidgeting on his bike. He had three sets of footrests and couldn't decide which gave him the most comfortable riding position. His name was Hatem. He looked like a teenager on his chopper, but later I learned he was thirty-two years old, in the Saudi military and married with three children.

From Jeddah to Al Haridhah, the road followed the coastal Tihama plains. By now, Frosty was riding with more confidence, so although I still kept a beady eye on the road ahead for hazards, I felt more relaxed with him, and I didn't have to endure the Thunderheader exhaust pipes. We stopped every hour and a half to refuel, stretch our legs and ease sore bums. Lunch was about halfway, at Al Lith, in a beachside restaurant catering for weekend scuba divers. The waiters served us excellent fish, rice and salad. We also had the treat of clean washrooms.

As I settled onto Maridadi for the next leg of our journey, I reflected again on how she had changed my life. I had been plucked from my safe, daily routine and forced to confront my fears about doing something that might further jeopardise my damaged body. The element of danger inherent in biking added a thrill to our new adventures, rekindled my rebel spirit and boosted my energy. My anger and distress, coupled with other people's opinions that the surgery had ruined my life, were being challenged. My philosophy was that it would be my own choices and attitude that would ruin my life, not the outcome of the surgery. But at times I faltered. I knew I would still be struggling with the concept if Diamond hadn't mentioned the ride to Oman. Now I accepted that although my disability had challenged me in every way, it hadn't ruined my life. It was an indelible aspect of *me*. And without it, we might never have bought Maridadi.

By the time we pulled up at our destination, it was late afternoon. Instead of being on the beach, our hotel was a cluster of cream-coloured stone buildings, set back from the main road. The sea was nowhere in sight. And this wasn't a proper hotel – our accommodation comprised self-catering apartments, used by local tourists escaping the cold in the mountains of Abha. They had been closed for some weeks. At the request of the prince, it reopened with a skeleton staff. There was no one at the reception to greet us, and no rooms had been allocated.

Chaos erupted because it seemed at first they didn't have enough space for everyone. When Saudis get agitated, they're like Italians – arms wave around; there's lots of shouting; no one listens to anyone. The man with his family was furious.

'What is this? This isn't a bloody beach hotel! This is nothing.'

'Why did you make us come here?' his wife demanded. 'We wanted to stay in Jeddah.'

'Right. We are going back. Now!'

He loaded his family back into the van, put his bike onto the trailer and headed for Jeddah. After their eight-hour drive, his wife and children now faced a night-long ordeal cooped up in the car. Another disillusioned biker followed behind them.

While rooms were being allocated, Peter and Kay arrived.

'How about we share one of the cottages,' I suggested to them. 'At least that will solve one problem for them.'

It also put a little distance between us and the Saudis, who I felt sure would stay up late playing cards and being noisy. The beds seemed comfortable and the place clean. At least a meal was ready for us, so we all sat down to an early dinner in the restaurant.

A few hours later we rode in convoy towards the sea where the festival was taking place. After parking the Harleys, we joined the hundreds of people seated around a central stage. It was an all-male gathering, save for us four expatriate women: Egyptian, Danish, British and Australian. Second-row seats behind the dignitaries were reserved for the HOGs. We were right in front of the stage and could observe and listen to poetry readings in Arabic. Because of its close association with the Koran, this literary art form is a revered Arab tradition.

As the last poem ended, we heard the voice of the muezzin resonate from the minaret, calling the people to prayer.

'*Allahu akbar*,' echoed several times in the night air.

In Jeddah, all the men would have gone off to pray. Here in the Asir, only a handful stood up and made for the mosque. The rest remained, chatting.

After this came the traditional men's sword dance, the *ardha*, which originated as a celebration of military achievements and victory in battle. The sword wasn't part of men's traditions in the Asir, so instead, the four groups dancing wore a belt and dagger, an essential part of their daily dress. Camera at the ready, I watched them parade onto the stage to the sound of loud drumming. Their ages ranged from boys to elderly men. The groups were of the Qahtani tribe of the Asir, men who were short, sometimes stocky. Traditional floral wreaths adorned their heads, and they wore bright, striped sarong-like wraps tied around their waists with their shirts hanging out over them. Because of their wreaths of yellow marigolds and aromatic herbs, the Qahtani had earned the moniker, the flower men. In rhythm to the primitive and hypnotic drumbeat, they stepped back and forth, stamping their feet and waving their daggers in the air.

The third group were older men, dressed in conventional white *thobes*. Besides their daggers, they carried old, long-barrelled muskets.

'Frosty, I am going to the front to get better pictures,' I whispered.

'Are you sure? Don't you think you'll be a bit conspicuous out there in front of everyone?'

'No, I think it'll be fine.'

I made my way to the front left of the stage and huddled down in position. Watching the men through my viewfinder, I snapped a few pictures as they moved back and forth, holding their muskets in front of them.

Bang! Bang! Bang! Shots blasted out. I jerked back, eyes wide with fright, heart thudding. My first thought was a terrorist attack. I just managed to stop myself from crashing over backwards. Embarrassed by my reaction, and feeling silly, I realised it was the old muskets being fired. I could smell the gunpowder from the puffs of smoke floating away and hoped no one had seen me. I settled back in position, heart still thumping and hands shaking as I turned my eyes back to the stage.

The following morning at breakfast there was more mayhem. The Forwards, Frosty and I were settled at our table in the restaurant when the only waiter came to take our order. We ordered some omelettes and tea and chatted while we waited for them to arrive. Fifteen minutes passed, and a group of Saudis seated nearby lost patience. They headed for the kitchen. We followed a few minutes later to see what was going on.

'Sorry, madam,' the waiter apologised, 'but they have eaten the omelettes I cooked for you.'

He pointed across to the group of Saudis at the kitchen counter. They had seen our eggs cooking, hijacked them and devoured the lot.

'Don't worry,' said Peter, taking control. 'We can cook our own breakfast. Have you got any more eggs?'

After breakfast, the Saudis and expatriate Arabs declared they'd had enough. They had seen what was on offer for tourists and weren't impressed.

'We're going back to Jeddah,' one of them said. 'But Saīd rang and told us that last night they went through a bad sandstorm.'

'Do any of you have Vaseline or anything to protect your bikes?' asked Frosty. 'You need to protect your paintwork and chrome with something.'

'No, we haven't, but we'll go anyway.'

'Okay, I hope it isn't too bad. The rest of us are going to carry on into the mountains. We'll see you in Jeddah.'

Frosty and I had toured the Asir Mountains several times before in our Nissan Patrol, either camping or staying in hotels. We suggested to the group left behind that we ride up to Al Baha, spend a night or two there and ride back to Jeddah. This way we might also avoid the sandstorm. Peter and Kay opted out, deciding to see how the festival developed. They needed time to reorganise themselves before they headed for Sudan.

Our extended tour attracted a like-minded international group that we began to ride with regularly. Ahmed, our chapter director, was the one Saudi who stayed with us, and he assumed the role of road captain. We ditched seven of the eight police cars and the plain one. Now a single vehicle led the way.

11

AL BAHA AND THE ASIR MOUNTAINS

By the time we left Al Haridhah, the tail end of the sandstorm had reached us. We set off in swirling dust.

Before we moved to Saudi Arabia, I had imagined it to be one enormous desert, mostly flat, but with areas of huge sand dunes. What I hadn't expected was the Sarawat mountain range running two thousand kilometres along the western edge of the country, starting in Yemen in the south, and continuing almost to the Gulf of Aqaba in Jordan. The highest point in Saudi is Jebel Sawda at 3,133 metres, a few kilometres west of the town of Abha. In this southern part of the country, the range is known as the *Asir*, meaning difficult. Further north, the midsection east of Jeddah is called the Hejaz. The word stems from the Arabic meaning to separate, as it divides the central Nejd region from the Tihama in the west.

When planning our first long safari to Najran in 1986, a friend whose work took him all over the Kingdom had told us about the alternative routes up and down the range between Jeddah and Abha. After that, whenever we took a trip to the south, we explored these possibilities as well as the options on the Tihama plains and the roads that wound along the foothills.

Now we headed inland to Muhayil on a road nearly as straight as the one along the Tihama. The next section to Al Makhwah ran parallel to the mountains, winding through the foothills in a series of sweeping S-bends.

As we rode through small villages, we passed blindfolded camels working in the shade of crude, corrugated-iron shelters. They extracted oil from sesame seeds by turning a giant wooden pestle inside its mortar. The pestle was attached to a rough-hewn wooden framework, weighted with large stones and attached by ropes to a camel. An attendant – expatriate Asian, not Saudi – watched over the beast as it walked in eternal circles. Another camel sat in the shade, ruminating and waiting for his shift. I had heard this practice had stopped, but we passed several more camels hard at work.

We were heading towards the land of one-thousand-and-one-watchtowers, a characteristic unique to the Asir. These tall, drystone towers, *qasaba*, dotted the hilltops from Taïf to Abha, a distance of 550 kilometres. Built from the local grey stone, they rose like natural features out of the landscape. Zigzag lines of white flint stone, another distinctive element of the area, decorated the turrets at the top.

With one police vehicle leading the way, our ride was relaxed. Every fifty kilometres, another was waiting on the roadside to take over, their relays smooth and efficient. Each officer set his own pace, so sometimes we roared along at 130 kilometres per hour; at others we bumbled at eighty kilometres per hour.

Several times large signs warned us of checkpoints, and policemen emerged from their roadside concrete cabin or cars beside the barrier. Ahmed got off his bike and had a courtesy chat, but they never requested our ID cards or motorcycle documents. Having him as our road captain and a police escort eliminated any harassment. There was no question of being told motorbikes weren't allowed or women pillion riders forbidden.

By the time we reached Al Makhwah and the turning for the winding road to Al Baha, the ochre-yellow cloud of the sandstorm had spread across the Tihama plains. At the base of the escarpment, we passed the drystone village of Dhee Ayn, set against a backdrop of rugged mountains. Expatriates knew it as the Marble Village as the picturesque pyramid of houses sat on top of an exposed seam of white granite. It is one of the few complete stone villages left in Saudi Arabia, reputed to be four hundred years old.

Our convoy meandered up the contours of the escarpment, riders leaning into the perfectly cambered corners. There was little traffic on the road. Large red signs warned us of "Dangerous Curves", but our biggest threat was the occasional oncoming vehicle whose driver ignored the central white line and came speeding around these bends on our side of the road. On one side of us, the rocky hillside towered almost vertically, while on the other the drop became more dramatic the higher we went. High above us, I caught glimpses of the bridges we would ride across on our way up. They were supported by long, concrete legs, carrying the road as it leapt across the chasms between the ridges. Numerous tunnels carved their way through the granite mountainside, embracing us in their blackness, then surrendering us to daylight the other end.

Other tunnels were constructed over the road to protect traffic from rockfalls. The longer ones had large, outward-facing portholes whose glare flashed past like strobe lights. Sunshine streamed through them, casting a succession of oval shapes onto the asphalt.

As we rode, I captured images of the bikes exiting these dark tubes, framed by the structure's arc. Having a new digital camera meant that I could check each shot. With practice I got the right exposure compensation to override the gloom inside and retain detail in the bright landscape outside. By resting the camera on my right shoulder with the lens facing backwards, I also perfected a knack of capturing the bikes coming up behind us, headlights blazing in the darkness.

The journey up the mountains took us from the scorching heat of the lowlands to temperatures that were twenty Celsius lower at the top.

After a night in Al Baha at the Palace Hotel, the police escort was waiting to lead us to Taïf. Our route to the east of the mountains took us through misty, yellow air caused by the persistent southern wind churning up the sand.

When we arrived at the bottom of Al Hada escarpment, we caught up with the dense sandstorm that the others had ridden through. By now, it had been blowing for three days. Anticipating this might happen, after our lunch stop in Taïf, Frosty had covered Maridadi's chrome and paintwork with a layer of Vaseline.

This was our first experience of riding through a proper sandstorm. Low flurries of sand rippled across the road, and visibility around us was reduced by the churned-up grains dancing in the air. The sinking afternoon sun ahead of us shone through the dust particles, suffusing the scene with a golden light.

The card in my digital camera was full, but I had my old Nikon F4 film camera hanging around my neck. With the sand swirling around me, I huddled over it to load a roll of transparency film, hoping the camera wouldn't fill with damaging grit as I did so. Practising the over-shoulder shots with my digital Nikon had paid off, and I captured photos of the bikes behind and ahead of us riding through the murkiness. Mini dunes were piling up along the side of the road. As I peered over Frosty's shoulder, the couple in front skidded on a heap of sand that had built up across the tarmac.

I loved the drama of riding in these conditions, of being out in the open, battling through this gritty cloud in the same way Bedouins and their camels had done for centuries. As though in response to my thoughts, I looked to our right and saw a long line of camels ambling across the desert towards us through the haze. A Bedouin, head and face wrapped in his red and white *shammagh* with only his eyes showing, rode his camel alongside them. Our seven Harleys continued passed a flock of sheep, bunched together against the wind. Two shepherds, sheltering in their midst, bobbed up to watch us go by.

As we approached Jeddah, the city loomed ahead shrouded in an orange mist. I knew when I took my helmet off, my face would have the abrasive texture of an emery board. Then we'd find a fine layer of sand over everything in the house. Despite closed windows, it found its way in through the tiniest cracks.

Our police escort had been brilliant with their relays this time. We pulled in at the dealership to say our goodbyes, with everyone keen to arrange another weekend ride together.

12

NOT ALL MUSLIMS ARE TERRORISTS

As 2006 progressed, I had to be in and out of Jeddah almost monthly. This was either to see my ailing mother in Kenya or to fly to London where we were refurbishing an apartment. Every time I returned, I had to overcome my negative reactions to the controlling Saudi atmosphere. After one short London trip in April 2006, when the aircraft was on its final descent to Jeddah, I looked out at the twinkling night landscape and thought, *I wouldn't mind if I never saw the city or this country again.*

I knew this crushing dislike of Saudi Arabia would transform once I was back in the swing of work and the spirit of our expatriate community. But I couldn't shake off the complicated oscillation between my aversion and enthusiasm for the Kingdom. We had a good social life with an international circle of friends. Because of the Islamic laws, we shared the thrill of New York society during the 1920's prohibition, brewing alcohol and holding illicit parties in our own "speakeasy" bars. Expatriate life also had a touch of glamour with the black-tie balls held several times a year at the British Consulate. We were invited to functions at other European consulates as well, including concerts with touring European musicians. When Frosty was away, I would sometimes take a limousine to my favourite haunts, the Old Town of Jeddah or the Corniche. The former was an endless source of fascination; the latter provided refreshing evening wheelchair walks and an escape from the compound. Both were great areas for street photography, one of my favourite genres. And then there were our trips around the country and my freelance work with the *Saudi Gazette*, although every time I returned it was like starting all over again. But that is the nature of freelance work. It doesn't fall into your lap. You have to make it happen.

But the dark side began with the autocratic political system and the fundamentalist Wahhabi version of Islam which the Saudis exported worldwide with impunity. It was the basis for Al-Qaeda, the Taliban and other Islamist organisations. The sharia legal system (with cases often conducted without defence representation), the renowned human rights abuses, the way the government treated all expatriates as though they were prisoners – although they called us guests – the treatment of the expatriate workers, the hypocrisy and the misogyny were all elements that grated against everything I believed in. At times, we felt we were wasting our lives and prostituting ourselves by working in the Kingdom.

The increasing Islamist attacks around the country, mainly against Western expatriates, added to the stress of living in Saudi Arabia. The rise in anti-Western – and especially anti-US – sentiment began after the 1991 Gulf War when some fundamentalist Saudis became angry at the presence of US forces in Saudi Arabia. The first attack, a car bomb in Riyadh, came in 1995, killing five US citizens and two Indians. In 1996, nineteen US airmen were killed when the Khobar Towers complex was blasted by a large truck bomb. Following 9/11, Islam and Saudi Arabia became firmly connected with the terrorist activity of Al-Qaeda. In 2003, a group of Al-Qaeda militants attacked three expatriate compounds in Riyadh, using several vehicle bombs and killing thirty-nine people. Deaths in 2004 included BBC cameraman Simon Cumbers, and journalist

Frank Gardner was severely injured and left paraplegic. And so it continued.

The security around our Western expatriate compounds in Jeddah escalated. Strands of razor wire fencing appeared, rising high above the original walls, and a protective row of concrete blocks was set up all the way around the external perimeter roads. Armoured military vehicles like Humvees, with armed Saudi soldiers, were parked at compound entrances. One was parked outside our flat as we were the first duplex inside our security gate. These measures were to protect us, but the compound was beginning to feel more like a prison.

In the past, when visiting friends in other compounds, the security check at the entrance had been more of a formality. As long as our names had been registered with the guards, the barrier was lifted, and we were allowed to drive through. With the new measures, we had to negotiate our way around preliminary concrete block chicanes, stopping at the first security check. Security guards inspected our vehicles inside and out, including engines, boots and underneath using mirrors. We had to leave our vehicle in a car park outside the next security gate, check in there and walk into the compound. For the likes of me with my walking disability, some compounds provided electric buggies to take us to the specified house. Buses were supplied when big functions were held. These procedures made it difficult for expatriates to visit each other, but we had to accept them. I often felt we were the ones being treated like the troublemakers.

The isolation and oppression that I felt inside our compound were worse when Frosty was away on flights. We had a spacious apartment, but I craved outside space, the big vistas and vast skies of Kenya. Once Frosty was home, an evening ride on Maridadi along the Corniche rejuvenated me mentally and spiritually. The sight and smell of the sea, the sun setting over the water and the atmosphere of people relaxing unfettered by fences and any threat of terrorism, restored a sense of normality. Since my back operation, I had given up my dinghy sailing and windsurfing at the beach and rarely went out scuba diving, so our Friday morning rides also refreshed our weekend social life.

Even so, my sense of freedom provided by Maridadi was dependent on Frosty. Like most women in the Kingdom, I had to play the waiting game regarding any form of transport. Only a privileged few had personal drivers.

Although we lived with these restrictions and tensions in Saudi Arabia, whenever jobs elsewhere came up for Frosty, we decided to stay put. We were locked in by what were known as the "golden handcuffs". His salary and contractual benefits with Saudia, and the substantial entitlement of his leave and time off, were too good to relinquish. The weird thing about my own emotions was that every time these offers came up, I thought of all the things I loved about Saudi Arabia and would miss: my work as a journalist, a BBQ at the beach with friends, my evenings on the Corniche and visits to the Old Town, the interesting consular activities, the lunches with my girlfriends, our Friday rides on Maridadi and especially those into the mountains. I didn't want to give any of them up and paradoxically wanted to stay. I even got a perverse pleasure from living in this exotic, closed country that didn't invite tourists in, that you could only see and get to know by working there.

That April, the same Harley group arranged another weekend in the mountains, with a two-night stop at the Palace Hotel in Al Baha. Once again, Maridadi and the open road would give me an adrenalin fix and blow away my blues. Because of Frosty's flying schedule, we had to leave later than the others, giving us our first long solo ride together. As we left the city behind and headed down the flat Tihama plains, my spirits lifted. I thought, *wouldn't it be great if we could keep going and not turn back.*

After 350 kilometres without a police escort, I saw a Nissan Patrol with a bar of flashing lights on the roof waiting by the roadside. Our solo ride was over. A cheerful policeman waved at us to pull up, greeted us and shook hands with Frosty, then led the way for the next fifty kilometres. Another equally cheerful one took over, and a third led us up the mountains, past the Marble Village, on to Al Baha and the Palace Hotel. Our escort officers seemed to enjoy this break from their routine days on the road. If there were two in the vehicle, the passenger officer would take photos of us with his mobile phone.

Among the biking group were a few extras this time, with some who had come in cars for a fun weekend out of Jeddah. Hatem, the military Saudi on his chopper bike, was there with a colleague, Mohammed, who had a similar crazy Harley. Mohammed's cousin and a friend had come along in a short-wheel-based Toyota Land Cruiser fitted with a V8 Chevrolet engine and a sound system with huge speakers in the back. Two English brothers, Kevin and Ken, were in their big 4x4 with English nurses, Gill and Jenny. A Saudi couple, Abdulatif and his wife Monen, came in their car. Jens-Ole and Bente had brought their daughter Helene with them, visiting from Denmark.

In the morning, once someone had woken Hatem and Mohammed, the group of nine bikes and three vehicles set off for a ride that Frosty and I had suggested. We had driven down this obscure, narrow escarpment road in 1986. The Grande Lavoro – Big Work – descended from just outside Baljurashi, a small town a few kilometres south of Al Baha. An Italian company had built the road to help the local population get up and down the mountains without having to drive miles to use the main Al Baha route.

With two police cars escorting us, we were in a social bubble of our own, exempt from the normal rules and regulations of the Kingdom. This was the only time I felt safe taking photos of policemen, police vehicles and anything around us. Not once did they object. The two nurses took advantage of our police protection and hopped onto Hatem and Mohammed's pillion seats. Neither choppers appeared to have rear footrests, but the two Saudi bikers had cheeky ideas about how to deal with this minor problem. They showed the girls how to swing their legs up and around their rider's waist, hooking their feet over his thighs. The men then leant back against the girls, using them as backrests. I could see they were loving the novelty of taking these Western women on their Harleys. Taking their wives with them was unthinkable. Reclining against the chrome sissy bar backrests, the girls were having just as much fun. This was what they had hoped for: a pillion ride on a Harley.

In the eyes of Saudi religious fanatics, their behaviour would be deemed immoral. In Jeddah or Riyadh, it could have led to arrest and imprisonment.

As our convoy slowed to a halt at the checkpoint at the top of the escarpment, the barrier lifted to allow us through without anyone having to show their documents. A large, yellow road sign warned, "Dangerous Descent – Use Low Gear". The narrow strip of tarmac began its plunge down the mountain, squiggling its way along the contours with no guard rails, tunnels or bridges. It roughly followed the ancient camel trail of steps carved into the rock of the escarpment by local tribesmen. This section of the mountains was forested with juniper trees and the occasional splash of cerise of a desert rose.

From the inside of our Nissan Patrol in 1986, the route had seemed precarious. Now, from Maridadi's pillion seat, the world appeared to drop away from the edge of the road into a hazy abyss far below. The fizz of fear coupled with the bracing mountain air was exhilarating. Red brake lights ahead flashed on and off as riders negotiated their way around hairpin bends, sometimes scattered with rubble from fallen rocks. Through my helmet, I could hear Arabic music pumping out from the big speakers in the Land Cruiser. One of the men was standing up in the open back with a video camera.

After dropping a thousand metres, we stopped at the base of the escarpment road, two-thirds of the way down to the plains. We pulled over to let a few camels cross and to stretch our legs before tackling the ride back up. That was all we had come for, the challenge of riding down and then up this little-known escarpment road. There were no restaurants, cafés or pubs where we could hang out, just the many amazing and empty roads through the Asir Mountains.

In the evening, some of Mohammed's relatives had invited the group to have dinner in one of the local forested tourist parks in Al Baha. Night had fallen by the time we set off. We parked our Harleys in a large, open space among the juniper trees. Nearby, several white plastic tables and chairs were set out with large platters of white and orange saffron rice mixed with chunks of mutton. Paraffin lamps sat on the tables and were dotted about on the ground, casting a soft glow of warm light. Rugs were spread out on the ground in a large square with the traditional rectangular cushions placed around the edges.

Ahmed, who had been riding as our road captain again, signalled for us to gather round.

'There are a few Muslim mullahs here,' he said, 'After we have eaten, they want to have a religious discussion with you to find out how you view Islam.'

A mullah is the equivalent of a priest. The Westerners in our group neither expected nor welcomed an evening of religious discussion. We knew it could never be an open discussion, so were more concerned that they would use it as an opportunity to tell us "infidels" – as devout Saudis sometimes referred to Christians – about how wonderful Islam was. There was also another issue we were concerned about.

In September 2005, a Danish newspaper had published a series of cartoons depicting the Prophet Muhammad in various ways (*Charlie Hebdo* republished them in February 2006, plus more of its own cartoons). The images offended many Muslims, who deemed them to be insulting and blasphemous. Anger swept through many Islamic countries and Muslim communities worldwide, resulting in attacks on several Western embassies. Saudi Arabia recalled its ambassador to Denmark and boycotted Danish products. Among our group was a Danish family, Jens-Ole, Bente and their daughter. Jens-Ole was particularly anxious, not wanting to be singled out in the discussion.

'You know we are Danish, don't you?' he asked.

'Don't worry,' Ahmed reassured him. 'I am sure it will be fine.'

After our dinner, we were invited to relax on the rugs to hear what the mullahs had to say. These three bearded priests sat with the few other Saudi hosts. They were all dressed in white *thobes*, a few with red and white *shammagh* headscarves, others with plain white *ghutras*. The men exchanged greetings and shook hands. In keeping with tradition, everyone removed their shoes and we sat or reclined on the rugs.

One of the Saudis poured each of us a tiny, thimble-like cup of *gahwah* coffee from a thermos flask. When I had first tasted this traditional green, spicy coffee, I found it disgusting. Over the years, I'd grown to like its unique flavour. Green coffee beans were first roasted over an open flame on a *ta-waa*, a giant flat metal spoon. When ready, they were ground up with cardamom seeds and cloves, then mixed into boiling water. No sugar was added, so it was always served with dates.

One of the mullahs welcomed us, then began his speech. After a while, he paused and glanced at Ahmed to interpret.

'They want to make the point that just because eleven of the 9/11 terrorists were from Al Baha, the people here are not all the same,' Ahmed told us. 'They believe the terrorists are not representatives of Islam. The mullah is saying that what the terrorists did, and are still doing, is wrong. None of them here agree with what they are doing. They don't want your view of Islam to be tarnished by what the terrorists do.'

Relief flooded through us at the non-confrontational tone of their message. The mullahs hadn't finished though. They took the opportunity to tell us about the Koran and chant some verses. One talked at length about the Prophet Noah, who is revered in Islam. He is said to have lived 950 years or more, preaching to the people to change their ways from idolatry to worship one God.

After a pause, they invited the men in our group to speak. A few of them, including Frosty, told the group how they came to be in Saudi Arabia and how long they had been there. Jens-Ole, a tall, handsome man, got to his feet last.

'I am Danish,' he said in his deep, steady voice. The Saudis and mullahs stared at him, eyes alert with surprise, a flash of hostility blazing from them. 'I have been in Saudi Arabia with my family for a total of twenty years. We left halfway through that for eight years but decided to come back. All of us felt that our years here have been some of the most beautiful of our lives.'

He paused while Ahmed interpreted for him. I could see the expressions on the faces of the mullahs softening as he spoke. Even they were receptive to compliments about their country.

'Our children spent half their lives here,' he continued. 'They are more Saudi than Danish. We spent many wonderful weekends camping out under the stars in your deserts and mountains. When my daughter arrived back for this visit, she said to me, "You know, Papa, when I come to Saudi Arabia, I always feel like I have come home."'

'Mashallah, as God wills it,' the mullahs said, nodding their approval.

To end his speech, Jens-Ole couldn't resist an echo of the message they had given about not all the people of Al Baha being terrorists.

'You know,' he said with a twinkle in his eyes, 'it is not all Danes that are good at drawing cartoons.'

The mullahs nodded again, this time chuckling, their hostility gone.

Most Saudis were oblivious to the fact that many expatriates regarded the Kingdom as home. They had dedicated years of their lives to living, working and raising their families in the country, always knowing that one day their usefulness would be over, and then they would have to leave.

After Frosty and a few other men in our group had thanked the Saudis on our behalf for the evening, we made our way back to the hotel.

Harley men in Saudi have a tradition of cigar and hookah water pipe smoking after dinner. The shisha molasses-based tobacco used in the hookahs was sometimes flavoured with fruit, such as apple or strawberry. The smoke had a sweet smell which I found sickly. As neither Frosty nor I smoked, we weren't in the mood to join the others in a room filled with cigar and shisha fumes. We sneaked off to our room to settle down with the bottle of homemade wine we'd smuggled into our luggage.

13

THUNDERSTORM IN THE ASIR

In the morning, it was time to head back to Jeddah. Our Saudi boy mascots, Hatem and Mohammed, again delayed our departure. Despite being in the military, the two struggled to be on time in the morning. Neither spoke any English, and the Westerners among us knew only basic Arabic. Yet these young men liked to hang out with us. Our two police escort vehicles had no problem timekeeping and were ready to leave with us at 9.00am.

Our ride to Taïf this time was along the top of the mountains, the Tourist Route. We had first driven here in 1985 in our Nissan, escaping from compound life for a few days' camping with our children. Ahead of us now, we had two hundred kilometres of another empty road, one of the best for motorcycling in the country. While Frosty focused on riding the sweeping S-bends, curling around, as well as up and down, the hills, I took photos over his shoulder. At times we were close to the edge of the mountains, catching glimpses of panoramic views over the hazy Asir range and into the Tihama plains below. On other sections we disappeared into long tunnels, dimly lit from above. Cat's eyes glinted along the centre line of the road, reflecting the glow of our headlights.

As usual, I scanned the landscape for the drystone villages and watchtowers. The grey houses, most of them deserted, nestled in the hills, merging with their environment. I wondered how long it would have taken to construct the buildings, a jigsaw of uneven pieces that somehow became a perfect fit with straight walls and the corners at sharp right angles. A few owners had integrated their old homes with new, painted concrete ones. Drystone walls, similar to the ancient ones found all over Europe, were also used in the farm fields and terraces in these mountains of Saudi Arabia.

About halfway to Taïf, Ahmed pulled over to announce that he wanted to show us an area in the heart of the mountains where the Prophet Muhammad had lived as a boy. We turned off down a dirt track, winding through barren, rolling hills. Maridadi was slipping on the gravel surface, and this was the only time I ever opted to go in one of the vehicles. I didn't want to fall on this stony ground.

After fourteen kilometres we stopped. As non-Muslims, we weren't allowed to see Makkah, the town of Muhammad's birth, but nothing prevented us from coming to this wilderness to see where he had lived, played and herded the family sheep. I felt honoured our Muslim friends were sharing this with us, Christians, atheists and agnostics. They weren't trying to convert us, simply showing us the landscape where their beloved prophet had spent his childhood.

A few dry tufts of grass were growing through the hard ground, but there wasn't a tree in sight or any signs of where there might be water. Nothing here would have changed since the time of Muhammad 1,400 years ago. The harsh lives of the desert Bedouins were much the same today. On our previous travels, we had come across scenes of youngsters, girls as well as boys, herding flocks in similar surroundings. I could easily imagine Muhammad as a child roaming these hills.

Back on the main road, the sky in front had grown heavy with gunmetal-grey clouds. Flashes of lightning lit up the sky, and a wall of rain was pouring down some distance ahead. We couldn't avoid it, but none of us were dressed for rain.

A few kilometres outside Taïf, the first fat drops splattered against our helmets. We stopped to ask Ken and Kevin if either of them had anything waterproof I could borrow. I was lucky, and Kevin handed me a Gore-Tex jacket. Frosty was wearing his tough, leather jacket which would keep the worst of the wet out. Neither Mohammed nor Hatem had jackets on. They were riding in long-sleeved T-shirts with cotton shirts over the top and a leather Harley waistcoat.

By the time we reached the outskirts of town, we were riding through a heavy downpour. Although only 5.00pm, it was almost dark. It must have been raining for a couple of hours because further ahead, a torrent of water was rushing across the three lanes and over the central reservation. I assumed that Ahmed and Jens-Ole in the lead would stop to assess this, but they carried straight on. In Jeddah, manhole covers on the roads were often left off, leaving a gaping, two-foot square hole, dangerous enough in dry weather. As we followed the leaders into the foot-deep stream, I peered wide-eyed over Frosty's shoulder, looking for telltale swirling in the water, an indication of an open cavity.

I still had my camera out, wrapped in a plastic bag, and continued to take photos as we rode through several kilometres of the murky water. Once through it, we persevered along the glistening, wet road with its reflections of the orange, red and white lights of the vehicles ahead of us.

Once through town, we pulled over. All of us were soaked through, including our boots which were squelching out water. I don't think Mohammed and Hatem had ever been so cold. Both of them were shivering, their teeth chattering. They commandeered a change of clothing from dry colleagues in their cars, and we continued towards Jeddah. Because the escarpment road was closed for maintenance, we were using what was known as the truck route. Instead of a steep road with hairpin bends, we went down a long, steady gradient with sweeping turns around the foothills, with farms on either side.

The rain wasn't giving up on us, and another heavy deluge bucketed down. The plastic bag over my camera was no longer effective so, against my instincts, I signalled to Kevin and Ken to stop so I could hand it to them through the window. I knew what was going to happen – I was going to miss the shot of the day. I could see it developing as the sun peeped through the clouds from time to time. The orb emerged low in the sky ahead, painting the clouds and the wet road with a golden glow. A low, metal barrier became a bright strip of gold, outlining the long curve of the road. I had to make do with a mental snapshot.

For the final stretch into Jeddah, a police escort was waiting for us. He sped away at 120 kilometres per hour down the fast lane of the highway, packed with traffic dashing home from their Friday prayers in Makkah.

Not comfortable with our speed amid the unpredictable Saudi drivers, I shouted over the noise at Frosty.

'Why are we going so fast?'

'I don't know,' he shouted back. 'I don't like it either.'

Despite Peter Forward's advice that "it's always my ride", we didn't do what we should have done: slow down, leave the ride and move to the middle lane. As we came down a hill towards an intersection, I could see a green traffic light with another police vehicle parked on the road beside it. Half of our convoy went through the junction. Then the light turned red. Like Doug and Anneli ahead of us, Frosty assumed the officers were stopping the cross-traffic, as they usually did with our escorted rides. As we continued through the red light, the three lanes of cars began to cross in front of us. Doug and Frosty jinked the bikes into the closing gaps between the vehicles. My hands were gripping the bars beside my saddle, my eyes wide, teeth clenched, my body tensed for a crash. Another jink and we were safely across.

'Fuck, that was close!' I yelled so Frosty could hear. My heart was pounding, its thud-thud-thud echoing in my ears.

Another lesson learned. I had also assumed the police car had stopped the traffic.

We pulled in at the dealership feeling shaken, to hear that everyone had found the night ride into town too fast, but no one had done anything about it.

Not long after this, we dropped in at the dealership for a social visit. My article about our trip to the Muscat rally had appeared in *HOG Tales*, the international Harley-Davidson magazine. A few Saudi bikers were there, browsing through the article. Lisa, Marwan and Monther were delighted to have Saudi Arabia featured in the magazine for the first time, but these men were angry about one of my photographs.

'Why did you put this picture in the article?' one of them demanded, glaring at me.

The man was pointing at the photo I had taken of Diamond and Houria riding ahead of us on the highway out of Jeddah. Above them was the large road sign for Makkah that read "Muslims Only", instructing non-Muslims to turn right.

'I didn't put it in,' I replied. 'I just sent a selection of photos to the editor, and she chose that one.'

'Well, you shouldn't have sent it.'

I regretted not asking why but deduced it was because Muslims were accusing the West of being Islamophobic. This sign showed Saudis discriminating against non-Muslims, and perhaps it embarrassed them. I left feeling irritated by their attitude, unaware that my writing was the glue that would get me back onto a Harley after a devastating accident.

14

UP CLOSE AND PERSONAL WITH A LAMBORGHINI

One moment I was on the pillion seat of Essam's Road King and the next I was on the road, rolling like an out-of-control barrel down the centre lane of the three-lane Madinah Road highway. As I rotated again, I snatched a glimpse of a motorbike ahead of me, hurtling high through the air from right to left in a cloud of dust. Thoughts flashed through my mind. *Oh fuck, we've had a crash! When am I going to stop?*

I seemed to roll for a long time, but it was only a few seconds. I stopped abruptly, curled up in the foetal position on my right side, facing forwards. In my peripheral vision, I saw the metre-high wheels of trucks trundle by on either side of me. My head was within inches of being crushed and squashed into the road. I lay still, frozen in the moment, brain numbed with shock.

I had no idea what had happened. There had been no warning, no sixth sense that something awful was about to go wrong.

It was Ramadan again, and the Jeddah HOGs were on another Thursday Iftar dinner ride to a private beach compound. Frosty and I had decided to go to this last one of Ramadan, Thursday 4 October 2007. He was operating a short return flight so had ridden to the airport on Maridadi, with a plan to join us later. As always it was a family event, with wives and children coming in cars with drivers. There were to be prizes for the best-dressed bikers and the best salads. I had prepared an exotic dish, and donned my Harley jewellery and leather waistcoat, complete with all its badges, for the occasion. I called a compound limousine and met the rest of the chapter at the dealership.

Our good friends Ken and Jo McIntosh were coming in their car but instead of going with them, I had wanted to hitch a pillion ride to take photos for my HOG newsletter. While I was waiting to find one, I noticed a convertible black Lamborghini among the parked cars. A dark-skinned Saudi dressed in a white *thobe* was hanging around beside it.

'Well,' I said to Jo, 'if I can't find a pillion ride, maybe I can cadge a lift in the Lamborghini.'

A few minutes before we left, Essam Istanbouli, a Saudi we'd ridden with on our trips to Muscat, offered me a lift on his motorbike, a fabulous anniversary-model Road King. He also worked for Saudia, and his wife and family were joining him with their driver. In the briefing, which was in English, the road captain stressed that the accompanying vehicles had to either go behind or ahead of the bikes. He didn't want any of them alongside for safety reasons.

Our ride of thirty motorcycles streamed out of the dealership car park. On the way, another set of ten joined us. Instead of being broken up into smaller groups, we were one long line of Harleys. This meant that we blocked a whole lane for about a hundred metres. Essam and I were in the heart of the pack where I could take photos showing riders behind and in front of us.

The staggered two-line formation was becoming chaotic, with a few men not keeping their positions. One guy in particular was making a nuisance of himself. He was a short, tubby man riding a red bike with fat tyres. One minute he was coming past us, the next pulling back.

The police at the checkpoint on the Madinah Road dual carriageway had been forewarned of our arrival, so we rode through without any problems. From there we continued down the centre lane, cruising at a hundred kilometres per hour. We were a few kilometres beyond it when I found myself off Essam's bike, rolling along the road. My brain didn't register the instant I flew off the saddle or the pain when I slammed onto the road.

Within moments, I was surrounded by fellow bikers and black-clad Arab women I didn't recognise. Their anxious faces peered down at me, relaxing into relief when I said, 'I'm okay.' What I meant was, 'I'm alive.'

'Essam? Is he okay?' I asked.

'Yes,' someone reassured me, 'he's okay; he's off the road.'

My next question came from the photojournalist in me. 'Where's my camera?' Someone found it and handed it to me. It was badly damaged, unusable. 'Please can you ask someone else to take some pictures?' I asked the faces around me.

Excruciating pain around my hips kicked in as soon as I tried to move. *Oh god*, I thought, *my pelvis is broken*. The thought of such an injury and the recovery involved was daunting. More months of rehab.

Ken and Jo appeared through the other faces.

'Bizzie, are you okay?' asked Jo, her eyes wide. 'We were worried sick when we heard Essam and you had been hit.'

'I'm in godawful pain, Jo, but I'm alive. I should've come with you. What the hell happened?'

'You were hit by the Lamborghini.'

'If I hadn't been on Essam's bike, I might have been in the Lamborghini. Who else was hit? I saw one bike flying through the air.'

'That was Ali Alireza. I'm not sure how he is. And another guy came off his bike as well.'

From where I was curled up on the road, I could see people

milling around everywhere. Cars and trucks had slowed down to crawl past me, drivers and passengers staring at the scene.

The police arrived soon afterwards, and now the bikers froze in panic. How were they going to explain my presence on the Madinah Road when I wasn't with my husband? They couldn't say I'd been riding pillion with Essam. They decided to say I was riding my own bike. We later discovered this caused major problems for the checkpoint police. Women were forbidden to drive cars or ride motorcycles, so the police officers were imprisoned for ten days over the Eid ul-Fitr holiday for not checking the bikes and riders.

Ambulances were on the scene soon after the police. As the medics bent over me, one of them demanded my identity card.

'Sorry, no ID. At home.' It hadn't crossed my mind to bring it with me for this beach ride.

A conversation ensued in Arabic, and someone said to me, 'They say they can't take you without your ID.'

I wondered what they planned to do, leave me lying injured in the middle of the road?

Colonel Haitham Attar, a retired pilot from the Saudi Royal Air Force, was riding with us and overheard the discussion. Stepping forward, he flashed his ID at the medics and snapped, 'You *will* take her!'

A stretcher was brought over, and the ambulance crew started to lift me onto it. As their hands moved under my body, a bolt of pain like a hot knife shot through my pelvis.

'Please, please, be careful,' I begged them, trying not to cry.

Once I was in place, lying on my back, they tried to force me to straighten my legs. Another vicious stab of pain shot through my thighs and buttocks.

'Don't touch my legs. I can't straighten them. Please, leave them.'

'Must straight to put straps,' one of them said.

Haitham exerted his authority again. 'Leave her as she is.'

I was lifted into the ambulance with Jo and the others looking on. Essam was loaded in beside me.

Siren wailing, the ambulance rushed us to the government King Fahd Hospital. Despite our pleas, they refused to take us to a private hospital. Their instructions were to take all traffic accident victims to government hospitals. Unlike the ambulance staff in Western countries who are qualified paramedics, these men were basic first aiders. They had no authority to give any analgesics. I didn't know how badly Essam was hurt, or how much pain he was in. Neither of us spoke on the journey – we were too traumatised.

My phone rang. It was Frosty.

'Hi, Biz. I've just got back so I'll be with you in about forty-five minutes.'

'We're not at the beach. There's been a terrible accident.'

I barely remembered our conversation, but he told me later I sounded so calm he assumed I was accompanying someone else in the ambulance, not injured myself. It must have been an echo of my nursing training from thirty years ago. We were taught to stay calm in emergencies.

'I'll have to drop Maridadi at home, then I'll come straight to the hospital,' he said and hung up.

With the influence of his high-profile family position, Ali ordered his ambulance crew to go straight to the Saudi German Hospital. Essam and I arrived at the government King Fahd Hospital where traffic accident victims were meant to go. We were transferred onto their trolleys and each movement sent more hot stabs of pain through my pelvis.

Essam was taken to the male emergency section, and I was wheeled to the female side. Several pairs of eyes greeted me, peering out from the slit in their black niqab face veils as I was lifted off the trolley and onto one of the emergency beds. White women were a curiosity as they didn't arrive here very often. Each move jarred the pain. I lay there in shock, sweating, taking deep breaths, trying to keep myself calm, unable to assimilate what had transpired. Just then two Saudi HOG faces appeared around the door. I knew them both. We had done a lot of riding together, and they had followed our ambulance.

'Hi, Bizzie,' said Mamdouh, one of the guys who had been with us in Muscat and Al Haridhah. 'Don't worry, you aren't staying here. The Saudi German Hospital is sending an ambulance for you.'

He was a tall, black Saudi with an outgoing nature, and we had nicknamed him *Zarafa*, the Arabic for giraffe. It turned out that as soon as Ali had arrived at the Saudi German Hospital, someone paid the ambulance driver to come and pick us up.

Once more Essam and I endured the pain of being lifted from bed to trolley to ambulance. We still hadn't been offered any medication. When we stopped at the Saudi German Hospital, the transfer process was repeated for the third time. It was torture.

Appointments for X-rays were made, and by the time I was lifted onto the X-ray table, Frosty could follow the sound of my screaming as he walked along the corridor to find me.

'Oh, Bizzie Bee. Poor you. I can't believe you're back in hospital.'

'I know,' I said, tears pouring down my cheeks, 'and the pain is terrible.'

He looked dazed. We were supposed to be at the beach having a sunset Iftar barbecue, not here.

The images revealed that my only fracture was on the little finger of my right hand. My pelvis, hips and leg bones were intact. More painful transfers on and off trolleys and at last I was wheeled into a private room and transferred to a bed. Still no pain relief was offered. I must have been in too much shock to ask for any. From my experience of my back surgery in 1999, I already knew Saudi hospitals didn't dish out analgesics if they could help it. You had to beg for them.

Word had spread around the Saudi community like an oil slick because of Ali's high-profile position. His family owned the oldest automobile distributor in Saudi Arabia. I now witnessed another difference between our two cultures. The drama triggered the Saudi families and friends to rush to the hospital to see the victims. Conversely, our expatriate friends made polite calls, said they were relieved to hear I was okay, sent phone messages and emails, and asked when it would be convenient to visit.

From the moment I was settled into my room, a continuous stream of well-wishing Saudis called in to pay their respects. Whether Frosty was in the room or not, the men still came in, sometimes bringing their wives and daughters, sisters, aunts, mums and dads. At about midnight, nearing exhaustion, I asked the nurses to put a "Do Not Disturb" sign on my door. It was ignored. The Saudis were in Ramadan late-night mode, and they still came in. They sat and chatted, expressing their dismay at what had happened and hoping I would make a speedy recovery. I was surprised that some of the men, unaccompanied by women, felt it was acceptable to come into my room when Frosty wasn't there, when I was in bed wearing a hospital gown.

Despite my exhaustion, these intrusions were heart-warming. Our Harley family was devastated by the accident, and I was one of them. They wanted to see the victims, to make sure we were okay.

Through their visits, I discovered how the accident had happened. The tubby Yemeni on the red bike was a newcomer to the Harley group. He didn't speak English and apparently hadn't understood the briefing. The Lamborghini belonged to one of his bosses from a high-profile company. The Yemeni had instructed the driver of the Lamborghini to race with him once the group had passed through the Madinah Road checkpoint.

Travelling at around two hundred kilometres per hour, the Lamborghini driver had lost control on the left side hard shoulder. Spinning across the road, the car smacked into Essam's Road King. I was taking photographs and didn't see it coming. Someone told me I shot off the pillion seat like a fighter pilot from his ejector seat. One of the Harley riders behind went under me while I flew high above him. From my severe bruising, I deduced I had landed on my backside on the hard tarmac, then bounced onto my left side before rolling along the road.

Essam, still holding onto his handlebars, had been flung into the desert on the right, landing about fifteen metres from the road. The sports car careered into a metal post on the right side of the road, which sent the vehicle spinning back across the line of bikers. On the way, it smashed into Ali, who was ahead of us. His was the bike that I had seen catapulting through the air. A third man, Mohannad AlKayyali from Jordan, had been knocked off his Harley when hit by flying debris from the concrete base of the post. He was lucky and got away with no injuries. It was a miracle that no cars or other vehicles were involved.

When the car hit Essam's left leg, it ripped off his boot and smashed his ankle. Ali came off the worst. After his bike hit the ground, he had been hurled against the camel fence on the central reservation dividing the highway and had been caught up between the strands of wire. When his colleagues rushed over, they found him unconscious and with a blocked airway. He was so tangled up that he had to be separated from the fence by pulling him through to the other side. Our dealership manager, Jamil Ayas, had recently completed a first aid course and managed to resuscitate him. Ali's right knee was shattered, and he'd also suffered a compound fracture of his right leg.

Thirty-seven other bikers had to pull up and find their way off the road, while traffic on either side and behind us slowed to avoid me lying in the middle lane. Thank goodness there had been the twenty bikes behind us to restrain the traffic and prevent vehicles from running over me.

With its broad chassis, the Lamborghini had spun rather than rolled. It had come to a standstill beside the fence where Ali's bike lay on the sand. Photos I saw later showed the car with the dazed driver still in his seat. Damage was minimal, the front end and sides unblemished. The rear bumper was lying on the ground, the boot open and the rear end staved in. The Yemeni on his red bike, the cause of all the damage, was unharmed.

Ali was the first to go into surgery, followed by Essam. It was 1.00am by the time my turn came to have a pin put in my right hand. My heavy Nikon had smashed my hand against the hard asphalt, breaking the bone near my little finger. By now, severe pain was throbbing through my bruised body. As I was being wheeled to theatre, the same two Saudi bikers who had been at the government hospital were standing in the corridor.

'What are they going to do to you?'

I couldn't resist a joke and said, 'I am going to have a sex change so I can ride my own Harley.'

They laughed. 'Good luck, Bizzie. We hope it is successful,' one of them answered.

I welcomed the anaesthetic and temporary oblivion, at last free of pain.

The following day the same two guys popped in to see me. They both had cheeky smiles on their faces as one of them asked, 'Was the sex change successful?'

'Wait and see. If you find me riding my own Harley, then you will know.'

Frosty popped in at midday on his way to a lunch party. 'I'll be back later,' he assured me, 'probably around 5.00pm.'

5.00pm came and went, but no Frosty appeared.

The flow of Saudi visitors continued, including Khaled Al Maeena, editor-in-chief of the *Arab News*, and his wife. Haitham, the air force colonel who had come to my rescue as I lay on the road, also called in. Massive bouquets were delivered from Harley-Davidson in Jeddah, Riyadh and Bahrain. Most of my visitors brought me chocolates packaged in expensive containers ranging from crystal bowls to suede-covered boxes. We ate the last of them three months later and still have some of the containers.

'Where is your husband?' the Saudis wanted to know. 'Why isn't he with you? When is he coming?'

'I don't know. I can't find him.'

I had tried calling Frosty several times, but he didn't answer. Then I called a few of our friends, but no one knew where he was. Now my imagination was running wild, thinking he might have had an accident as well.

The following day he showed up with a monumental hangover.

'What the hell happened to you last night?' I greeted him, my irritation clear. 'I was worried sick something had happened to you.'

'Well, it was a good party,' he said. 'In the end, someone had to drive me home. I couldn't even remember where our house was, so they had to ask security.'

'I don't think that's funny. Why didn't you call me to tell me you weren't coming back?'

'I forgot.'

'Well, thanks a lot. If you're ever in hospital, you know what kind of sympathy you're going to get from me.'

'Okay, okay. I know I should have called you, but this is stressful for me too, you know.'

After thirty years of marriage, I had learned there was no point in carrying on with the argument. During my time in hospital after my back surgery and the weeks in rehab afterwards, Frosty had been amazing – he hadn't missed a single visit when home from flying. I was mad for a while but let it go.

The benefit of him not showing up was that the hospital had wanted to discharge me that night. I knew I wasn't ready, so because he wasn't there to take me home, I had to stay. Before leaving, we visited Essam and Ali in their rooms.

Essam said his injury should heal without too many problems. Ali's multiple knee and leg fractures were more complicated. He was planning to fly to Switzerland for further surgery. Both men shook their heads when I asked if they would ride in Saudi Arabia again. Essam's wife had ruled that his motorcycling days were over, and Ali was too important in the family business to risk that kind of danger again on Saudi roads. I later discovered that he still rode his Harley in Europe.

Although I had no serious broken bones, the medical staff paid no attention to the severe bruising in my buttock muscles, left leg and pelvic bones. The Egyptian surgeon who'd set my hand discharged me without any pain medication or advice on how to care for my injuries. He gave no indication of how long my recovery would take, leaving me feeling disillusioned and angry that doctors in Jeddah had let me down again.

15

RECOVERY AND HEALING WITH THE PHARAOHS

Meanwhile, the first Saudi HOG rally was soon to take place at the Durrat Al Arus resort, an hour's ride from Jeddah. While I was recuperating, Frosty was involved in the preparations for the function, working with Diamond and others from the chapter. I should have been involved too but, as well as being out of action, I had lost interest in Harleys. In fact, I hated them and all motorbikes. They were dangerous, and now I knew we shouldn't have bought one.

Despite the name Saudi German Hospital, all the doctors I saw were Egyptian. My surgeon admitted to not having a holistic approach and that he was only interested in my fractured hand. The accident had hurled me back into a world of pain, helplessness and despair. With no medical advice for my deep contusions and severe pain, I didn't know where to turn for help. When I tried to stand up, my gluteus muscles contracted into an agonising spasm. Mothers know that level of pain from giving birth. I was back to being tearful, unable to walk and having to use my wheelchair. My behind and all down my left side – shoulder, arm, hips and leg – had turned a deep shade of purple. I thought Frosty had developed caring nursing skills when he offered to massage some skin healing cream into my grazes. As he rubbed it in, I yelped.

'Frosty, that stuff is stinging like crazy. What the hell is it?'

He paused to check the ointment tube.

'Oops,' he said, 'it's your Sensodyne toothpaste.'

The crazy thing was I later discovered posts on the internet about the healing power of toothpaste on bruises.

We turned to our Saudia Medical Centre and the Egyptian doctor there. He was kind and sympathetic, but my unbearable pain continued unabated despite his daily Tramadol injections. When he changed the treatment to tablets, I read the package leaflet. I discovered he hadn't cross-checked the reactions of Tramadol with my regular neuropathic pain drugs. The literature stated that Carbamazepine neutralised the effect of Tramadol.

I decided to find an alternative remedy. Through a Lebanese friend who ran a hospital spa, I found a Filipina woman who knew the art of meridian massage. This Chinese healing is based on acupuncture and acupressure points and energy pathways. The massage stimulates and restores the free flow of qi, the body's vital life force. She came to our flat every day for the next two weeks to massage me for an hour, with amazing results. My bruises cleared up, muscles stopped their vicious spasms, and I could stand once more without crying out from the pain.

News of the accident filtered through to the airline crew scheduling staff. Frosty never had to ask for any extra time off to look after me or take me for medical appointments because they pre-empted him by covering all his flights. Whenever he was due to fly somewhere, they called up a few hours earlier and said, 'Captain Richard, no need to come to work. Your flight covered. We see you next time.' This went on for a month.

Frosty then took me back to the hospital to check the pin in my hand. First, I had an X-ray. After checking it, the Egyptian doctor said, 'The bone has healed, so we can remove the pin. Don't worry; it won't hurt.'

It became obvious he had never had a pin removed from his hand. I yelled out as a red-hot sensation tore through the side of my right hand. It felt as though he was ripping the bone out along with the pin.

'That did hurt! You shouldn't do that to people,' I snapped. The unexpected rush of pain had me in tears – again.

'You have another problem now,' he continued, businesslike. 'You have lost a lot of bone density since your X-ray a month ago. Have a look at these two images.' He placed the two X-rays side by side on a lightbox on the wall. 'You see this one,' he said, pointing to the one on the left, 'the bones here are a dense white. But on this one,' he now pointed to the new image on the right, 'you can see the bones have become very pale.'

'So what does this mean?'

'It means you have osteoporosis. You will have to take treatment to restore your bone density.'

'How long will that take?'

'A few years.'

I couldn't believe that one month of being immobile could have such a devastating effect. On top of my other problems, I could now be prone to hip and wrist fractures. My body had become even more fragile than it had been before. I had also become weak and wobbly on my legs.

The time had come to return to the Abdul Latif Jameel Center for Rehabilitation (ALJ) where I had done my rehab in 1999 after being paralysed down my right side. This time around, I attended three days a week, for three months of physiotherapy.

It was a revelation to see the changes that had taken place in eight years. The previous time, the Saudi women who had been with me in rehab hadn't engaged with their exercise programmes at all. Sport for women didn't exist in their culture. Now they were allowed to use the new, larger gym, and I looked on in amazement at how an enthusiastic spirit had ousted the old apathy. Dowdy clothes had been replaced by trendy tracksuits and bright-coloured trainers, bought for them by their daughters or granddaughters. Elderly women who had suffered strokes were learning how to pump iron, work out on treadmills and use other equipment too. They were now actively contributing towards their recovery and, judging by their lively expressions, were feeling the psychological benefits.

Although the driver of the Lamborghini had been imprisoned, the anger of the HOGs wasn't directed at him. It was directed at the Yemeni biker, who didn't face any charges for what he had precipitated. He had the grace to buy me a new camera (but questioned the cost of a professional Nikon D3), a new helmet and a few other items. Frosty collected the cheque from Jamil, who asked him to sign a document to say the matter was closed and he wouldn't pursue the man for any further costs. We had to foot the expense of the masseuse and rehab. Claiming from the Lamborghini owner's insurance was impossible for me and no doubt problematic for Essam and Ali. In Saudi Arabia, blame for traffic accidents is apportioned fifty-fifty: fifty per cent for the one who caused it and fifty per cent to the other party, as the accident wouldn't have happened if they hadn't been there.

The rally day dawned, and I stayed at home while Frosty went to join the boys. I had no plans to attend but Lisa Schlensker, the Bahrain-based manager and driving force behind HOG Middle East and Africa, was having none of that. We had got to know each other through meeting at the Muscat rallies and through my work on the committee.

'Bizzie, we're sending a car to pick you up. You have to be here,' she commanded. 'Monther and Marwan are both here, and they want to see you – in fact, we all want to see you!'

It was time to don my Harley finery again, including my badge-covered leather waistcoat. The driver arrived in a large, comfortable vehicle. He loaded my wheelchair into the back, and we set off for Durrat Al Arus, an hour away. My reluctance to attend was dispelled by the hero's welcome I received from Lisa and the AlMutlaq brothers, Amer AlKhaldi, Diamond and our friends in the Harley group, together with others who didn't know me so well. Diamond later gave me an enlarged photo taken of us all together that day.

Despite seeing everyone again and watching the fun they were having, the last thing I wanted was to get back onto a Harley-Davidson. Shock caused by the accident was still radiating through every part of me. Recovering from this monumental crash, where I was inches from losing my life, was going to take time. What I had feared most had happened – I had been involved in a horrific collision. My body was already damaged beyond repair, and I couldn't risk putting it back into situations that attracted trauma. Whenever Frosty suggested a ride on Maridadi, I was almost reduced to tears.

'No. I never want to go on a motorbike again. I don't understand why you are even asking me. I think you should sell Maridadi.'

I felt angry with him that he didn't suggest this, having seen the result of the motorcycling crash. But he hadn't witnessed it so wasn't affected in the same way as those who had.

Several of the Saudis who had been on that fateful ride, including big Suleiman and a pilot colleague of Frosty's, said their riding days were over. I hoped this would make Frosty change his mind, but it didn't. The calamity was the 9/11 of our biking community and broke it up. No one wanted to risk riding with bikers they didn't know and trust. The Yemeni and his Harley disappeared off the Jeddah HOG radar.

'You see? It's not only me,' I snapped at Frosty. 'Even some of the men don't want to ride motorbikes now and they weren't in the accident!'

The months passed, and my fear didn't diminish. But one man was confident my biking days weren't over: Jamil. Frosty said to him one day, 'That's it for Bizzie, she's never going to come riding again.'

Jamil looked at him with a wise eye and said, 'You don't know your wife.'

He wasn't alone in his assessment. Lisa also appeared to know me better than I knew myself. She and the AlMutlaq brothers loved my articles. They appeared in the *Arab News*, the *Saudi Gazette*, *Ahlan Wasahlan* (the Saudia in-flight magazine), and the international *HOG Tales* magazine. There were no other journalists in Saudi interested in giving the Harley-Davidson brand this kind of publicity.

One day in early 2008, a few months after the accident, the phone rang. It was Lisa.

'Hi, Bizzie, how are you doing?'

'Not bad, Lisa, I'm getting there. At least I'm walking now.'

'So when are you going to get back on your Harley?'

'Never. Don't bother to ask me again, Lisa – I'm through with motorbikes. My body's already too buggered up. I can't afford to have another accident.'

'Okay, I understand. Take care, I'll talk to you soon.'

A few weeks later, she was back on the blower, asking the same question.

'No, Lisa, I'm not getting back onto a Harley. My biking days are over.'

The third time she struck lucky.

'Bizzie, we're having a press launch in April to celebrate 105 years of Harley-Davidson,' she told me. 'We're doing this in Dubai. We need you there to write it up.'

'I'm really not keen, Lisa.'

'Bizzie, you'll love it. There are thirteen brand-new Harleys, including the new 2008 touring bikes. Frosty can come too.'

I was running out of resistance. Lisa's pressure tactics were working.

'Okay, Lisa, you win. I'll come. What are the dates? Frosty may be flying.'

'If he is, you can ride with Jamil as he's coming too.'

'I'll have to get a new helmet first – my beautiful one matching Maridadi was damaged in the crash.'

I discovered Frosty was scheduled to be away over those few days. We decided I should try a short ride on Maridadi before leaving to make sure I could handle being back on a bike. My whole being resisted and was clogged with fear as I settled onto the pillion seat. My mouth was dry, my hands cold and shaky. Why was I risking this again?

As we rode out of the compound and into the traffic, I became super-alert, watching everything in front, alongside and behind. If a car came too close, I pointed at the driver and made an emphatic pushing movement with my hand. It worked, but I still felt sick with fear. Half an hour later we were safely home. Although I was back in the saddle, I wasn't sure if I was being brave or foolish.

Jamil was a tall, good-looking Lebanese and had been working for Harley-Davidson for seventeen years, two of them in the UK. He had perfect manners and always looked smart in his jeans and designer Harley shirt. We liked him a lot, and I had absolute faith in his ability – he'd been riding since the age of eighteen. He was part of the Friday bike rides, and we had sometimes been on the group night rides around the city with him.

We flew to Dubai together on 20 April and were delivered to the Ritz Carlton. Thirteen brand-new Harleys, in the anniversary colours of black and metallic copper, were lined up outside the hotel.

The following morning, despite my faith in Jamil as a rider, I had a dry mouth and sense of nausea again, and my body felt tight with apprehension. We were allocated the anniversary Screamin' Eagle Electra Glide Ultra Classic, the most powerful of the range. It came with a big price tag and was the sort of motorcycle most enthusiasts could only dream about. When he let out the clutch and accelerated away behind the others, my heart lurched, and butterflies fizzed from my stomach up through my throat. I didn't mind that sensation when it spelt excitement, but this time it was pure fear. Although there were other pillion riders there, I was the sole female among the representatives and journalists from around the Gulf Cooperation Council (GCC) countries, the UK and South Africa.

Our first day's ride was around the city of Dubai itself. Due to a raised highway being constructed through it, I felt as though I was riding through a vast, dusty building site. The next day, we started off in searing white heat and a low-grade sandstorm, now on a longer ride towards the Oman border. We were in the usual staggered formation most of the way, but when we got closer to the winding roads through the hills around Hatta, the group pulled up for a quick discussion.

'We'd like to go faster,' said one of the men. 'We're not testing the capabilities of these bikes by crawling along like this.'

'Jamil, I don't want to go any faster. Please can we stay behind?'

'Don't worry, Bizzie,' he reassured me. 'We'll go at our own pace.'

They sped off one by one. Jamil held back and we caught up with them at the Hatta Fort Hotel for lunch.

Back in Jeddah, the men didn't mind riding without their jackets in the summer heat, but for this promotion ride everyone wore their protective clothing. I knew mine had saved me from terrible grazing injuries so no matter how high the temperature, I kept it on. Despite the intense, consuming heat that day, when we got back to the hotel, I had to admit to myself that it was good to be back on a Harley. My confidence was on the way to being restored, defying the undercurrent of fear fizzing in my belly the whole way. And the Ultra Classic was gorgeous.

My report on the weekend and the new range of Harleys was published in the *Saudi Gazette*, which is what Lisa had wanted. But her pivotal achievement was getting me back into motorcycling.

After that Dubai trip, local rides around Jeddah with Frosty increased my confidence. By the following year, I was ready for a weekend in the mountains around Al Baha for the second Saudi National HOG Rally. Lisa was there, with Marwan AlMutlaq and Colonel Attar, the air force pilot who had ordered the ambulance men to take me to hospital. Along with other Saudi bikers, they wanted to know how I was getting on since the accident. A few of our friends from previous trips to the mountains were also there.

'So, Bizzie, how does it feel to be back on a Harley?' Lisa asked.

'It scares the hell out of me, Lisa, but it's a lot better than spending the weekend alone in Jeddah.'

My passion for biking adventures was decisively reignited when Lisa invited me to go to Egypt that November to cover the press launch of another range of new Harleys. Frosty was invited too, all expenses paid for both of us.

We flew to Marsa Alam, a new five-star beach complex on the Red Sea, where we met other journalists from the UK, South Africa and the Middle East. The new Harleys were lined up outside the hotel. A tag was hanging off the handlebars of a regal, dark-blue Ultra Classic. I turned it over and read "ELIZABETH FROST". I smiled. Lisa knew exactly how to woo me back into biking.

It was the first time Frosty and I had been on one of these luxurious touring bikes together. Our group had a backup vehicle, a police escort and its own small fuel tanker provided by Shell.

Bikers from the Cairo Chapter led us 365 kilometres inland to Luxor, a small city on the River Nile, full of character and history. Once known as Thebes, it had been the capital of the ancient Egyptian pharaohs. It was my fourth visit there, giving me a welcome opportunity to revisit my favourite archaeological sites. After riding through the town's chaotic traffic alongside picturesque horse-drawn carriages, cars and tourist coaches, we stopped at the Luxor Temple to take photos. We parked our new Harleys against a backdrop of towering columns that had stood in the heart of the town for 3,400 years.

Later, we went to see the Sound and Light Show at the magnificent temples of Karnak, three kilometres away. I treasure every visit to this four thousand-year-old complex and its Great Hypostyle Hall, with its forest of 134 immense sandstone pillars, all carved with hieroglyphics. To this day mystery surrounds how the ancient Egyptians built such structures and raised the massive stone architraves, weighing some seventy tons, to sit atop columns that are up to twenty-one metres high. Each time I have visited the temple, my skin tingles as goosebumps come up on my arms. All I do for the first few minutes is gaze upwards in awe. In its atmosphere of reverential silence, I then meander between the columns, marvelling at their ten-metre circumference, soaking up the grandeur and mystique of my pharaonic surroundings.

Another highlight of the two days was our ride across the River Nile to the Valley of the Kings. Our parked line of shiny chrome and steel was against a backdrop of brown rugged hills where the legendary Tutankhamun and numerous other pharaohs were entombed between three and four thousand years ago.

Those long rides in Egypt on traffic-free, winding roads through mountains and deserts under vast blue skies, had me hooked on biking once more. Lisa's persistence had paid off, and now my gut-gripping fear of riding had been quashed by my thirst for more adventures.

16

GURAYAT TO DAMASCUS

October 2009, HOG Rally in Beirut and 3rd Saudi National HOG Rally in Abha. Total distance ridden: 4,614 km. Scale idea: Aqaba to Jeddah 1,115 km

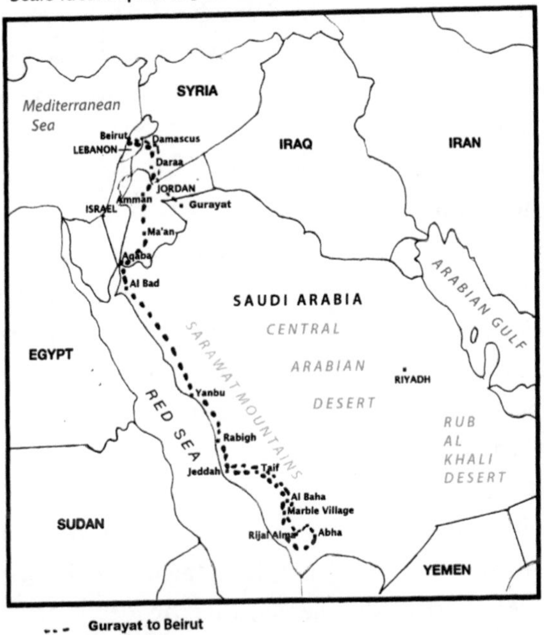

In 2009, the Lebanon HOG Chapter announced their first Harley rally was scheduled for the beginning of October. The country had recovered from fifteen years of civil war from 1975 to 1990 and

its capital, Beirut, was still renowned for French influence, style, culture and fun. It was one of the most popular cities in the Middle East. Members from the Harley groups in Jeddah, Riyadh and Dammam were planning an extended tour around the event.

Frosty and I were both keen to ride all the way. As most of the Jeddah bikers were trucking their machines to Beirut, we contacted Amer AlKhaldi in Riyadh. Sixteen of them were going but first transporting their Harleys to Gurayat, a small town thirty kilometres from the Saudi-Jordanian border. They would continue through Jordan and Syria, spending a night in Damascus before riding on to Beirut.

'Would it be okay if we joined you guys?' Frosty asked.

'Of course, you are welcome,' said Amer. 'The best thing would be for you to truck your bike to Riyadh, and we can put it on our transport to Gurayat.'

'Great, I'll do that. We'll come to Riyadh the night before and fly to Gurayat with the group.'

Neither of us had been to these three Arab countries before, and the very names Jordan and Damascus belonged to a biblical world I had first heard about in Sunday school. We would be travelling through the mystical lands of Moses, the Three Wise Men and Jesus. Another attraction was that our close friend, Mae Moussa, lived in Beirut. Like our first tour to Oman, this was a trip we weren't going to miss.

It would be our third long ride with the Riyadh Chapter. We liked the men, their rides were disciplined, and I felt safe with them. Unlike the Jeddah Chapter, they divided their rides into smaller groups of around ten bikes, each with its own road captain and sweeper.

While Frosty organised the transport, I contacted my features editor, Ramesh, at the *Saudi Gazette*. I had given up writing for the *Arab News*. Promises of better pay hadn't come through. The *Gazette* had welcomed me back, agreeing to a good rate for all my features.

I explained the details of the trip to Ramesh and added, 'Would you be interested in a daily blog?'

'Bizzie, that would be great. Give me around four hundred words a day and a photo. And you know this will be our last project together because I'll be leaving as soon as you get back.'

Apart from my short break at the *Arab News*, Ramesh and I had worked together for twenty years.

'It's time for me to go home to India,' he said. 'But you know, I regret not pushing you harder – you could have become a Middle East correspondent.'

'You had more confidence in me than I had in myself. I will miss you, Ramesh – thank you so much for your encouragement.' His support had shaped my career and helped rebuild my self-esteem following my operation. He had once offered me a position as a staff writer, but if I'd taken this full-time job with my own work permit, I would have lost the airline privileges that came with Frosty's job, as well as the flexibility of a freelancer.

Frosty's job now was to organise the paperwork and the dealership had given him some notes to work with.

'Frosty, have you read these?'

'Not yet. Why?'

'Well, they advise you not to have a passenger during the ride from Jordan to Lebanon, and you should let me fly there.'

'Well, we know we're going to ignore that one. What else does it say?'

'Saudis have to get a travel permit from the government for their wives to be allowed to fly to Lebanon.'

I read out the rest of the list to him. We needed multiple entry visas for Jordan, Syria and Lebanon, and he had to get a *carnet de passage* customs document for Maridadi. This document is compulsory for vehicles going through several countries in case you want to sell it, return through a different border control, or your vehicle breaks down and needs to be reimported to your country of origin.

'You'd better get moving, Frosty – you've got a lot to do.'

Deciding what to pack was, as usual, dictated by the limited space. I would hit the Middle East capital of chic with only my biker kit. My few concessions to anything like style were my Harley earrings and necklace and, of course, my leather waistcoat festooned with badges.

Our night in Riyadh was a "signin' on for the ride" bad sleep that Diamond had described to us on the day we set off for Muscat in 2005. We were both overexcited and wide awake at 2.00am. I dozed off again until our alarm jingled at 5.00am, but Frosty was still wide awake. His mind was churning about his future with the airline. Expatriate pilots were being terminated at age sixty-three instead of the internationally approved sixty-five. This would mean a loss of two years' income before our retirement, critical when you don't have a pension. A long Harley ride would do him good.

We were staying in the airport's Sahara Hotel, so after breakfast we made our way to the terminal to catch the flight to Gurayat. The Riyadh Chapter, along with Amer, were already there. I couldn't help liking him, with his friendly manner and contagious cheerfulness. And he loved riding. Unlike the other bikers, Amer always dressed like a cowboy with black leather chaps over his blue jeans.

'Hi, sis,' he greeted me with a big smile. 'Good to see you again.'

We had a long-standing joke between us because when I had first joined the Jeddah Committee, the men from our two chapters greeted each other in communications as brothers. I had fun emailing him back and telling him there was now a sister on the Jeddah HOG Committee.

We took a group photo on arrival at Gurayat Airport, and there I stood, a lone woman among this group of eighteen bikers – expatriates and Saudis. Since the accident and getting back onto the pillion seat, I had sensed a new respect and warmth from both the Jeddah and Riyadh Arab HOGs. None of them questioned why I hadn't flown to Beirut.

A minibus took us to the truck depot where the eighteen Harley-Davidsons had been offloaded. They were still strapped to their pallets and covered with dust. The owners took out dusters and spent fifteen minutes cleaning their precious bikes.

'Come and say hello to Maridadi,' said Frosty. He always liked me to greet her before a long ride and thank her after we arrived. I joined him beside our Road King and patted her fuel tank.

'Morning, Maridadi.' Our bike seemed to smile back at me, like an inanimate character out of a child's storybook.

After Amer's briefing, we got onto our machines. It always impressed me how my man heaved the leaning and loaded Maridadi to a stable upright position with me already on board. He kicked away the stand and started her up.

By 9.50am we were at the Omari border crossing, checking out of Saudi Arabia and into the Hashemite Kingdom of Jordan. Despite being the poorer of the two countries, the Jordanian border building was smarter than the Saudi one and the officers more pleasant.

'Welcome to Jordan,' they greeted us.

It was a slow process going through the Jordanian side. The *carnet de passage* was the crucial document for each bike, and everyone had to buy temporary insurance for riding through the Kingdom. The Saudi HOGs obtained special permission for us to ride through the country because large motorbikes were officially banned – except for King Abdullah, who owned several. The Kingdom of Jordan Chapter and Harley ownership existed at the discretion of His Majesty. Even the Jordanian nationals had to request a special permit from their government to ride through their own country. Large motorcycles had a bad reputation in Jordan, Syria and Lebanon – they had been used as vehicles for drive-by assassinations and other crimes.

To pass the time I wandered up and down the line of Harleys, as usual parked in a neat row. Jackets and helmets had been left on the saddles or were hanging off handlebars. I paused to read and photograph the captions on the embroidered badges.

"Ride It Like You Stole It", and on one sleeve, "BADD – Bikers Against Dumb Drivers". A black helmet was decorated with a band of shark-like teeth. Numerous stickers took up the rest of the space: "Instant asshole, just add alcohol"; "If I have to explain, you won't understand"; "My favourite colour is chrome"; "Out of mind back in five minutes"; "Is there life after death? Touch this bike and find out!".

None of the Muslims on the ride bothered about prayer time. When they were on the road, prayers could wait until a more convenient time.

Three hours later we were out of Saudi Arabia and into Jordan. Like our previous crossings into the UAE, I noticed the release of tension in the group, especially among the Saudis. Jordan was a far more tolerant and liberal state, and although the principal religion was Islam, it had some of the world's oldest Christian communities. At the time, it was also one of only two Arab nations that had signed a peace treaty with Israel. They shared a common boundary, which people crossed daily. Most were tourists visiting Petra, one of the best-known historical sites in the Middle East. Without the benefit of oil wealth, Jordan depended on its tourist industry.

Because of this relative poverty, Jordan's roads weren't up to the same standard as those in Saudi Arabia. Except for a few stretches of dual carriageway, we faced two-way traffic on a narrow strip with no hard shoulder. On some sections there was a scary four-foot drop off the edge. For the first fifty kilometres, the surface was rough and potholed, damaged by the constant flow of heavy trucks. We slowed to pass a fuel tanker, which had rolled onto its side and lay there like a giant dead insect, its black belly and wheels exposed. A huge red fire truck stood beside it.

Our group growled along at a steady one hundred kilometres per hour, on this flat, straight road that stretched ahead to the horizon. Unlike the pristine highways of the UAE and Oman, rubbish lay scattered on the roadside.

Barren, gravelly desert spread into the distance on either side of us. Village houses we passed resembled those in Saudi Arabia: white concrete shoeboxes with holes cut for windows and flat roofs like shoebox lids. Blocks of flats were unfinished but inhabited, with steel rebars sticking out the top.

At our first fuel stop, we gasped at the price: four times that of Saudi Arabia. The washrooms were equally horrible, but now the facilities for men and women were in the same room.

When we arrived at the Syrian border, a police escort and twenty-six bikers from Damascus were waiting to welcome us. Their motorcycles were a variety of brands, all of them powerful, expensive machines.

'I thought big motorbikes weren't allowed in Syria,' I said to Amer.

'They aren't, but these guys are very influential. I've met them a few times, and I don't want to know who some of them are.'

'Who's that man over there, talking on his mobile phone? He looks like he's in charge.'

'That's Louay Kazzaz.'

Louay was a big man, over six feet tall, round-faced and clean-shaven. He had a blue and white bandana covering his bald head. We found out later that his father and President Assad's father had been friends since their years in the Syrian Air Force. The families had lived on the same air force base, so Louay and the Syrian president had known each other since childhood. His authority became clear when he arranged for someone to collect everyone's passports and documents to be dealt with en masse. Instead of hanging around outside, we were shown to a VIP lounge with comfortable armchairs and sofas. Frosty took the opportunity to have a catnap. The Syrians waited with us for the two hours it took for everything to be processed.

Before moving on, we all gathered onto the outside steps for a group photo, holding up the flags of three HOG chapters: Riyadh, Jeddah and Qatar. I handed my camera to one of the men so I could be included. Again, I was a lone female figure among those men, most of whom were Arabs. Yet I felt comfortable, and they didn't appear to find my presence odd.

The sun was setting by the time we left the border with the Syrian group and the police escort. Instead of breaking up into smaller groups, we rode in a long, double line of forty-eight bikes: Syrians, Jordanians, Saudis, five Western expatriates, two men from Qatar and two from Kuwait. For the first few kilometres of dual carriageway, we passed a continuous queue of trucks that must have stopped for the night at the border. We discovered Louay had a radio giving him direct access to the police escort, which kept us moving at a fast pace.

On the edge of Damascus, we hit the heavy evening traffic, including hordes of minibus public transport. Our police escort, now with two motorbikes as well as a car, commandeered a way through, blocking off every junction. They took us into the modern city centre where we parked in a tree-lined avenue. On either side were four-storey blocks of flats with women's fashion shops on the ground floor. The arrival of forty-eight powerful motorbikes caused a stir, and people in the well-lit streets stopped to watch us go by. Once we'd parked, they gathered round for a closer look. We felt like celebrities as journalists interviewed us for television and took photographs for magazines.

A distinct difference from Saudi Arabia was the dress code for the men. Following the example of President Assad, who always wore a well-cut suit, they all wore Western-style clothing. King Abdullah of Jordan switched between the two styles, suits and the traditional *thobe* with the red and white *shammagh* headscarf, while the Saudis, Emiratis, Kuwaitis and Omanis stuck to their traditional clothing.

Our Syrian hosts had booked out the small Casa restaurant and treated us to a typical Middle Eastern mezze dinner. Afterwards, the police escort led us on a night Thunder Parade up and down the central three-lane highway in Damascus. I noticed a large billboard advertising "The Pub" as a typical English pub with live entertainment. Road signs pointed towards the renowned ancient part of Damascus, but we hadn't allowed time for sightseeing in Syria. By the time we arrived at the Sheraton Hotel, it was 10.00pm.

Once Frosty had parked Maridadi, he said, 'Only 310 kilometres. Not far when you think we've been through three countries.'

Like several others among our group, we were now thirsting for a cold beer – the Casa restaurant hadn't served alcohol.

I had my commitment to write my daily blog, so while Frosty carried on chatting to HOGs in the bar, I found the hotel's business centre. By the time I had downloaded a suitable photo from my Nikon D3, reduced it to an email-friendly size, written my blog and sent it to the *Gazette* on a tortoise of a computer and slow internet, it was 1.00am. Frosty had long since left the bar and was fast asleep.

17

KEEP YOUR EYES ON THE ROAD: BEIRUT

In the morning we had a leisurely start, a relief after my late night. The Harleys were waiting for us under the covered driveway outside the entrance to the Sheraton. We found most of the men already there, polishing off yesterday's dust. The day before, I had researched among the group who was the eldest – Frosty, followed by me – and who the youngest: a Saudi of twenty-four called Bilal. Ten-year-old Maridadi was also the oldest bike among them.

Our police escort, including officers on white Honda motorcycles, led us out of Damascus on a wide dual carriageway lined with trees. There were no skyscrapers, just unremarkable modern blocks of flats and offices on either side, some with shops on the ground floor. I was impressed by the quality of the road, the trees and greenery and how smart and clean everything looked. On the way we passed the occasional small 100cc motorbike. There seemed to be no rules about how many people they carried. On one, I saw a family of four huddled up together with no crash helmets.

The road led us through the ochre-coloured barren hills surrounding the city and on to the Jdeidat Yabous border exit from Syria. This time we didn't have a VIP luxury lounge to wait in.

Instead, we parked our Harleys under the full force of the midday sun and waited there for two hours while our passports were processed. Our Syrian police escort stayed with us, a prolonged, boring shift for them. The Saudis' documents were dealt with first, so they zoomed on ahead.

At last, we were released and entered the eight kilometres of no man's land neutral territory between Syria and Lebanon. For the first time, we saw a strong military presence at a Middle Eastern border – we rode past a succession of armoured vehicles and soldiers manning machine guns. Although we had tight security around our expatriate compounds, we weren't used to this combative atmosphere. After their long civil war, the Lebanese people understood it well.

The Lebanese border control at Masnaa was crowded and scruffy. Once again, we had to wait out in the scorching heat while immigration processed our papers. Looking around, I saw rubbish everywhere. Thinking out loud, I asked Frosty, 'Why don't they make borders more pleasant?'

He shrugged. 'This is how they are. They don't see it and don't care.'

The entire way between the borders we had ridden past a continuous line of trucks. One of the expatriates, Dan Prevost, was the general manager of the Naqel trucking company based in Riyadh.

'Our trucks go through unbelievable headaches to get through these borders,' he told us. 'It's surprising the drivers don't abandon their trucks. I've sometimes had to send them food because they get stuck for so many days.'

Most of the cars we saw were old and carried at least six people. Minibuses were running a service for local people to cross the border. There were also a few tourist coaches, one with Westerners in it. I went over to chat to them.

'What are you doing here?' I asked one woman.

'We are supposed to be visiting a historic site in Lebanon for the day, but we've already been at this border for three hours,' she replied. 'I thought travelling was supposed to be fun, but I'm not so sure anymore.'

Two and a half hours later, we were in Lebanon, renowned for being a nation of party people.

'They live each day as though it's their last,' Amer AlKhaldi had told us.

Within a few kilometres, we were greeted by a billboard displaying the country's difference in attitude to all the other Arab countries we had visited. The image showed the upper half of a young woman in a bikini top, side view, sitting up, looking over her shoulder, her head tossed back and hair flying. Large words to her right said, "READY TO PARTY". She was the attraction for XXL Vodka Party Flavours. Either one of these images, let alone the combination, was taboo elsewhere. The next billboard, even larger, had two faces – one a handsome man and the other a pretty young woman – with the statement, "I know she's after my money". Beside the caption was a large bottle of Label 5 Scotch Whisky with the words, "Live Your Way". More billboards depicting saucy images of women advertising jeans and dresses followed at regular intervals.

Our ride to Beirut wound up through densely populated mountains, barren to begin with but giving way to tree-lined avenues through the villages. We faced frenetic two-way traffic with numerous beat-up old cars, many of them 1980's Mercedes Benz taxis. Frequent bumps and holes in the tarmac, and sections where the top layer of asphalt had been scraped off, pummelled Maridadi's suspension and my body. There were no marked lanes, and everyone drove wherever they wanted to. We had also been warned drivers took no notice of red traffic lights, so policemen controlled some junctions instead.

In all the villages we passed roadside stalls abundant with fresh fruit and vegetables. From time to time, I noticed buildings pockmarked from bullet strikes, sometimes with collapsed walls and deserted. This was my first encounter with real-life evidence of a recent war – I had only ever experienced war in the cinema and on television. I shuddered, imagining the noise of the bullets battering them and the fear they instilled in the people inside. What the country had been through was sinking in.

It was a long, steady climb up the evergreen treed hills until we reached the top with a view over the whole of Beirut, with the Mediterranean Sea beyond. My first impression was how big the city was, fanning out down the mountain and for kilometres along the coast to the north and south.

At the first sweeping bend of our descent, the view of the city became a panoramic backdrop for another massive billboard. We faced a large horizontal image depicting a curvy young woman wearing black bra and pants, lying on her side, propped up on one elbow. She was advertising a brand of lingerie. Above her was the caption, "KEEP YOUR EYES ON THE ROAD".

This big disparity between the Lebanese culture and the other Arab countries took me by surprise. All the advertising agencies in Saudi Arabia were run by Lebanese men, but the Wahhabi atmosphere must have stifled their creative juices and mischievous humour.

After riding only 110 kilometres that day, we pulled into the Monroe Hotel where we parked the Harleys in a secure underground car park. Our room had a sweeping view of the Mediterranean, taking in the bombed-out shell of the Saint Georges Hotel. It was draped with a massive piece of fabric with a blood-red, hexagonal sign and "STOP SOLIDERE" in contrasting white letters.

In the evening we met our friend of many years, Mae, at the Phoenicia Intercontinental for dinner. Here was another building that had been bombed during the war. Standing beside it was the grey, towering, concrete skeleton of the Holiday Inn. There were no windows; the walls were pockmarked with shell wounds, the building deserted. Everywhere around us bore these haunting scars and reminders of the recent war.

From its shared status with the Saint Georges as the most prestigious hotels in Beirut, the five-star Phoenicia had been reduced to a burnt-out ruin in what was known as the Battle of the Hotels from 1975 to 1976. For the next twenty years it stood abandoned. After a $100 million refurbishment, the Phoenicia reopened in 2000, regaining its reputation.

Over dinner, Mae's friend Georgette told us what it was like to live in Beirut during the conflict.

'This hotel marks the Green Line which separated the Christian and Muslim sides of the city during the war. When it was time to take the kids to school, the soldiers would have a ceasefire so we could do this safely. Some families had to cross the Green Line twice a day because their home and school were on opposite sides. As soon as they were in school, the shooting would begin again. At the end of the day when we collected the kids, they would have another ceasefire. They were crazy times.'

'And what's the story behind that building with the big stop sign on it?' I asked.

'That hotel, the Saint Georges, has a sorry history,' she continued. 'It was badly bombed during the war. The story goes that President Rafic Hariri refused to allow the owner, a woman, to have it rebuilt because he wanted to buy it. In the end, he gave in, and she was allowed to rebuild. No sooner had she done so, Hariri was killed in a car-bombing right outside it, and the hotel was blasted to a wreck once again. Now history is repeating itself. Hariri's son is said to be trying the same tactic, refusing to give the owner permission for her to rebuild because *he* wants to buy it.'

'And yet from our hotel we can see its beautiful swimming pool and marina still in action, with lots of people there,' Frosty commented.

'Yes, she's allowed to keep all that outdoor area going. It's a popular and trendy place. The big stop sign is her protest.'

Despite hearing these stories relating to the fifteen-year history of the Lebanese civil war, I went to sleep thinking how refreshing it was to be in a country where, for the first time in an Arab state, I saw a mosque and a church standing side by side, the cross on the top of the steeple of one and the crescent moon on the minaret of the other.

After breakfast the following morning, our group rode over to a large car park to join the 280 Harley-Davidson motorcycles to tour the country. What I now observed in this Arab country was the number of women with us. Of the 333 participants, there were fifty-six women, most riding pillion. They wore tight, sleeveless tops, clothing that was taboo in the Kingdom. I could see why the Saudis liked coming here.

Everyone had to register for the event; then we waited with our bikes, again under the searing sun, while we were sorted into groups of sixty bikes. Arabic music blared from several Ultra Classics, creating a festive atmosphere. The separate chapters gathered together for group photographs, holding their large flags. They photobombed each other's groups, bringing their own flags, until we had members of the Jeddah, Riyadh, Qatar and Lebanon chapters crowded in together.

After a while, boredom set in. A cacophony of revving engines and horn blowing let the organisers know we were itching to get going.

A murky layer of smog hung in the air as we eased onto the three-lane highway out of Beirut, heading north towards Tripoli. With such a big event, we had the usual police security with us in several vehicles and on motorbikes. The coastal road seemed to go on and on through heavily built-up suburbs, so it was a relief when we turned off near Batroun and headed inland towards the mountains. What the Lebanese loved to say about their country was, 'You can snowski in the morning and waterski in the afternoon', but October was too early for snow.

The road now was narrower, with two-way traffic and a broken-up surface. When the occasional truck came towards us, we had to squeeze past, our handlebars almost scraping the sides of the big vehicles. We twisted and turned into the forested hills, from time to time going through a small town or village. People hung out of their windows and lined the streets to watch us go by, waving and smiling, most of them men and boys. When we reached the canyon of Wadi Tannourine, the empty road wound along the edge of the canyon, tucked against a steep, golden-ochre rock face to our left and a drop into the dark-green valley of the Cedar Forest Nature Reserve to our right.

Representing resilience, immortality, strength and elevation, the cedar tree is the national emblem of Lebanon and appears on its flag.

We stopped for a late lunch at Al Mrouj restaurant in Laqlouq. The single-storey rustic building, with water-stained white paint peeling off, sat in a rural area with only a few farm buildings for miles around. Two hundred and fifty bikes spread out to find somewhere to park along the lanes, and then 350 hungry, thirsty people poured in. This unassuming restaurant took it in its stride, serving up an excellent Lebanese mezze meal on several long tables, with seating for everyone. The atmosphere was noisy and cheerful. As well as catching up with our Jeddah Chapter friends, we found people we had met on other Harley rides.

'Indji,' I called out, spotting the Egyptian girl we had met on our Luxor trip. 'How great to see you here. Are you on your own Harley?'

'Hi, Bizzie. Yes, I am. I rode here with sixteen others from Cairo, nearly 1,200 kilometres. And we'll be riding back.'

Among the riders, Indji was one of three women on her own Harley. Another surprise was to meet Amer AlKhaldi's wife Amal, who had flown from Riyadh to meet him in Lebanon. She was now riding pillion with him. She had abandoned her black abaya but still covered her hair, wearing a funky combination of a long, light-blue scarf and a baseball cap.

When I saw Lisa Schlensker later, I asked her, 'When Saudi women ride pillion here, why do you think they don't in Jeddah and Riyadh?'

'Come on, Bizzie, think about it,' Lisa drawled, giving me a look that said I should be able to work this out. Like a true Texan, she shot with both barrels with her answer. 'When you ride pillion, you've got your legs wide apart, and your crotch pushed up against a man's back. Of course the police and *mutaween* aren't going to like it. And look at their butts from behind, all those curves.'

Our afternoon ride took us further into the mountains, meandering up and down and through villages with tree-lined avenues. The narrow road left them behind and led us higher and higher until we were above the treeline, riding along a strip of road that wound its way across barren wilderness. We had the world to ourselves; there was no other traffic. When I thought the landscape couldn't get any better, we came around a wide corner, and a hazy panorama of a vast valley spread out to our left. The road captain in front of us made a sweeping gesture with his left arm as if to say, *there you are. This is what we brought you here to see. Our beautiful Lebanon.*

This was the Bekaa Valley. Lying between two mountain ranges, the Lebanon Mountains in the west and the Anti-Lebanon Mountains in the east, it is the beginning of the spectacular Great Rift Valley which runs seven thousand kilometres southwards through Israel, Jordan, the Red Sea and on through Eastern Africa, including Kenya, to Mozambique.

Our journey took us along kilometre after kilometre of winding mountain road, the only sign of habitation the occasional Bedouin encampment. It seemed we were riding forever to nowhere through the soft, late afternoon light.

The sun had set by the time our group stopped on a section of road running along the edge of a mountain. We got off our bikes to watch the headlights of a long line of Harleys as they crept along the valley floor in the gloom, like an army of glow worms. The twinkling convoy wound around a hairpin bend and made its way up the hillside towards us. The bikes were too far away for us to hear their growl; the only sound was the slight breeze.

By the time we moved on it was dark, and we continued the rest of the way under a full moon, the temperature cool but not yet cold. Our Lebanese hosts had treated us to a ride through their country we might not have found ourselves – we found out later this was the old, rarely used road to the Faraya Mzaar Ski Resort on Mount Lebanon. We pulled up in the resort's Intercontinental Mzaar Hotel car park en masse at 7.00pm, with that kind of happy tiredness when you are glad to arrive, but you couldn't have hoped for a better day.

While the rest of the group queued for coaches to take them to a restaurant, we spent our evening in the bar bonding with an eclectic group of men – Saudi, Indian, Canadian, American and Swedish – and being entertained by a male singer playing a keyboard.

Our next day's ride was to the historic Bekaa Valley.

18

WHERE ROMANS ONCE DRANK WINE: THE BEKAA VALLEY

After breakfast, our first stop was a small fuel station with four pumps, where 280 bikes waited in an untidy queue to funnel through. The prices were a shock – what would have set us back

US$3 for twenty-two litres in Saudi Arabia was a hefty US$21 here in Lebanon.

Fuelled up, we rode back along the meandering road through the barren, ochre-coloured hills. Being in that vast, uncluttered space with nothing to do but appreciate the scenery and take photos cleared my mind. My pain and fear forgotten, I was back in that headspace of the freedom of the open road, living in the moment. The only sign of life was the occasional shepherd with his flock.

After a few kilometres, we turned off onto a road that took us down into the expanse of the Bekaa Valley. During the era of the Roman Empire, it was a major agricultural source. It is still Lebanon's most important farming region.

As we descended, the cool mountain air gave way to a gruelling forty Celsius on the valley floor. Our long convoy crept along the narrow roads. In the full midday sunshine, the temperature was more like fifty Celsius, and we baked in our dark clothes. The heat radiated back up from the asphalt where crude repairs had created a patchwork of bumps on the surface. A steady flow of tractors, trailers, pickup trucks and donkey carts had to pull over to make way for us. At one point I saw a huge bundle of pink on the back of something ahead of us. It turned out to be a small motorbike carrying a five-foot circular bunch of individually packed helpings of candy floss.

On the way, we passed potato and onion crops, and I wondered how they managed to grow without shrivelling up like I was. A lot of people took their jackets off and rode in T-shirts, but after my accident, there was no way I was going to ride without mine. Whenever we stopped, my black clothing absorbed more heat, locking me into its oven.

For part of the way, a couple of policemen on white, beat-up Harley-Davidsons accompanied us, and two ambulances stayed with us all day. Local drivers had to pull over and wait for our lengthy convoys to pass. In all the villages, I waved back at smiling people lining the road, taking pictures of us and this novelty event. At most Harley rallies, there is a Thunder Parade through the host town, but this was a 495-kilometre Thunder Parade around a large chunk of Lebanon. I was told that the police were only willing to close the roads for a single day, which was why we all had to ride together.

We zigzagged through numerous chicane checkpoints, made from metre-high concrete blocks and guarded by armed soldiers. They were constant reminders of the country's fragile oscillation between war and peace. This northern part of the valley we drove through in the morning looked unkempt and poor, with litter on both sides of the road. We were told later it was the Muslim section.

When we stopped for a late lunch, I felt withered by the heat, not at all like a "Born to be Wild" biker.

'Riding with these big groups is too much,' I said to Frosty.

'I agree, never again. We need to go at our own pace. That was hard work.'

If you want to learn how to run a restaurant that doesn't turn a hair when 350 people stop by for lunch, go to Lebanon. As with our lunch stop the previous day, the riverside Al Bahsasa Restaurant welcomed us without any fuss. Everything was ready and we settled at the tables, cooled by their big water wheels and shade. Dishes of mezze flew out of the kitchen in the hands of energetic waiters. Judging by their smiles and lively eyes, they liked their work, or perhaps it was because our big group represented good money, and they were serving up an easy meal. We devoured the tasty variety of meat, cheese and salad platters while we chatted.

Towards the end of the meal, the hookah water pipes came out, with several positioned at every table. They are part of life in the Arab world, and smoking in restaurants in Lebanon was allowed.

Leaving it behind, I went out to take photos of the long lines of Harleys, parked up against the yellow stone wall along the road outside the restaurant. There were at least thirty in each direction, all the front wheels in a neat line to the left. The others had found space under a section of the restaurant that was raised on high stilts, or in whatever parking space they could find. At the annual rally in Sturgis, USA, they have up to 750,000 motorcycles, something I found difficult to imagine. This was a big enough gathering of high revs for me.

Our afternoon ride switched back northwards along empty roads through more rolling ochre-coloured hills, unproductive except for a few olive groves. It led us to the wealthier central section of the Bekaa Valley which was covered in vineyards. Winemaking here was a tradition going back six thousand years, and we passed several signs advertising wineries. No wonder the Romans had valued the area. A prominent double-steepled church nestled among pine trees announced that this was the Christian section. Everything, from the quality of the road to the tended fields and vineyards, looked well cared for. The litter had also disappeared.

Our night stop was in Hammana, a small town back in the cooler, tree-covered hills east of Beirut. The Lebanese members of the tour knew which of the two booked hotels to head for: the luxury five-star Pinelands Hotel and Health Resort. It didn't have enough rooms for everyone, so someone directed us and the Riyadh group to a small, scruffy hotel whose name I didn't even notice. We were checked in by Michel, who turned out to be the general Mr Fix-It, as well as the waiter, night manager, room service and housekeeper. He was amusing in all of these roles, and I had great fun bargaining over a cup of tea for which he tried to charge me US$7.50.

After supper, Frosty went straight to bed, exhausted from the heat. We had ridden 124 kilometres, but it felt like five times that. I still had my blog to write, but with no business centre in our two-star hotel, our Canadian friend Dan lent me his notebook computer. Like Frosty, I was worn out, and as soon as I had done the job, I fell into bed. It was almost midnight.

Me on my motorbike, Kitu Ngini, on cliffs near Land's End, Cornwall, in June 1974.

Amer Kashoggi, who rode with us to Muscat.

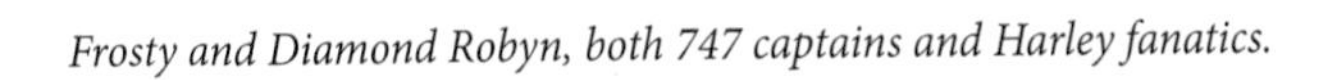

Frosty and Diamond Robyn, both 747 captains and Harley fanatics.

Bikers arrive at the beach for Iftar 2005.

Diamond and Houria at the Makkah junction: Non-Muslims turn right.

The policeman who stopped us for three hours on our way to Riyadh.

The desert surrounding the Christian Bypass.

Thunder Parade through Muscat with 250 bikes, Dec 2005.

Al Qahtani tribesmen perform the traditional sword dance.

Riding from Taïf to Jeddah in a sandstorm.

Caravan of camels appears in the sandstorm on Christian Bypass.

A camel in a village on the Tihama grinding oil from sesame seeds.

The escarpment road up the Asir Mountains from Dhee Ain to AlBaha.

A typical Asir qasaba drystone watch tower.

Frosty and me in the mountains where the Prophet Muhammad grew up.

The drystone village of Dhee Ain, nestled in the foothills of the Asir Mountains.

Caught in a rare heavy rainstorm and riding through flooded streets of Taïf.

The accident on the Madinah Road with Ali AliReza's Harley lying beside the Lamborghini that struck Essam and me as well.

Essam Istanbouli on his Anniversary Road King on which I was riding pillion at the time of the accident.

At the first Saudi National HOG Rally with Amr Al Khaldi, Ahmed Halawani, Marwan Al Mutlaq, Lisa, Monther AlMutlaq, Frosty, me and Diamond.

Cruising on the open road in Egypt in 2008 and fully recovered from the devastating crash.

Right: Lisa Schlensker, Manager of HOG Middle East, who persuaded me to ride again.

Below: Keep your eyes on the road – billboard seen in Beirut.

Riding down into the Bekaa Valley in Lebanon.

Frosty beside the Syrian flag where we broke down outside Damascus.

A highway patrol relay takes over.

Above: The 2442 road snaking down the Asir Mountains from Jebel Sawda to Rijal Almaa.

Left: Frosty, me and Mike by the Makkah Region sign.

Below: The two of us with Maridadi on the escapment road to Al Baha.

The road from Tabuk to the Jordanian border.

Right: Maridadi on the road from Tabuk to the Jordanian border.

Below left: The 1.2-kilometre siq leading into the rock city of Petra.

Below right: Me on Coco at The Monastery in Petra.

Above: Actors arrive at Wadi Rum Station to carry out a WWI simulation for tourists in the old Hejaz Railway.

Left: Frosty and me with Atallah in Wadi Run Village.

Frosty and Faïz on top of one of the rock bridges in Wadi Rum.

Tanya and me on the boat tour around the Farasan Islands.

The preserved drystone village of Rijal Alma.

A hut in the "mud nest" settlement near Jizan.

Some original artwork in one of the houses at Rijal Alma.

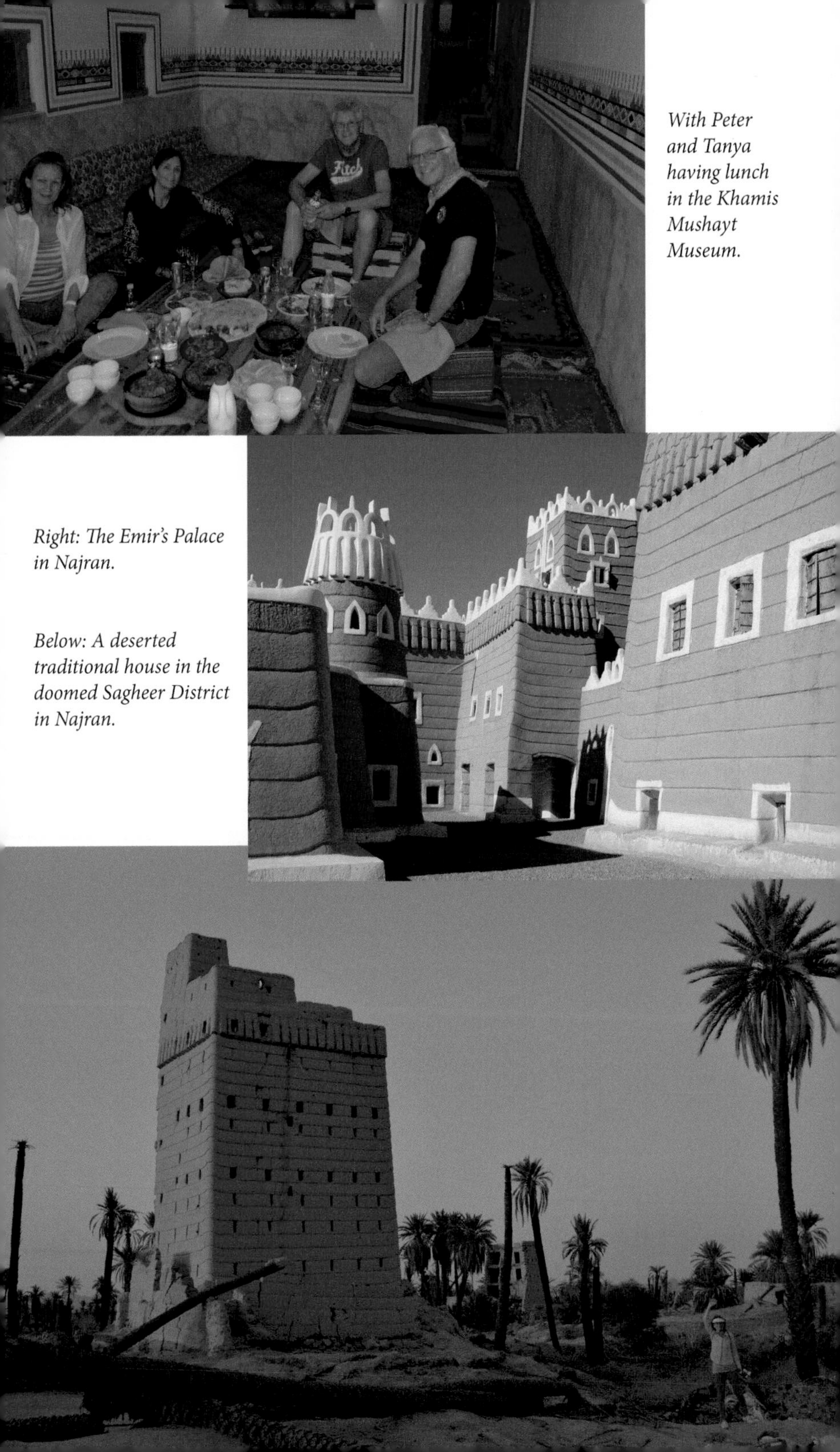

With Peter and Tanya having lunch in the Khamis Mushayt Museum.

Right: The Emir's Palace in Najran.

Below: A deserted traditional house in the doomed Sagheer District in Najran.

Maridadi breaks down as we leave Najran for Al Kharj.

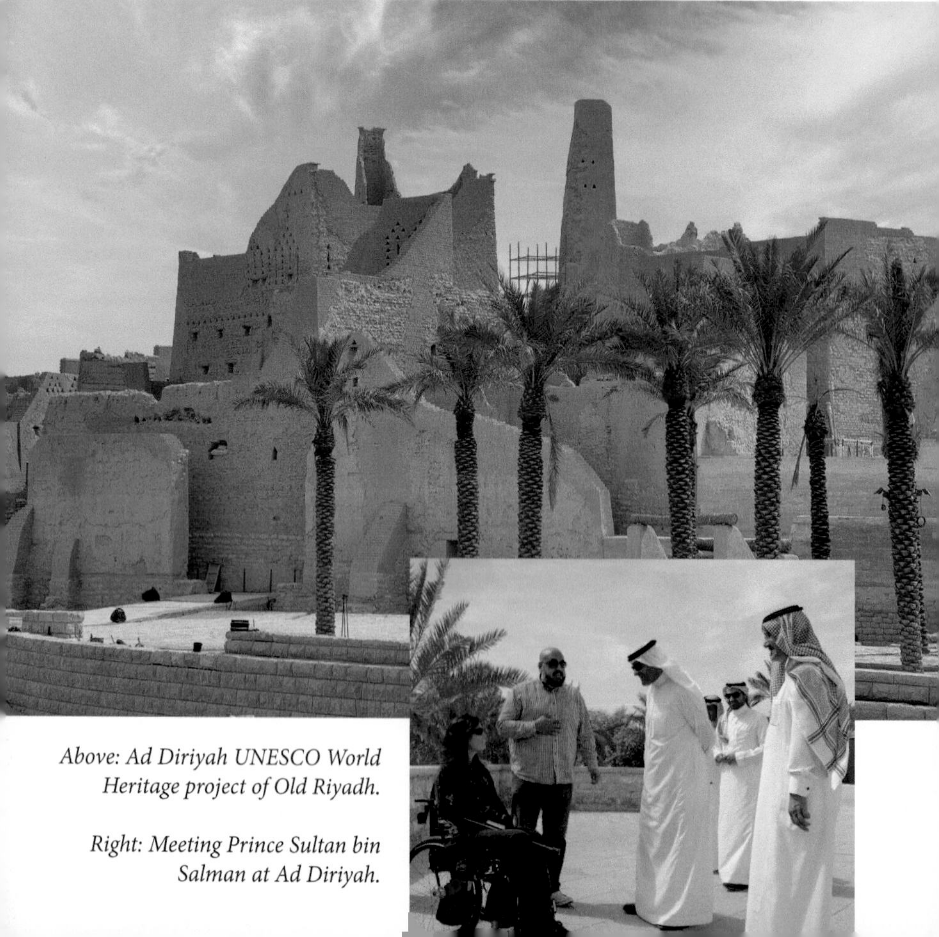

Above: Ad Diriyah UNESCO World Heritage project of Old Riyadh.

Right: Meeting Prince Sultan bin Salman at Ad Diriyah.

Camels watch us overtake as we head from Sakaka towards Al Ula.

Right: Frosty and me at Mada'in Saleh with the Qasr al Farid tomb behind us.

Below: The Qasr al Bint tombs at Mada'in Saleh.

One of the men who chased us for a chat in Dumat Al Jandal.

Rock formations in the desert near Mada'in Saleh.

Creative roofing of a petrol station.

Our final police esc
into Jeddah.

We arrive back in Jeddah on a very dusty Black Beauty.

The Riyadh Chapter was always on time, so we were the first at the meeting point at 9.00am. I closed my eyes and took a long, deep breath of the invigorating, cool morning air of the hills. While we waited, I heard a voice calling my name.

'Hi, Bizzie.' It was Indji again. 'Come and meet the other girls who are riding their own Harleys here.'

I had become obsessed with any sign of women's liberation in the Arab world.

The three girls posed for a photo, with Indji sitting in the middle on her Harley. Wearing tight black tops, blue jeans and dark glasses, they were a paragon of confident, independent women. Their feisty attitude to be among the first female bikers in a macho Arab atmosphere reminded me of myself and my biking days in London thirty-four years earlier.

Our ride that morning went south through small towns and along shaded lanes in hilly areas with lots of trees. I looked up at a house with bright-red window shutters where an elderly woman stood on the balcony, wearing a light-blue blouse and headscarf. She was looking straight at me, smiling and waving. Other families, their ages ranging from about five years old to eighty, were also on their balconies, watching the Thunder Parade go by.

We stopped for lunch in the Sakhret Al Shallal restaurant perched on the edge of a sheer rock face in Jezzine. It overlooked a deep gorge with a panoramic view over the rest of the valley and mountains beyond. Once again, long tables had been set out for us, with an anticipated menu: the ubiquitous mezze. Most people, including me, are happy to eat these tasty dishes for three days in a row.

I stopped at the table for a chat with our Jeddah Chapter, feeling guilty for not hanging out with them more and for sticking with the Riyadh Chapter instead. Jamil was there with his wife and several others who had been with us on that fateful Iftar ride in 2007. I liked all the guys, and they were always friendly, kind and courteous to me, but we rarely went on rides with them anymore. They were too unpredictable. The chapter didn't practise the high standard of safe riding that the Riyadh Chapter did. Following the accident, safety was my priority. On local rides, we preferred to ride with a small group of like-minded friends.

I moved on to join Frosty at the table with Amer and Amal and Louay Kazzaz, who we had met at the Syrian border, and his wife Dania.

'How are you getting back to Jeddah?' Dania asked me.

'We're riding back, going through Syria and Jordan again. We'll be stopping for a night in Amman, then going on to Gurayat in Saudi Arabia.'

'Well, in case you have any problems while you're in Syria, here is my card and Louay's as well. If anything goes wrong, please call us.'

Like the other lunch stops over the three days, the atmosphere with this gathering of Arabs from all over the Middle East was lively and noisy. But now, on the last day of the rally, they were in an even more festive mood. Unlike in Saudi Arabia where meals are rushed, no one here was in a hurry to leave the table. Loud Arabic music blared from the sound system, smoke from the hookah water pipes wafted in the air, and a few people got up to dance. This was Lebanon, a country that had lived through fifteen years of civil war but hadn't forgotten how to party.

With my blog in mind, I tracked down Norbert Ferber, a Frenchman and the oldest biker at the rally.

'Excuse me,' I said, approaching him where he sat at a table, 'I am a journalist writing about this trip, and I've heard that you are the oldest man here?'

'Ah, *bonjour*,' he said, standing up with old-world courtesy. 'Yes, I believe I am. I am now seventy-three.'

'How have you ended up here?'

'Well, my son-in-law works in Amman with Harley-Davidson,' he replied with a strong French accent, 'and he told me about this trip. I came from my home in Lyons to ride here with him and my daughter. He has lent me an Ultra Classic.'

'That's a huge bike. Don't you find it too heavy?' Although I was thinking *at your age*, I didn't say it.

'No, not at all – it is easy to ride. It's a very nice bike.'

'Have you done any other long motorcycle rides?'

'Oh yes, much further than this one. When I retired from being a chef, I joined some others riding from Paris to Dakar in Senegal. We had to cross the Sahara Desert on the way.'

Norbert Ferber was sixty-nine when he undertook a journey that most men of his age would think was mad. He became forever a role model for us.

'Please give me a moment, Norbert,' I asked him, 'while I find Bilal. He is a twenty-four-year-old Saudi and the youngest at this rally.'

My photo of the two men shows a fresh-faced young Arab with dark eyes and a black bandana and a blue-eyed Frenchman with unruly grey hair and a goatee beard, both of them sunburned after our three days of riding. Norbert was old enough to be Bilal's grandfather, but the age gap didn't matter – their passion for riding Harleys united them.

On the final stretch back to Beirut, the 280 Harleys pulled over and parked in a large viewpoint area. A bay of blue sea spread out in front of us, stretching across to the city, hazy in the distance. We were about forty-five minutes' ride away and bikers wanted a last chance to socialise and to rearrange themselves into their chapters for the evening parade into Martyrs' Square.

19

DRAMA IN DAMASCUS

On this coastal route, we rode through several towns, passing more bullet-ridden, derelict buildings. Lebanon was an open-air museum of scars left by war. Most of the cars on the highway looked the worse for wear too. Where dents had been removed, the grey undercoat hadn't been sprayed over to match the car's colour. Drivers and passengers weren't wearing seat belts either. We passed a saloon car with four young women with long, dark hair sitting out of the windows, their bottoms perched on the windowsills. I was told this cavalier attitude to safety in vehicles was attributed to the war – it seemed to be the excuse for every lapse or irregularity, a comment for all occasions.

Our long caterpillar of Harleys crawled into downtown Beirut at dusk. We were bunched up in the street, each bike's headlight almost touching the vivid red rear light of the one in front. The roar of our revving engines echoed in the confined space of the large apartment and office blocks on either side of us, and by the time we arrived near Martyrs' Square, spectators had gathered on the roadside. A stage had been set up in the square with spotlights and a band, and each chapter was announced on arrival. Riders parked their machines, and in the centre of this international gathering of bikers, a single outsize flag was raised on a pole above their heads, the green standard of Saudi Arabia.

After a few speeches, prize-giving and thank-yous, the rally was over. The square emptied.

The Jeddah, Jordan and Cairo bikers left for home the next morning but, along with the rest of the Riyadh Chapter, we stayed on for a few days to explore the city. While Frosty took himself off to play golf, I took a taxi to visit Mae. Her flat was in the cool, hilly village of Roumieh, surrounded by pine forests and with a panoramic view over Beirut. Although in an upmarket area, muddled bundles of electricity cables were strung across the streets between tall posts. From there, they fed into the houses and other buildings.

'Our mains electricity is cut off for at least six hours a day,' Mae told me, 'so some people have set up massive generators in our area. If you want constant power, you can get connected to this other supply. So we have two sets of wiring and two bills to pay at the end of the month.'

Later, we drove to the next-door village of Brummana to see Mae's handicraft workshop. This predominantly Christian part of Beirut emanated a strong European influence. Terraced houses and flats, built from cream-coloured stone, had traditional French window shutters. Flowering plants cascaded from their window boxes.

'This is a very wealthy part of Beirut,' Mae said, 'and popular with Gulf and Saudi tourists. You may have heard of Brummana High School? It's one of the best in Lebanon, a co-ed boarding school.'

Despite being a long-established British Quaker school, she explained, some high-profile Muslims were alumni. Among them were some of the Bin Laden brothers, including Osama.

Frosty picked me up on Maridadi the following day, and we dropped her off to have an oil change before our journey home. Still hungry to see more of the city, we took a taxi with a driver called Sami.

'I see you have big camera,' he said. 'You like take picture?'

'Yes.'

'I show you nice place. We go to Gemmayze.'

Gemmayze is renowned as the artistic quarter of Beirut, full of cafés, restaurants and art galleries. We inched our way through the traffic along a narrow street with cars parked on either side. We peered out of the car windows, catching glimpses of the three- and four-storey houses lining the route. They were a fusion of French and Ottoman architecture, each one different. Some were in natural stone, others painted in pastel shades of blue, purple or green, with a darker tone for door and window frames, and louvred shutters. Decorative fanlights topped tall, elegant windows, and elaborate wrought-iron balconies adorned the first and second floors of most buildings. As in Brummana, thick bundles of electricity cables carried power from house to house, with single strands leaping overhead to the houses on the other side. Sami pointed to various buildings we passed.

'This one, too much bomb-bomb. Now good. But not new build. Just make old new.'

Without stopping to take photos, we left this bohemian section and Sami dropped me off at El Maarad street in the central area. He continued with Frosty to the Harley dealership to collect Maridadi.

The grand buildings here traced their origins to the French mandate era (1923–1946) and were inspired by the Rue de Rivoli in Paris. During the civil war, central Beirut suffered horrendous damage, with some buildings almost reduced to rubble. Like the historical houses in Gemmayze, these had been faithfully reconstructed by the Solidere Construction Company, a joint-stock company formed specifically for this purpose. The long, cobbled streets were now traffic-free zones. I didn't have my wheelchair, but I managed to walk the length of the pedestrian precinct – past the shopping arcades, alfresco cafés and restaurants – to where several streets converged on Nejmeh Square with its art-deco clock tower in the centre. Surrounded by gracious three-storey buildings with elegant arches on the ground floor, and balconies with wrought-iron railings on the upper levels, I felt as though I was in a European city.

As the sun was setting, I heard the simultaneous echoes of the Muslim prayer call and the sonorous ringing of church bells. I worked my way towards the sounds, through a narrow lane, until I stood at the railing overlooking the Saint George Maronite Cathedral and the blue-domed Mohammad Al Amin Mosque, with the Roman ruins spread out in front of them. I listened, savouring the unfamiliar fusion of the calls to prayer of two great religions.

Later that evening, I mentioned this experience in my blog, expecting the dual prayer calls to be edited out in the Saudi paper. They weren't.

Fast forward to 4 August 2020, when a stockpile of 2,750 tons of ammonium nitrate, stored in a warehouse in the Beirut port since 2014, exploded. The blast was felt 240 kilometres away on the island of Cyprus. More than two hundred were killed, over six thousand wounded and some 350,000 left homeless. Destruction to the city during the civil war paled in comparison to the devastation caused by this single explosion. The fault lay mainly with the judiciary and the government. They had done nothing to ensure the safe storage of the explosives, despite repeated requests from the port authorities.

My first thought was of Mae, and I contacted her straight away. She told me all the areas I had seen in central Beirut in October 2009, including the Saint Georges Hotel and the Phoenicia Intercontinental, had suffered terrible damage. I thought about our taxi driver, Sami, telling us about "too much bomb-bomb" during the civil war and how proud he was that the buildings had been reconstructed. On Facebook, I saw the devastation to the Harley-

Davidson dealership. Light poured in through a massive hole in the roof, and chunks of broken glass covered the floor. Marwan, the owner, assured me that none of the staff had been hurt.

Lebanon was already plagued by a financial crisis and the struggle with the Covid-19 pandemic. For them, this explosion equated to 9/11.

◈◈◈

Back to 2009 and our ride back to Saudi. We teamed up with our ski resort drinking buddies again, a small group of six bikes. When we saw O'Neil, the Indian guy, one of his upper arms was wrapped in a transparent bandage, like cling film. It looked horrible, with blood oozing out from what appeared to be a nasty wound underneath.

'O'Neil, what on earth has happened to your arm?' I asked him.

'It's a tattoo,' he said. 'A dragon. I like to have one done whenever I go to a new country.'

Our plan was to ride to Amman in Jordan and spend a night there with the rest of the Riyadh Chapter. The Jordanians were keen to show us around their city.

Shortly before 8.00am the next morning, we rumbled out of the hotel courtyard and started back up the steep climb out of Beirut. We left behind the hordes of naughty billboards with their seductive advertisements for alcohol, lingerie and fashion. We had found the city fascinating but expensive, from food to telephone calls. The Lebanese seemed to like to overcharge and bargain others down.

At the Lebanese border control, a man directed me to the most revolting concept of a toilet I had yet come across. I walked along a corridor and round a few corners, the stench growing worse with each step. As I came around the final corner, I stopped and almost gagged. There was no toilet there, just blobs of faeces dumped on the floor in front of the end wall. Hand pressed over my nose and mouth and holding my breath, I left. A man in a building opposite saw I was still searching and beckoned me in. He pointed up a flight of stairs.

'*Yameen*,' he said. Turn right. I was luckier this time, but even this squat-down loo wasn't clean.

After riding through the military-patrolled no man's land, we arrived at the Syrian border. Going through as a small group was much quicker, and we were soon on our way.

Two hours later, after refuelling, both of us felt a slight wobble in Maridadi's rear wheel. Suspecting a puncture, Frosty slowed and stopped. No puncture. We carried on, but there it was again, that disturbing wobbling. We all pulled up on the side of the road beside a huge billboard of the Syrian flag.

'I think our bearings have gone,' Frosty told the others. 'There's no way we can continue.'

'What are you going to do?' asked Dan.

'I've got Louay Kazzaz's card,' I chipped in. 'He was one of the guys who met us at the border on our way here. He and his wife said to call them if we had any problems.'

Frosty dialled Louay's number, and he answered straight away.

'Don't worry. I'll ask Hazem Alkadi if he can help you. He has a proper trailer for motorbikes.'

A few minutes later, Hazem called back.

'I'll be with you in about half an hour.'

While this was going on, two other motorcycles had pulled up beside us. The impressive BMW off-road machines were ridden by two big men and were kitted out for a long journey, with side panniers and two spare tyres each, strapped on top of bags on their pillion seats.

'Hi, can we help you?' the older man offered.

After explaining our situation, Frosty asked, 'Where are you two going?'

'We're on our way to Cape Town. We're riding from the northernmost point in Europe, in Norway, to the furthest point in South Africa.'

He removed his helmet.

'I'm Arnold Visser,' he introduced himself. 'I'm a captain with KLM Airlines. My son is on a gap year before going to university, so we thought we'd do something special together.'

With two interests in common, bikes and big jets, Frosty and Arnold could have chatted all afternoon. The Dutchmen were disappointed when Frosty told them they wouldn't be allowed to go through Saudi Arabia. They had planned to catch a ferry from Jeddah to Port Sudan.

'Saudi Arabia doesn't issue tourist visas unless you have connections,' Frosty said. 'We met some Australian bikers who managed to get visas, but they had to wait for three weeks in Bahrain to get them.'

We chatted a while longer, then we waved the Dutchmen off to Cape Town and our group to Amman.

After taking a photo of Frosty with the flag billboard behind him for my daily blog, he went and lay on some rocks. I took a few more photos of Maridadi with the billboard, then looked around at the brown, desolate landscape, with a few trees and buildings in the distance. Only a few vehicles went past, one of them a large, red truck. Its massive load of hay bales, covered with a green tarpaulin, was leaning dangerously to one side. I wondered how far it would get before the whole lot tumbled off, pulling the truck over with it.

I joined Frosty on his rocks and sat surfing through my pictures. We were both lost in our thoughts, midday sun burning down. Turning off my camera, I looked up and froze. Soldiers carrying guns. About eight metres away. Where the hell had they come from?

Wearing sand-coloured khaki uniforms, they seemed to have popped up out of the rocks. Their weapons were pointing at us.

'Oh shit, Frosty,' I muttered, 'we're in trouble. Have a look.'

Opening his eyes, he sat up.

'What the…?' He didn't finish the sentence.

We both stood up as the men approached. One of them barked a question at us in Arabic. Neither of us answered, not sure of what he had said.

'Why picture?' he then asked in English.

In our broken Arabic, we tried to explain to them that the bike had broken down and we were waiting for help. A younger soldier with a red armband must have been trying to impress his seniors because he was being the most officious.

'No good! No picture!' he snapped at me.

I noticed one of the men had two stars on his epaulette and appeared to be in charge. I tried to demonstrate I had been taking photos of the bike, but he didn't believe me.

'No good. No picture here,' he snarled back.

'Let me call Hazem and ask him to explain,' said Frosty.

Despite Hazem's explanation, the soldiers still weren't satisfied.

'They say you have to go to the Military Police Headquarters,' explained Hazem. 'I'll be with you as soon as I can and hope we can sort this out.'

We hadn't realised Syria was a police state, oversensitive about people taking pictures. Why would they consider that Frosty, with his white hair, and me, a middle-aged woman with a walking stick, were a threat? We couldn't get away, and the photos I had taken were of far less consequence than anything taken by satellites or Google Maps.

Beckoning the soldier with the two stars over to our immobilised motorbike, Frosty said, '*Dabbab mushkila katir.*' My motorbike has a big problem.

He wasn't interested.

We went back to our rocks and waited for Hazem to show up. Photography was regarded with suspicion in Saudi Arabia and had got me into trouble there a few times, but I hadn't expected it to be a problem here, on a straight road in the Syrian desert.

After another fifteen minutes, a Toyota Land Cruiser towing a trailer appeared. Hazem had arrived, along with his mechanic. He pulled up in front of Maridadi, the bright-orange trailer lined up to load her. After greeting us, he went over to the soldiers and tried again to explain our situation.

'They don't believe the story and still want us to go to their headquarters. Let's get your bike onto the trailer.'

He lowered the ramp for Frosty to ride Maridadi up onto the trailer, where a single strap was used to secure her. A young soldier was ordered to get onto it to hold the bike steady.

We both got into the back of Hazem's Toyota, and the soldier with the two stars got in front with the mechanic and Hazem. We set off, a jeep full of soldiers following behind. After a few kilometres the officer indicated for Hazem to turn left, and we followed a bumpy dirt road for another twenty minutes. Whenever I looked out of the back window, I saw the soldier struggling to hold his beret on while simultaneously trying to keep Maridadi upright – Hazem hadn't had time to secure her properly.

Our rough track ended outside the Military Police Headquarters, stuck in the middle of a stony, desert landscape. I had an uncomfortable feeling that people could disappear here, and no one would ever know what had happened to them.

By the time we got out of the Toyota, I was bursting for a pee. This wasn't a good time to want a loo, in an all-male, isolated Arab military barracks. We followed the soldiers through open gates into a large, barren courtyard, surrounded by bleak, single-storey brown buildings. At my request for a *hammam*, one of the men escorted me to a door at the far-right corner. It opened into a dark, stinking little room. The porcelain footrests on either side of the squat-down toilet were soiled, the floor surrounding it wet. I couldn't understand why these soldiers accepted such squalor and thought it was acceptable for me.

Afterwards, the soldier with his two stars took us to the boss's office. When I looked at the neat man behind the desk in its ordered surroundings, with a large photo of President Assad on the wall behind him, I wanted to ask, *why did your men show me to their foul shit hole? You must have a more hygienic toilet that I could have used.*

He was clean-shaven, wore a well-cut suit and stood up to greet us. After shaking hands with Hazem and Frosty, he invited us to take a seat.

'Would you like some tea?' he asked us in Arabic.

'*Shukran*, yes, thank you,' Frosty replied.

'Where are you from?' Hazem was now translating our conversation.

'We are British,' said Frosty, 'but we live in Saudi Arabia.' Taking out his airline ID, he passed it across to the officer. 'I am a captain with Saudia.'

The conversation eased into the saga of how we came to be with our broken-down Maridadi.

'And your wife was taking photographs?' the officer asked.

'Yes, I am a travel photographer,' I replied. 'I am writing an article about our trip to Beirut. Would you like to see the photographs?'

'Thank you, please show me.'

I took my camera around to his side of the desk and scrolled through the photos taken in Syria.

'I take photographs of all kinds of things we see on our journey,' I told him.

He chuckled as he saw an image of an open van loaded with furniture with two men holding it all in place. Next came a few pictures of our small Riyadh group, the two Dutchmen and Frosty with Maridadi beside the flag billboard. He chuckled again at the final shot of the red truck loaded with hay bales.

'There is no problem with any of these photographs,' he said, 'I am sorry to have bothered you. But our soldiers have to go through their procedure.'

We parted the best of friends but wary of what can happen in Syria.

En route to the city, Hazem told us he had a packaging factory for transporting fruit and vegetables. By the time we arrived at his warehouse, Louay was waiting for us.

20

DAMASCUS TO JEDDAH

Hazem backed Maridadi off the trailer and his team of mechanics handled her with well-practised efficiency. Hidden away at the back of the warehouse, a door slid open to reveal a purpose-built bike garage, with several Harleys parked inside. Maridadi was attached to a hoist and lifted off the ground, ready to have her rear wheel removed and repaired.

'We'll leave your bike here,' said Louay, 'and you can come with me. Do you have a hotel booking?'

'No, we haven't had time to make one. We stayed at the Sheraton on our way here,' said Frosty.

Louay took control and called the hotel.

'I'd like a room for tonight,' he said. We didn't hear the reply, but it must have been negative. King Abdullah of Saudi Arabia was visiting Damascus, and his entourage had booked up most of the good hotels.

'This is Louay Kazzaz speaking. I am sure you have a room.' A pause. 'Good. Thank you. And please give my usual discount.'

We followed him to a gleaming, obsidian black convertible Mercedes Benz, the soft-top down. Louay drove well, with no need to show off the speed of his luxurious car. I love convertibles and revelled in the unexpected treat, the wind blowing through my hair as we headed towards downtown. Among the beat-up vehicles around us, this car was an explicit symbol of wealth. I relaxed into the moment of the stylish drive into Damascus.

Louay dropped us off, promising to return to take us out to dinner.

By 9.00pm, Hazem had delivered Maridadi.

'Your bearings were shredded!' he said.

'Thank you very much, Hazem. How much do I owe you?' asked Frosty.

Hazem refused any payment. Not only had he rescued and fixed Maridadi, but he had also returned her cleaned and polished.

Soon afterwards, Louay arrived in his Mercedes with Dania to take us on a tour of Damascus. Settled in the back of the Mercedes, still with the soft-top down, we drove through the balmy night to a viewing spot near the top of a hill. From there, a panorama of city lights twinkled back at us. At the heart of them all, bathed in a golden glow, was the Umayyad Mosque, one of the largest and oldest mosques in the world.

On our way to the old quarter of Damascus, Louay drove us through a wealthy residential section of the city.

'An apartment here will cost you US$3 million,' Louay told us. As we drove through another upmarket area, he pointed towards a woman we could see through a ground-floor apartment window. 'That's my ex-wife. I used to live there with her.'

We had a perfect view as Louay drove us down the long, covered bazaar of Al Hamidiyah. This was part of the Ancient City, one of the oldest, continuously inhabited cities in the world. By this time, the huge wooden doors of the shops were closed. How I wished we had time to see it the following day.

'We're going to the Naranj Restaurant,' Dania said. 'It is the best in Damascus.'

We walked into a large restaurant filled with the hubbub of conversation and laughter. All the tables, covered with crisp white tablecloths, were full. With its lofty pitched roof, central fountain and hanging plants, the space looked like an indoor courtyard. Louay was well-known here as well and was immediately approached by a waiter who showed us to a table on the upstairs balcony. Our view overlooked two huge buildings: a mosque, bathed in green light, and the Mariamite Cathedral, in purple.

One dish after another of Damascene cuisine was placed in front of us. Although similar to the variety of mezze we'd eaten in Lebanon, Syrian cuisine had its own distinctive flavours and ingredients. Kibbeh meatballs were served in a yoghurt sauce; *fatteh* flatbread was covered with a mix of yoghurt, chickpeas and garlic, then garnished with fresh coriander leaves and pomegranate seeds; and *mujaddara* lentils were mixed with cracked wheat and sprinkled with caramelised onions. Every mouthful was delicious. When we offered to pay the bill, Louay wouldn't hear of it.

By the time we got back to the Sheraton, it was 1.30am.

In the morning, when Frosty fired up Maridadi, it was strange to hear the rumble of only one Harley engine. Once on our way, we both felt the release and exhilaration of having 1,700 solo kilometres ahead, when we could ride at our own pace.

We left Damascus carrying a lasting impression of the warmth and generosity of our Syrian fellow bikers and hosts. Our brief visit had more than made up for missing out on Amman. One day, I hoped to return to spend more time in the Anicient City of Damascus and to see the UNESCO World Heritage site of Palmyra.

Now riding the section to the Jordanian border in daylight, we saw it went through flat, arid farmland. Despite the parched-looking soil, it was fertile enough to support vineyards, olive groves and cornfields. Huge electricity pylons marched beside us most of the way. We bypassed Daraa, a small town thirteen kilometres from the Jordanian border. It was to become known as the "cradle of the revolution" because it was here that unrest among students sparked the Syrian uprising in 2011.

As we exited Syria, I looked up at a large billboard with a photo of the current President Bashar Al Assad on the right and the previous president, his father, Hafez Al Assad on the left. Both wore suits and stern expressions. The Syrian flag fluttered between them. As we entered Jordan, a similar billboard had a photo of the late King Hussein on the left and his son and heir King Abdullah on the right. Again, both men wore suits, but these two men were smiling. Images of the country's tourist attractions spread out between them: Petra, the Roman ruins at Jerash and the Red Sea. Both countries were ruled by family dynasties, yet the former gave the impression of being in the grip of an uncompromising ruler, the latter in the hands of a benevolent monarch.

Now that we were a single motorcycle with only two of us, the border formalities took an hour and a half, an improvement on the three hours last time. We vowed not to ride through borders en masse again.

When we got to Amman, we lost our way looking for the road to Ma'an. Because everyone we asked pointed us in a different direction, we rode through what appeared to be the poorest sections of the city twice. Beige-coloured blocks of flats were stacked one behind the other, layered up the hillsides on either side of us. After a long search, we found route fifteen to Ma'an and realised the confusion had been people thinking we were looking for Amman and not Ma'an.

Now we had miles of open highway through the desert to ourselves, passing the occasional car and small, brightly painted trucks full of crates of tomatoes. From Ma'an to Aqaba, the dual carriageway was excellent, and there were several warnings for speed bumps. There was nothing special about the scenery until, at sunset, we rode over the crest of the Jordanian Highlands. We were at Ras an Naqab at an altitude of around 1,700 metres. A wide band of sky above the horizon ahead was painted with golden light, and a vast panorama spread out below us in the twilight. Like the Bekaa Valley, this Jordan River Valley was another trench of the Great Rift Valley, which has some of the most spectacular desert scenery in the Middle East. In the distance, craggy hills and huge outcrops of sandstone dotted the hazy landscape.

As Maridadi took us down the winding escarpment road, a sense of euphoria surged through me, as though I was weightless and released from the constraints of my damaged body. I always felt lucky that I could experience this kind of natural high purely from my response to a magnificent environment and being absorbed in the moment. I had grown up close to the Kenyan section of this Great Rift Valley, and every time I saw it, I felt this same sense of wonder at its ancient grandeur and would try to imagine the formidable earthquake that tore the landscape apart like this thirty-five million years ago.

Nestled somewhere in this Jordanian landscape was Petra, the ancient Nabataean capital. We had no time to spare and had to continue past it, as well as the desert of Wadi Rum where the legendary British officer, Lawrence of Arabia, had led his Bedouin troops on camels during the Arab Revolt in World War I.

I dug Frosty in the ribs.

'We've got to come back here one day to see Petra and Wadi Rum,' I shouted over the noise of the engine and wind. He nodded his assent.

The descent down the steep highway to Aqaba was only eighty kilometres, but it seemed to go on forever.

Tired after riding five hundred kilometres, and getting lost a few times, we were relieved to pull up at the Gulf Hotel.

We were up at 4.30am to tackle our 1,200-kilometre ride to Jeddah, the longest stretch we had ever attempted in a single day. It was still dark when we left the hotel. Half an hour later, we were at the border. The Jordanian officials were pleasant to us but had nothing good to say about the Saudis. A few minutes later at the Saudi border, a short and rather cocky immigration official greeted me.

'*Marhaba*,' he said. 'Welcome to Saudi Arabia. Are you Muslim? Islam *mia-mia* – one hundred per cent.'

The nearby officers turned to look at him, startled and frowning in embarrassment.

'No, I am Christian. Christianity *mia-mia* too,' I responded.

He laughed, then pointed towards a door.

'You go there. Security,' he instructed.

I walked through the door into a ladies-only room to be searched. They have one of these in all the airports as well. They are grubby little rooms with two or three bored, slovenly looking women, either in uniform or cloaked in black abayas, slouched in chairs. They don't greet you, just heave their heavy bodies out of their seats, feel you over with their hands and wave a black detector wand up and down your body. I resented this disdainful, unprofessional treatment of female travellers but in the end learned to accept it. Terrorists and suicide bombers had been discovered this way, disguised as women by wearing abayas and full-face veils.

As I came out, the officer was asking Frosty, 'Where you go now?'

'Jeddah. But first to Al Bad, then Yanbu, Rabigh, and Jeddah.'

We left the building without further fuss. Our border crossing from start to finish had taken an hour.

In Al Bad, we had to stop to ask the way again and discovered a highway patrol escort vehicle waiting for us. Some people had doubts about these uninvited escorts, feeling they were an intrusion, monitoring what they did and where they went. After random terrorist attacks on expatriates, our view was that the Saudi authorities went to great lengths to provide this protection service, free of charge. They never prevented us from taking our planned route.

Because we were travelling alone, I found their presence reassuring. About every fifty kilometres, another vehicle would be waiting. We barely slowed down for their seamless, relay handovers. Twice they took place in isolated areas in the foothills of the mountains.

Friends warned us "there is nothing to see" on this route, but being on Maridadi made it different. Riding on that open road through the wilderness gave me the heady sense of freedom that bikers get hooked on. Our route from the border to Umluj wound in sweeping curves through craggy foothills, following wide, dry riverbeds. Apart from the odd vehicle, we had the superb road to ourselves.

From the small town of Umluj on the Red Sea, Highway 55 ironed out flat and straight under a cloudless sky, pale on the horizon and darkening to a deep blue above us. I felt as though we were riding to the end of the world. The only other vehicle in sight was our escort, ahead of us. Whenever we stopped to refuel, we munched on snacks bought in a nearby shop, had a drink and the occasional ice cream.

Although the highway was well marked in English and Arabic, once it meandered through Yanbu, the signs were all in Arabic. Without our escort, we would have lost our way. Apart from this town detour, we continued on this straight road for 680 kilometres until we arrived in Jeddah. The hazy silhouettes of the Hejaz Mountains were always there to our left, and we caught occasional glimpses of the Red Sea. Our escort stuck with us, always giving us a wave as they gave way to the one taking over.

A few kilometres before we reached Rabigh, the last one in the series pulled over and we paused to thank them. Soon after at a checkpoint, an officer stopped us and demanded to see our passports. He had an unpleasant smirk on his face as he handed them back with attitude, as if to say, *I asked you not because I needed to but because I can.*

By this time, it was dark. During daylight, we had cruised at 120–140 kilometres per hour, but at night we had our own rule to slow to a hundred kilometres per hour. We had ridden through countries where the roads weren't as good as those in Saudi Arabia, forcing people to drive more slowly. As we got closer to Jeddah, traffic on the three-lane highway increased, and cars shot past us doing at least 180 kilometres per hour.

Whenever we had been away touring the Kingdom, Jeddah always impressed me when we returned. That evening, our home town looked smarter, more modern and more beautiful than it had done when we left. The northern side of the city was more upmarket anyway. We worked our way home via the familiar King Abdul Aziz Road with its seven lanes going in each direction.

It was 9.15pm by the time we parked Maridadi in our carport in Saudia City, outside our flat. We had ridden 2,838 kilometres over eleven days. My back and bottom were both tired and sore after our long day.

This section though, on our own from Damascus, gave us a taste for biking alone.

After two nights at home, we would be off again, this time to the Asir mountain towns of Al Baha and Abha, a round trip of at least 1,600 kilometres over five days. The Jeddah Chapter was holding the third Saudi National HOG Rally there, a brave move so soon after the vibrant one in Lebanon.

21

A HARLEY RALLY WHERE MUSIC IS BANNED

The day didn't start well. I couldn't find things I needed to pack for Abha. My biking jeans had been washed and put in the drier and were so tight I could hardly squeeze into them. The Jeddah Chapter had wanted to leave at 9.00am, but we couldn't join them – I had to go to a photography shop as I needed to buy a new UV lens filter. I had lost two on the trip to Lebanon as the vibration from Maridadi unscrewed them.

We completed our chores and left Jeddah at 10.30am with a friend, Mike Kontos. I was glad we were late as it meant we had another long ride without a big group, going at our own pace.

As we rode out of the city, the desert sun was unrelenting. The official temperature was thirty-eight Celsius, far lower than the intense heat we felt from the burning rays above, which bounced back off the tarmac. Our last ride up Al Hada escarpment had been at night, on our way to Muscat. Now, in daylight, we could take the ninety-three hairpin bends up the mountain without worrying. The police had been notified of the rally, so this time no one stopped us. Our reward at the top was the blissfully cool air, twenty degrees lower.

Although the signs on the highway were in English and Arabic, we discovered that the ones through the towns had been updated.

Now they were only in Arabic. In Yanbu our police escort had shown us the way, but in Taïf we were on our own. A car carrying four cheerful *shebabs* – young men – followed us for a while, smiling and waving, then directed us towards Al Baha.

A few kilometres outside the town, we turned right off the Riyadh highway onto the Tourist Route. We'd been along it before on Maridadi, coming from the other direction in torrential rain. Now we had the 220 kilometres of hills, valleys and sweeping bends, riding under a clear blue sky. One expatriate had described the route as "one of the best biking roads in the world". With only ourselves and Mike to consider, we cruised along at a sedate eighty kilometres per hour. I hugged Frosty, happy.

We wound along the top of the Hejaz Mountains, passing bright-yellow signs warning us of "Fog" and red ones warning of "Dangerous Curves". In one of the tunnels, a lone Asian worker, barely visible in his dark clothes and black woollen balaclava, was bent over in the gloom cleaning the cat's eyes. Sometimes we passed a gap in the hills revealing magnificent views of layers of hazy, blue mountains stretching into the distance. On one section, roadside fibreglass picnic shelters in garish colours flashed past, out of keeping with their environment.

About seventy kilometres before Al Baha, a large blue sign welcomed us to the region. The checkpoint officials stopped us.

'ID please,' said the official, his manner polite. After a quick look, he added, 'Please, you stop and have chai, some tea.'

We parked the motorcycles and sat with him and a few other officers on a rug outside their office, sipping small cups of sweet, hot tea. After a while, a highway escort Nissan Patrol arrived to take us the rest of the way to the Golden Tulip Hotel – previously called the Palace Hotel – in Al Baha for our first night-stop.

As we pulled into the hotel, three bikers from Dhahran came out to greet us: Frenchman Patrice Ligneul and brothers Farid and Sami Bukhari, who were half-Saudi, half-Indian. The Jeddah

Chapter still hadn't shown up, although they had left before us. It turned out they had stopped off in Taïf for an extended lunch in McDonald's and to meet the family of Ameen Thaqif. He was the sole biker from Taïf, and as soon as we saw him, we wondered what he was doing with the Harley group. His beard was bushy and untrimmed, a symbol of men who adhere to the fundamentalist sect of Wahhabi Islam. He looked like a *mutawa*, a religious policeman and a member of the Committee for Promotion of Virtue and Prevention of Vice.

A rally sponsorship van also arrived and a woman got out of the passenger seat.

'Hello,' she said in a strong French accent. 'I am Eliane.'

Hotel restaurants in rural Saudi Arabia lacked atmosphere, and if Saudi men were with their wives, they preferred room service. To escape the dreariness, Mike, Frosty and I teamed up with Eliane and went to a Turkish restaurant in town, driven there in the sponsor's van.

The rest of the Harley group disappeared to a men-only place serving what we irreverently called a goat-grab. This traditional Saudi meal, called *kabsa*, comprises flavoured rice with some kind of meat, served on a large platter. If goat or mutton is used, the head is sometimes placed on the top of the rice and meat. A guest of honour might be offered the eyes as a delicacy. The men sit on the floor around the large platter and eat from the same dish, with their right hand. In Islam, the left hand is reserved for cleaning yourself after going to the toilet.

In our Turkish restaurant, a waiter ushered us into the basement, which had individual stalls for families. This was either to hide us women or give us privacy, depending on which way you viewed it. We settled down to a tasty meal of grilled chicken, rice and salad. We also ate with our fingers but off our own plates.

'How come you are here, Eliane?' I asked her. 'We haven't seen you with the Harley group before.'

'I work for the French Consulate. It is very near the dealership, and I love Harleys. I met Jamil there, and when he said you were all coming to Abha for the rally, I asked him if I could come. And I know Patrice.'

Back at the hotel, we noticed a man wearing the traditional *thobe* and red and white headscarf, sitting alone in an easy chair in the lobby.

'I bet he's part of the secret police,' said Frosty.

After all our travels around the Kingdom, we had learned how to spot these men. I don't know if they were in hotels when only Saudis were staying, but they were there whenever a group of expatriates arrived on Harleys. When I'd interviewed the manager of a major shopping centre in Jeddah, he had told me that these officers also prowled their premises. On a walk-around, he'd pointed them out, so I had learned to recognise them. They often followed our motorcycle convoys in their ordinary-looking white saloon cars, stopping at fuel stations whenever we stopped but without acknowledging us.

In the morning we had an early breakfast with Mike, Patrice, Eliane and the Bukhari brothers. Patrice had been riding motorcycles since he was eighteen and now, aged sixty, was the senior HOG at the rally. He teased us with his low opinion of Harleys.

'Harleys are for agriculture. They are way behind in their technology – they are like tractors!'

The Bukhari brothers had learned to ride their uncle's motorbikes in Mumbai in their teens. This trio had been biking together for three years since meeting in Dhahran. Sami now owned a powerful new Road King, designated for the Saudi police. It was white, with the Harley-Davidson police insignia badge on the fuel tank.

'How come you've got a police bike?' Frosty asked, unable to hide his envy.

'They were ordered for the Saudi police, but they found the bikes too big and heavy. You know how small and skinny those guys are. The extras were sold through the dealership, so I bought one.'

With the body armour on the outside of his biker jacket, Sami looked like a Teenage Mutant Ninja Turtle riding a Harley.

We set off for Abha with the six others from Jeddah and the bearded Ameen from Taïf. Eliane had abandoned the sponsor's van and was riding pillion with Patrice. We took the escarpment road to Al Makhwah, which we had ridden down many times. Riding back and forth along the mountainside, through at least twenty-three tunnels and over bridges, we dropped 1,300 metres.

We had ridden through magnificent open landscapes of Lebanon and Jordan, but I was struck again by the grandeur of our Saudi mountains. They were forbidding, dramatic, craggy and steep with patches of forest and inhabited by soaring raptors, troops of baboons and endangered animals like the rare Arabian leopard, striped hyena and caracal.

Our Kingdom might not have the pizzazz of Lebanon, but we found it compensated with its network of superb, traffic-free roads going through hundreds of miles of the country's varied wilderness scenery. The fact that Saudi Arabia didn't allow foreign tourists added to its uniqueness. No travel brochures were advertising our favourite places to the rest of the world. I felt possessive about them, that they belonged to us, the people committed to living in the country. I resented any possibility that outsiders lacking this commitment might be allowed in to see them.

Once at the bottom we stopped for a group photo at the Marble Village of Dhee Ayn. The authorities had recently registered it for preservation, and I could see that renovations were underway. I hoped they weren't going to spoil it by installing a cable car, a favourite novelty of Saudi tourism.

At the Al Makhwah junction, we met up with another eight bikers from Jeddah and continued towards Abha. As the road wound around the foothills of the mountains, we left behind the fresh morning of Al Baha. The temperature soared again to a scorching forty degrees Celsius. We passed kilometre after kilometre of ploughed fields, ready for planting but parched by the sun. Houses painted bright green, yellow, orange, blue or shocking pink brightened up the monochromatic desert landscape. Even the mosques, normally white, were painted peppermint green, pale pink or light blue.

As we began our ride up to Abha, the dry valley narrowed. Once again, the road followed the contours, hugging the mountain and switching back numerous times. We faced a steady onslaught of cars and trucks on this two-way road, the main route up to Abha. Impatient car drivers behind the trucks coming down couldn't overtake because of the Harleys coming up. Conversely, the ones behind us couldn't overtake because of the trucks coming down. In typical Saudi fashion they became reckless, overtaking and cutting in when they felt like it, even on the hairpin bends. Our road captain had instructed us to ride in the staggered formation of two lines, but this was too dangerous for those of us who were towards the centre of the road.

We acted on Peter Forward's advice. It was our ride. We opted out, held back and stuck to the safe edge of our lane.

Our base was the Abha Palace Hotel, owned by Prince Khalid. He was the governor of the Asir Region and the same prince who had invited us to Al Haridhah festival a few years earlier. After the 280 bike entries at the Lebanese rally, the modest forty-bike turnout in Abha was a little embarrassing.

In the evening, we gathered for dinner in the dull atmosphere of the hotel restaurant. Mike Kontos's French wife Sylvie had flown in from Jeddah to join him.

'Mike, why did you make me fly all the way here for this non-event?'

The Bukhari brothers were with us, and Farid agreed with her description.

'When have you ever been at a Harley rally with no music?' he said. 'It really pisses me off. I'm going to sort it out.'

He left the table, strode up to the front of the room and placed his smartphone up against a microphone linked to the speaker system.

The classic Steppenwolf biker song "Born to be Wild" whispered out of the speakers around the large room.

'Well, it's not a rock concert, but it's better than nothing,' said Farid as he rejoined us.

'Oh-oh,' said his brother, Sami, 'look who doesn't like it.'

Thaqif walked to the podium and removed the offending phone. The music died and the joyless ambience of Wahhabism took over again. In that world, music was sinful and forbidden. Farid and Sami were rebels, and although Farid had a brief row with Thaqif when he went to retrieve his phone, he didn't put it back against the microphone. This was Saudi Arabia, where religion ruled, and the secret police were watching us from somewhere.

Another of the Saudis we knew from Jeddah came over to our table to offer apologies.

'I'm very sorry about this,' he said. 'We would all like to have some music.'

'Why did he buy a Harley if he doesn't like what we do?' I asked.

'Very weird,' added Frosty. 'Especially as this is a mixed gathering.'

'I can't answer your question, but sadly most of the young people in the Kingdom are like him,' said the Saudi.

After dinner, the bikers gathered on a veranda to smoke hookahs. With no beer or alcohol of any kind, it was going to be a social but not rowdy evening.

I headed for the business centre to write my blog. Despite possible controversy if I mentioned the presence of Ameen Thaqif amongst us and his aversion to music, I wrote about him anyway. Ramesh could edit the copy if he wanted to.

Again, he let my words go to press.

We were up at 7.00am and, two hours later, the Harleys were lined up to tour the local sites. A South African couple and their young son had driven from Jubail, 1,500 kilometres away. While the mother came along in the backup van, the son rode pillion with his father all day. Our convoy, escorted by the police as usual, now included an ambulance.

22

ABHA AND HOME TO JEDDAH

We meandered through the morning chill to Jebel Sawda, the highest peak in Saudi Arabia. The temperature was down to a bracing thirteen Celsius.

As soon as the Harleys were parked, the Lebanese and Saudis who had Ultra Glides with sound systems took their revenge on Ameen Thaqif. Music blared out from all of them. Thaqif prowled about, doing his utmost to get it turned off, but he had no power out here. He was put in his place, and the music cranked up louder. The few Lebanese women who had come along started dancing. Thaqif followed them with his video camera, watching this forbidden activity through his lens. I wondered what was going through his mind, why he was taking videos and what he was going to do with the footage.

In some ways, we preferred being at this smaller rally. Refuelling and parking forty bikes rather than the 280 in Lebanon was easier, and we didn't cause such bad traffic congestion. An easy bond had formed between Patrice, Eliane, the Bukhari brothers, Frosty and me, as well as Mike and Sylvie, who we had known for years. The languages between us switched between French and English. Others had found their own groups too. Jamil had brought his wife, sister and niece along, and was with some of the Lebanese guys. A group of young Saudis I hadn't seen before looked like they were having fun, and Mohannad, the Jordanian from the 2007 crash, was there with other expatriate Arab friends. A group of Filipino HOGs had also come from Jeddah, and Thaqif had his Saudi friends to hang out with.

After breakfast in the restaurant overlooking the Tihama plains 2,500 metres below us, bright blue gondolas on a cable lift took us on a scenic tour down the craggy mountainside. Our glass bubble descended almost vertically for ten minutes, taking us down a thousand metres. The aim of having the rally in Abha was to show everyone the country's mountain scenery, and we did.

This was our third visit to Abha. As we rode around the outskirts of the town to see the various sites, I was disappointed to see how few traditional houses were left. The city had expanded, losing its charm.

We were heading for Al Habala, known as the Hanging Village. This tiny settlement of drystone houses sat on a ledge halfway down a thousand-metre cliff. The only way to reach it was by a rope, *al habal.* At the time of the Ottoman Empire, the Qahtani tribe – the flower men – set it up as a refuge from persecution. The Qahtani had long since been evicted by the government, and it remained deserted. When we had first visited the area in 1986, all we had seen was pristine wilderness. We'd had to stand on the edge of the sheer cliff and peer over it to see the cluster of homes. Patches of green vegetation were evidence of a fresh-water spring, which enabled the villagers to live on this inhospitable ledge. Now, along with the picnic tables, there was another cable car to take tourists to view Al Habala ruins. There was even a café at the bottom serving tea and coffee. I was glad we had seen the area before it became commercialised.

In the evening, while I was writing my blog, a young Saudi came over and introduced himself.

'Hello, Mrs Bizzie, I'm sorry to disturb you. My name is Kamal.' His tone was respectful.

'Hi, Kamal, nice to meet you.'

'I know about the accident you had, and I saw you in Beirut. I wanted to say to you that I am honoured to meet you. I admire you very much.'

I wanted to hug him, but it would have been inappropriate. Instead, I placed the palm of my right hand against my heart, a gesture that Saudis often used. It conveyed a deeper meaning than simple appreciation for his words.

'Thank you so much, Kamal. I hope we can ride together again one day.'

He mirrored my gesture and added a brief bow of his head.

'Thank you, Mrs Bizzie. I hope so too.'

After he left, I sat and stared into space for a few minutes. I mused over who had spoken to him about me, to have elicited such high regard. The respect I sensed coming from the men in the Harley community since the accident wasn't my imagination.

By morning our rally buddies had left, except for Mike Kontos. We had proposed that we ride back together, taking a route down the mountains that we had driven in 2004 in our Nissan Patrol. It was one of the steepest escarpment roads out of the many we had been on.

'You must be crazy using that route,' one of the Saudis from Jeddah said. 'Surely you're not going with them, Mike?'

'Actually, I think I will,' Mike responded. We had done several trips together, and he seemed to trust our judgement.

Without a police escort to guide him, Frosty managed to get lost before we had left the car park. Then, after we turned around from the dead-end and found our way out, we got lost a second time at the top of Jebel Sawda. We ended up in a compound full of mobile phone pylons. Mike must have wondered about his decision.

We turned around and at the first fuel station pulled in to ask the way. A Saudi who overheard said, 'Follow me, I will show you the road.'

After a few kilometres, the Saudi pulled over and pointed to where a road peeled off to the left.

'There you are. Have a safe journey and take care – it is very steep.'

'*Shukran. Ma'assalama*,' Frosty called out.

Our route was the 2442, a narrow two-way strip built for local traffic, similar to the Grande Lavoro descent from Baljurashi, but better. A large sign announced, "Dangerous Descent – Use Low Gear". In perfect biking conditions – cool and sunny – we began to snake our way down the craggy mountainside, creeping along with Maridadi in first gear. At times I held my breath as we approached blind, hairpin bends down the steeply pitched road. All I could see ahead of us was a panoramic abyss, with layers of mountains beyond, disappearing into the distance. I felt as though we were about to ride off the edge into the endless space. Then the road would curl around the jutting ridge, taking us away from the danger of the near-vertical drop on one side. There were no protective barriers on the edge of the road, no tunnels or bridges to make the route easier. The bitumen surface was excellent though, and we met only two cars the whole way.

When we stopped to refuel at the first village, Mike removed his helmet. He was beaming.

'Wow, what an amazing ride.'

'We thought you might like it,' I said. 'It's one of our favourites in the Kingdom.'

'I reckon it's the best one we've done this whole rally. Out of Jordan, Syria and Lebanon, Saudi definitely has the best rides.'

From there, we were back in the sweltering forty-degree-Celsius heat as far as Al Makhwah. As if by magic, an escort vehicle was waiting at the roadside to take us up the escarpment to Al Baha. There was no escaping them. I had by now worked out the colour coding of the official vehicles. The highway patrol had a broad brown stripe around the centre of the white body; traffic police in the towns had a green one, the regular police a blue one. Those that escorted criminals to be beheaded had a black band.

Because it was the middle of the day on a Friday, male Muslims throughout the country were praying in the mosques, so there was little traffic. At the top of the mountain, a blue striped police vehicle took over and led us to the Golden Tulip Hotel. We requested our usual room, 604 on the sixth floor with a view over the mountains and escarpment road we had come up. The sun had just set, and clouds were pouring over the mountain rim like fluffy, beaten egg white, tumbling into the valley.

The two officers in our police escort vehicle weren't going to leave us unattended and remained parked outside the hotel entrance. Frosty asked them if they knew a good restaurant in town, and they led us to a fish shop with a restaurant. The place was clean, with a few tables for whoever wanted to eat there, including women. We weren't relegated to the basement family cubicles. There was even a clean sit-on loo and washbasin, with towels, a rarity in rural Saudi Arabia.

Like all the restaurants in the Kingdom, the chefs weren't Saudi. In Al Baha, they were often Turkish or Lebanese. We could see into the kitchen, and after selecting our fish fillets, already marinated in spices, we watched them being pan-fried.

The fillets, delicious and perfectly cooked, were served on a bed of flavoured rice, and we ate with our hands. Although we offered the policemen a drink, they refused. Their vehicle was parked right outside the picture window where they had a good view of us throughout our meal.

Back at the hotel, four men in crisp *thobes* and white *ghutra* headdresses were sitting in the lobby. They weren't conversing, and none were distracted by reading newspapers. They tried to look like hotel guests, but something about the way they were either staring past us across the room or looking at the table – anywhere but at each other or us – made us suspect that they were more secret police.

On a cool mountain morning, after seventeen days on Maridadi, we packed her for our final leg home to Jeddah. Our escort officers were outside, ready to leave when we were. I suspected they had spent the night there.

We were on our way at 8.00am, under yet another flawless deep-blue sky. The plain-clothes detectives watched our departure. Soon after, we noticed two lots following us in dust-covered small cars, trying to blend with the traffic.

Our ride home was along the Tourist Route again to Taïf, following Mike at an easy pace. We leaned into the graceful S-bends through familiar mountain scenery, passing the watchtowers and drystone villages and small farms, aware of how lucky we were to have the road to ourselves again.

At the checkpoint delineating the border between the Asir and Makkah Regions, we were stopped again, but this time the officials didn't offer us any tea. Our bikes were parked in front of a large sign declaring, "Welcome to the Makkah Region". I liked the idea of a photo showing us in the province with the same name as the city forbidden to non-Muslims. With our Syrian experience still fresh in my mind, I wasn't taking any chances, so I asked permission to take a photo with us in front of the sign. They agreed and, after taking a few snaps, we continued on our way.

By the time we were back on the Christian Bypass, the temperature had once again hit a sweltering forty-one Celsius. Inside my helmet, my head began to itch from the heat and sweat.

Our escort stuck with us in relays until a checkpoint on the outskirts of Jeddah. A light layer of brown smog hung over the city, a mix of smoke from the desalination plant chimneys and sand blown up by the southerly wind. The last half hour of our ride home involved intense concentration as we negotiated heavy afternoon traffic. After stopping to say goodbye to Mike, we continued our separate ways.

When Frosty parked Maridadi in our carport, a wave of relief washed away a background sense of dread that something might go wrong at the last minute. After riding 4,614 kilometres around Jordan, Syria, Lebanon and Saudi Arabia, we had arrived home safely.

Now I was ready for more – we still had unfinished business with Jordan.

23

PETRA AND WADI RUM

2013 Jordan trip to ride along the King's Highway and see Crusader castles, Petra and then Wadi Rum

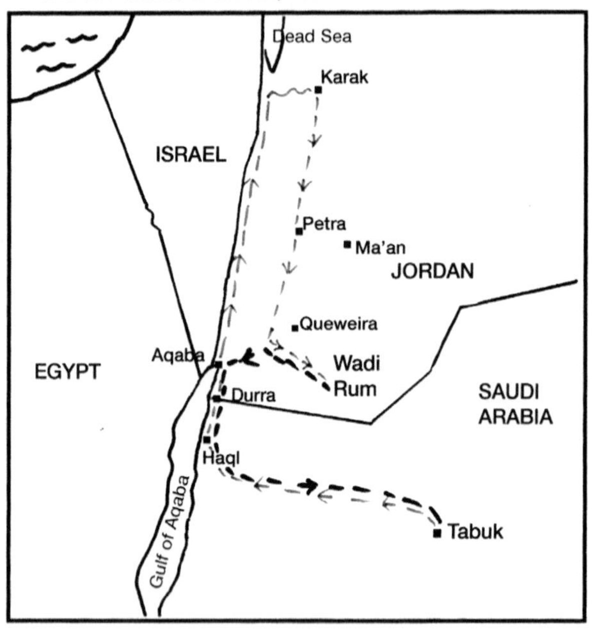

Another four years were to pass before we could fulfil our personal promise to revisit Jordan to see Petra, the World Heritage Nabataean rock city, and Wadi Rum. As the summer of 2013 came and went,

I suggested to Frosty that we plan a trip before the year was out. When he turned sixty-five on 22 March 2015, he'd have to retire as an airline captain, and we would leave Saudi Arabia for good.

By this time the Arab Spring movement, which originated in Tunisia, was spreading through other Middle Eastern countries. Unrest in Syria in 2011 had exploded into a civil war, so my dream to see Damascus again, and the ancient ruins of Palmyra, was over. Instead of tourists going in, refugees were pouring out, many of them to neighbouring Lebanon and Jordan. Apart from this influx of refugees, Jordan was unaffected by the contagious unrest.

We set aside a few days towards the end of November for our visit and decided to truck Maridadi to Tabuk in the far north-west of Saudi Arabia. We would fly there and then it was less than a two-hour ride to the Jordanian border. Frosty called our Riyadh friend, Dan Prevost, who booked Maridadi onto one of his Naqel trucks going to Tabuk.

When flying anywhere I usually travel with my own wheelchair, but we didn't have a backup truck to carry it with us to Jordan. I hated the uncomfortable steel contraptions typical of airports, big enough to accommodate people at least twice my size. They made me feel like a lumpy, grumpy old woman. While the attendant pushed me into the new, shiny arrivals foyer in Tabuk, I read the illuminated signs suspended from the roof: "Maids Gathering Area" and "Expatriate Women's Waiting Area". Lots of bearded men were milling around, wearing their headscarves without the black *igal*, indicating that they were advocates of the strict Wahhabi dogma. As I was dressed in black and sagging low in the oversized wheelchair, they probably didn't notice that I wasn't wearing an abaya.

After a night in Tabuk, we donned warm clothes for the cold ten-Celsius morning and took a taxi to the Naqel truck depot. Maridadi was waiting for us, resting on a pallet with her cover on.

Our ride to the border took us through a vast reddish sandy desert dotted with gigantic sandstone inselbergs. Each mass heaved out of an otherwise flat landscape, its surface eroded into intricate patterns by wind. I looked up to see condensation trails racing across the expanse of blue sky, gradually dispersing until they looked like linear cloud formations. Except for the occasional truck, there were no man-made objects to ruin the wilderness. Riding on our own was bliss. After an hour, we wound down through the foothills of the Sarawat Mountains, leading us to the Gulf of Aqaba and the border.

Going through the Durra border as solo bikers took an hour, and our visas were free of charge. No visas were issued to strangers coming the other way into Saudi Arabia. A small duty-free shop marked another difference between the two countries – in Saudi, alcohol was banned, but a few metres away in Jordan the small shop had shelves packed with whisky and champagne.

From the border to Aqaba, we found ourselves caught up in a queue of trucks in the industrial area making their way to the potash factory, the principal industry of southern Jordan. We skirted around the town to the Dead Sea Highway. This ran along the Jordan River Valley, most of which is below sea level, making it the lowest valley on the planet. To our left, a series of watchtowers demarcated Jordan's border with Israel.

Regular signs warned of camels crossing, and at one point, we had to slow down to get around a dead one lying in the middle of the road. The animal had just been hit, and several cars and men were standing around its large body, which blocked the road. One of their pickup vehicles was parked to one side on the gravel with its front bashed in.

Evidence of Jordan's biblical history appeared soon after, with brown tourist information signs, one announcing the "Museum at the Lowest Place on Earth, Site of Prophet Lot's Cave". The altitude was 405 metres below sea level. We continued past it, towards a layer of overhead smog coming from the potash industry. Like a grey blanket, it hovered above the Jordan Valley, unable to rise over the mountains on either side.

Our first night stop was Al Karak, a small town sitting on top of the hills, renowned for its Crusader castle. In 2014, the town's name hit the international news with the shocking story that one of its citizens, a young fighter pilot from the Royal Jordanian Air Force, was captured in Syria and burned alive in a cage by ISIS terrorists.

Al Karak lies halfway along the King's Highway, an ancient trading route between Syria and Arabia, dating back more than three thousand years. We peeled off the Dead Sea Highway to the right and took a narrow, patched-up tarmac road that wound up the escarpment towards the imposing castle, sitting on a cliff with a commanding view of the valley below.

With no idea how to find our hotel, we asked two cheerful young men the way.

'Come! We show you,' one said.

We followed their car, riding up and down the steep hills of the town until we pulled up outside the Hotel Cairwan. This quaint cottage-like place was once a private home but had been converted into Al Karak's version of a boutique hotel.

'Hello, welcome to Hotel Cairwan,' the manager greeted us. 'My name is Mike.'

'Mike?' I queried. 'Aren't you Jordanian?'

'Yes, I am. My proper name is Mwa-Awiya, but a guest couldn't remember my Jordanian name, so he called me Mike. I liked it, and it is easier for tourists.'

Mike was adamant that Maridadi be parked in his paved courtyard overnight for safekeeping. Although he offered to prepare dinner for us, we opted to take a taxi to Ker Heres, a restaurant he recommended and the only one in town selling alcohol. After our long day, we were looking forward to a cold beer. Most of the hotels and restaurants were close to the castle and family owned, not large chains, as the government was trying to encourage local business. There were no other guests in the small restaurant where the owner, Sadam, cooked our food himself.

'You know, business isn't good for us because of the war in Syria and the problems in Egypt,' he told us. 'Tourists are afraid to come here.'

The Arab Spring had also affected Egypt's stability. Their troubles began in 2011 and still hadn't settled down.

After a cold shower and breakfast the next morning, we took a taxi to the castle. When we arrived there at 8.00am, we realised it was Friday and opening time was later. Ignoring that, the helpful guardian let us in and, for several hours, we had the place to ourselves.

The Crusader King of Jerusalem had built the medieval castle in the twelfth century. It soon became the capital of the Crusader district of Oultrejourdain and controlled the trade and travellers along the King's Highway.

We entered the castle across its massive drawbridge, which spanned a dry moat. Once inside, walking with my stick down the steps and uneven ground proved difficult. While Frosty steamed on ahead to see more, I made my way as far as I could at my own speed. Collapsed protective barbed-wire fences lay in bedraggled heaps beside a chilling forty-metre drop down the near-vertical castle walls. After seeing the expansive views across the Jordan Valley from one side, and the hills on the other, I met Frosty at the entrance to a vaulted stone corridor, running underground for about one hundred metres. Soft light filtered into the ancient, dark tunnel via round holes cut into the roof. Our walk down the length of it took us past large rooms opening up on either side of the supporting arches, apparently barracks for soldiers.

As we left, three coach-loads of tourists arrived, good for the economy but a relief for us that we had missed them.

Maridadi carried us southwards along the narrow King's Highway, which took us through a few small towns but mostly wound through miles of the dry, brown Jordanian Highlands. A few sections snaked down precipitous escarpments into deep canyons, then continued up equally challenging roads on the other side. Despite the dryness, we saw acres of ploughed fields ready for planting the next season's crops. I figured they had wells somewhere to irrigate them because in the towns we passed huge displays of top-grade cauliflowers, aubergines, tomatoes, cabbages and other vegetables and fruit. I could see why the area was known as the food basket of Jordan.

After a few scenic detours, we rode through the steep main street of Wadi Musa, the base town for Petra, as the sun was setting. Hotels and tourist shops lined the road. Our hotel, the Petra Guest House, was smarter than it sounded and the closest to the entrance to Petra. We spent a mellow hour in the cellar bar which was inside an original Nabataean tomb. The hotel had no television, no internet, no business centre and no newspapers. This was my idea of heaven in a world where I sometimes felt overloaded with information and the pressure to check emails and Facebook posts.

Our alarm woke us at 5.45am, in time to view the rock city in the early morning light. Because of my mobility problems, we got special permission for a horse-drawn carriage to take us as far as Al Habis, the furthest point possible. Given that Petra covers 260 square kilometres, our one-day visit would cover a fraction of this capital of the Nabataean Kingdom, which dated from around 200 BCE.

By 7.15am we were sitting on the red velvet bench in our carriage, under its matching canopy. Our driver steered his pony towards a narrow gap in the rock face, created by the tectonic splitting of a massive, single inselberg. We entered the *siq* corridor with sandstone walls towering on either side of us, at times 180 metres high, almost blocking out the light. The rock face curved and bulged its way up, the shapes carved out by water and wind erosion.

As we made our way through the gloom, the only sounds were our horse's hooves clip-clopping on the rough paving stones. There were moments when I thought we'd barely squeeze through some of the narrow sections. Along the winding way, our guide pointed out features of spiritual significance, showing how the Nabataeans had turned the gorge into a sacred entrance to their Ancient City. On both sides, the remains of water conduits carved into the rock face, running the entire length of the corridor, were still evident. A faint whiff of horse manure hung in the air, and we passed a few workers sweeping up the droppings. At each blind bend in the passage, I expected to see a glare of light showing we had come to the end. But it wasn't there. This magical *siq* was 1,200 metres long.

Just before the end, we had our first peek of the forty-metre-high edifice of the Treasury, as though looking through a keyhole. The Nabataeans weren't builders; they were sculptors who carved their houses, monuments and tombs into the rose-coloured rock. This one is believed to have once held the body of the Nabataean King Aretas IV.

We emerged into bright sunlight, facing the two-thousand-year-old façade with its sculpted Corinthian columns and pediments. Camels squatted in the sand in front of it, dwarfed by the structure, waiting with their owners for customers. The animals looked as though they were dressed up for a festival. Multicoloured rugs were draped over their saddles, and they wore bright woven head collars, both of which were decorated with masses of tassels. Further on, donkeys were also waiting for tourists. Business didn't look promising.

From the Treasury, Frosty walked a couple of kilometres with a guide through the extensive Roman section of ruins: the colonnade street, the Great Temple and the amphitheatre. I looked on from my carriage as we clip-clopped along the sandy road, longing to be able to walk through them with him. My grumpy driver refused to stop so that I could listen to what was being pointed out to us, telling me he had commitments to other passengers for a later trip. He dropped me off at Al Habis, where I hired a donkey and her owner. This was my only option to get up the eight hundred steps of the steep gorge leading to the Monastery, another iconic monument of Petra that we wanted to see.

I had ridden horses many times, but this was my first donkey ride. With my legs dangling on either side of the little beast, I felt insecure and hoped like hell I wasn't going to fall off. The steps were irregular, some narrow, others wide and often quite high. At times, they ran right along the edge of a deep crevasse. Confident, sure-footed and unbelievably strong, my donkey – called Coco – handled the hazards with stoic ease. All day, we saw small children and elderly women, looking relaxed as they tottered along on their donkeys, whereas I clung onto Coco's saddle, terrified she would slip.

At the top, Coco carried me through a gap in the rocks. I felt the hair on my arms stand on end as we emerged into an immense courtyard-like area surrounded by sandstone hills. To our right, the majestic façade of the Monastery towered over this space, thought to have been levelled by human hands to accommodate large gatherings for religious ceremonies.

It was worth every scary step on Coco to see and feel the aura emanating from this immense hand-sculpted monument. I took one look at the huge step to enter the interior and decided it was too much for me – I needed all my energy for the return trip. Leaving Coco to rest with her owner, Frosty and I took a break in the cave café opposite. From there, we could admire the magnificent structure and marvel at how architectural features, such as the broken pediments at the top, had withstood over two thousand years of weathering and numerous earthquakes.

My anxiety levels soared again as I faced the ride back on Coco. On the way up, her steps had been slow and deliberate as she heaved my weight upwards, but as her momentum increased down the rough path, she was almost stumbling into a trot. I clutched the front of the saddle with both hands and gripped with my legs, expecting her to trip any minute. She never faltered. Coco must have done the journey hundreds of times before and knew exactly where to place her small hooves.

The next morning, we were up early again as we had to be at the Wadi Rum Visitors' Centre by 9.30am. It was another cold ten Celsius ride on Maridadi, following the southern section of the King's Highway across some bleak landscape. At the Visitors' Centre, a young man from the Bedouin Lifestyle Camp was waiting to greet us. After we had paid our entry fees, he gave us directions to Wadi Rum village.

'It is another seventy kilometres, and the speciality for dinner this evening is scorpions.'

'Scorpions? Seventy kilometres?' I queried, eyebrows raised. 'The book says it's a short distance.'

'Don't worry – I am joking,' he said, laughing. 'It is five kilometres, and you won't get scorpions for dinner.'

A taxi met us on the outskirts of the small, scruffy settlement in the desert and led us to the house of Atallah, the manager of the Bedouin Lifestyle Camp.

'You can leave your motorbike here in my compound,' he said, 'and we will take the camels to Lawrence's Well.'

Wadi Rum, also known as Wadi Al Qamar, the Valley of the Moon, sits on a high plateau. I was incredulous when I discovered the altitude of Rum village was the same as the Jordanian Highlands, 1,609 metres. During our ride, I'd noticed our descent from Karnak but not our gradual increase in altitude.

Once Maridadi was safely parked, we met the camel handler and the two camels that would carry us for the forty-five-minute ride to the well, named after T.E. Lawrence, aka Lawrence of Arabia. It was his link with Wadi Rum during the World War I that had made the area famous in the West. He was awestruck by this red desert with its huge sandstone outcrops, which he crossed by camel with his Howaitat Bedouin troops on his way to attack the Turks in Aqaba in 1917.

'What a shame it's such a short ride,' I said to Frosty. 'Wouldn't it be great to spend the whole day on camels exploring the area, imagining we're with Lawrence?'

Once in my saddle, I held on tight as the camel first lurched forwards, then backwards, in its ungainly effort to stand up. People always seem to look comfortable on camels, but five minutes into our ride, my fantasy of a day on one of these creatures was binned. My saddle was downright uncomfortable. We both agreed a forty-five-minute ride was going to be ample.

At Lawrence's Well, we swapped the camels for cushioned benches in the open back of a 4x4 pickup driven by Faïz, who also served as our excellent guide and cook. He drove us through scenery similar to that in northern Saudi Arabia: open stretches of reddish sand intersected by massive outcrops of weathered sandstone. Here in Wadi Rum, they seemed even more splendid, with elaborate patterns of nooks and crannies carved out by wind and sand. Over the centuries, weakened sheets of rock had fallen away from the gigantic main body, leaving behind soaring, sheer rock faces. Colours of the stone ranged from black to brown, cream, ochre-rust and shades of pink. Sometimes the erosion was so great that a hole was sculpted right through an inselberg, leaving behind a high bridge.

While he cooked our lunch over an open fire, Faïz told us about the Bedouins of the area.

'Our tribe – the Howaitat – originally comes from the south, near Yemen. We used to wander freely all the way up to Syria. When the countries were split up, so were our people. We ended up here in Jordan, others in Tabuk, and some are still in the south.'

'So, you have family in Saudi Arabia?' I asked.

'Yes, we have cousins there. But we don't like them. The Saudi education and attitude to Islam are not like ours. We have become separate people.'

He went on to tell us how the tribal customs of Wadi Rum also differed from those of the Bedouin tribe living in Petra, a short distance away.

'In Petra, you would have seen women working in the tourist stalls. But here in Wadi Rum, our women have to stay at home.'

Later, while we watched the desert and outcrops turn a deep golden orange in the sunset, Faïz took himself away from us to sit on the bonnet of his vehicle and watch the scene alone. This would normally be the time for the Muslim evening prayer, but perhaps these minutes of contemplation were his way of praying.

Following the relative luxury of the Petra Guest House, the Bedouin Lifestyle Camp was the next best thing to real camping: no electricity, no en-suite bathroom, only a central block with two toilets and showers. Inside our black, woollen Bedouin tent, we found two beds and bedside tables. A torch was essential, but you had to have your own.

We joined a few other guests in the large mess tent where a fire burned in the centre, heating syrupy sweet tea in one kettle and sugarless tea in the other. Our meal was cooked in an underground cavity in the sand, using hot coals, in the traditional Bedouin style. Afterwards, we were entertained by two musicians, and Atallah – the camp manager who'd met us earlier – made sure everyone got up to dance around the fire. He had wanted the guests to join in and sing something from their own country, but no one did. I love singing and to this day, I regret not contributing at least one song to this evening around the fire.

Once we were settled into our beds, torches off, I listened to the desert night. There were no mosquitos, crickets, frogs, rustling leaves or other sounds. The Arabian deserts are the only places where I have ever heard such profound silence.

In the morning, we collected Maridadi and started her up for our return journey to Tabuk. We had one more nearby stop in mind: Wadi Rum Station. A century-old steam engine complete with carriages was based there, a relic that used to carry pilgrims and Turkish troops from Damascus to Madinah in Saudi Arabia. The Hejaz Railway first opened in 1908 and was put out of action by T.E. Lawrence and his Bedouin troops during World War I. They blew up the tracks in several remote places in Saudi Arabia, along with engines and carriages that happened to be travelling on them at the time. The line was too expensive and difficult to rebuild. As we had seen large sections of the defunct railway in Saudi, we wanted to have a look at this Jordanian branch.

As we were exploring the carriages, two camels and a few men showed up, dressed in replica Turkish military uniforms and carrying old rifles. They turned out to be actors.

'If a group of thirty or more tourists book the train,' one of them told us, 'we fire up the old engine and take them for a ride. On their journey, we show them what a World War I battle against T.E. Lawrence might have been like.'

On the section of our ride back from the border to Tabuk, through the sandy desert with its giant sandstone outcrops, I realised the landscape here was as dramatic as the renowned Wadi Rum. If Saudi Arabia ever opened to tourism, this would be the ideal area to set up similar Bedouin camps, like the one we had stayed in. But in my heart, I hoped it would never happen.

24

OUR FAREWELL TOUR OF SAUDI ARABIA BEGINS

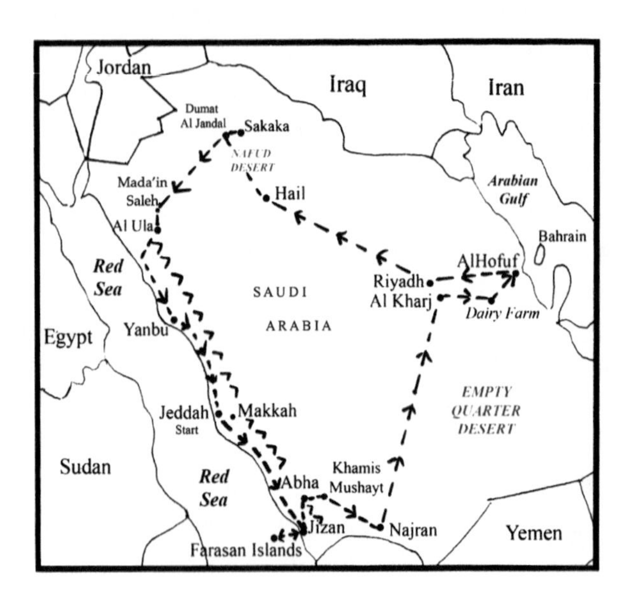

As the first couple of months of 2014 slid past, I became acutely aware that we had only one year left in Saudi Arabia. By the time Frosty retired, the city would have been our home for thirty-one years. In 2015 we would be issued with exit-only visas, and it would be nigh on impossible for us to return for a visit.

Before leaving, I wanted to see a few places we hadn't been to, like the Farasan Islands and *al ousha attiniya* – mud nest settlements – with their African-style huts, in Jizan. There were other favourite locations I wanted to revisit to see how they might have changed. But most of all, I didn't want to leave the country that had been my home for half my life by simply walking out of our flat and taking a taxi to the airport. Despite the times when I'd found the country distressing and depressing, overall I had a deep attachment to it. I had to say a proper goodbye to Saudi Arabia.

'Frosty,' I said one day, 'what do you think about doing a farewell tour around the Kingdom on Maridadi?'

He loved my idea of a long journey on our beloved Road King. I spent the next months studying maps, searching the internet and thinking about what I wanted to get out of this epic final safari. I drew up a table with a detailed itinerary, and a friend gave me the number of Rashid, a Saudi travel agent. He provided me with contact numbers for Saudi guides in Jizan and Abha and said to contact him any time we needed help.

Another friend suggested that we visit Almarai Al Danah Dairy Farm in Al Kharj in the Eastern Province. The company was a household name and had some of the biggest dairy farms in the world. It supplied most of the fresh milk and dairy products in the Kingdom. Frosty's nephew was working on one of Almarai farms in the north which grew lucerne and other fodder, so I called him to ask if he could arrange a visit.

He called me back a few days later.

'The name of the general manager is Paddy McKeague. He's a really nice Irishman. In fact, the whole place is run by Irishmen. He says you are welcome to stay there a couple of nights and he'll arrange a tour of the farm.'

A journalist colleague Roger Harrison gave me another tip, about Riyadh.

'Bizzie, you must go and see how they are renovating the old city of Ad Diriyah. I know the team doing the work, so I can give you an introduction. It's not open to the public yet, but I'm sure they'll let you in.'

One evening, when we were talking to our friends Peter and Tanya Linton about the trip, Tanya began to look excited. She was half-Russian, half-Hungarian, with a passionate personality. I sensed she was itching to say something.

'Bizzie,' she blurted out, 'we'd love to come with you!'

'What? You mean to the Farasan Islands?' She was a keen scuba diver, and the Farasan Islands were known for their unspoilt dive areas.

'No, Bizzie, I mean the whole way.'

'Wow. I didn't think anyone else would want to do a trip like this. Are you sure?'

'Yes, we are. Aren't we, Peter?' This was the first time she had consulted Peter about the idea. He was the opposite of Tanya, a down-to-earth Yorkshireman from Leeds.

'Yes, Tanya, I agree – I think it's a wonderful idea.'

'Okay, but give us a day or two to discuss it and we'll let you know,' I said.

Peter and Tanya had lived in Saudi Arabia longer than us, were veteran explorers of the Kingdom and loved travelling. We had Kenya in common too, as they had met there and spent the first few years of their married life in Nairobi. Tanya was also one of my closest friends. As they would come in their Nissan Patrol, I could take my wheelchair. This would make a big difference for sightseeing in many of the places on my schedule.

'My only concern,' I said to Frosty, 'is that they don't try to change our itinerary. If they come, they have to follow our plan or break away to do what they want to do.'

'I agree,' he replied.

I called Tanya the next morning and put forward our conditions for them joining us.

'That's fine, Bizzie, we'll be happy to go along with whatever plans you have made. The main thing is that we can come with you.'

Having decided where we wanted to stop off for nights on the way, Peter and I spent a couple of afternoons researching and booking accommodation. Most of the towns had hotels, but some only had serviced apartments. I also called Paddy McKeague at Al Danah Dairy Farm to give him our dates.

Before packing up the house, we threw a farewell party with all our friends. We had a long-established reputation for a costume ball we held every year to raise funds for Kenya conservation and wildlife, so it was fitting that the theme for this one was Back to Africa. In Saudi Arabia, where all forms of public entertainment were banned and only parents allowed to visit, our friends meant everything to us. They had become our extended family. Our expatriate social lives revolved around dinners and parties in each other's homes and contributions they made to the community events. This wasn't just a farewell party – it was also a big thank-you for everything they had done to make our lives interesting and fun during our years in Jeddah.

I advertised household items for sale on a Facebook page, and slowly the house emptied. When a family came to collect our much-loved cottage piano, the reality of leaving hit home. As a few men carried it down the stairs, I followed, feeling choked up, and then burst into tears.

'Don't be sad, my dear,' said the Egyptian woman who had bought it for her young daughter. She put her hand gently on my arm. 'We will look after it. And before you leave, you can come and hear my daughter play.'

'Thank you,' I said, hugging her. 'I'd love that.'

A few days later, I called the packers for our container shipment to Kenya. Boxes destined for London would come with us by air on Saudia. I joined Frosty on his last flight pairing to Sri Lanka with two nights in Colombo. I was with him in the Boeing 747 cockpit for his final landing in Jeddah. He always preferred to do a manual landing, and I sensed the concentration of both pilots as they went through their checklist.

My heart was racing as the glowing rectangle of runway lights came closer and closer.

As one of his pilot friends had said, 'You know you've had a good flying career when you've done the same number of landings as take-offs.' When the wheels touched down on the runway, and the reverse thrust of the engines roared to slow the huge aircraft down, I relaxed into my seat.

It was a big moment in his life, in both our lives. The years of my husband coming and going in the middle of the night were over. He was here to stay.

Frosty finalised his paperwork with Saudia and, after forty-five years in aviation, he became a retired airline captain. We celebrated his birthday and retirement with a few friends in another in-compound restaurant, where we consumed lots of home brew and good food.

On the afternoon before we set off on our tour, I called Tanya. She had a notorious reputation for being late for almost every occasion.

'We're leaving at 6.30am, Tanya, so please don't be late. If you're not here, we'll leave anyway, and you can catch up.'

It was still dark on the morning of 24 March 2015 when I joined Frosty in our carport to finish packing Maridadi. Under the glow of the strip light, I looked at the two of them, wondering if I was dreaming. Were we really going on the tour I'd spent a year planning? Me, the one who hadn't wanted him to buy a motorbike, who was now as much in love with our Road King as he was.

'Say hello to Maridadi,' he instructed me.

'Morning, Maridadi,' I said, patting her fuel tank. I savoured the moment of light-headedness, the butterflies in my stomach, the start of this journey. Once we were underway, the excitement would settle down.

'Are you sure you've got everything? Your drugs? Camera batteries? Phone charger?' Frosty asked.

'Yup, they're all there. They're the first things I pack.'

Peter and Tanya arrived in good time for us to leave together at dawn. We took the lead on Maridadi and headed south out of Jeddah on route fifty-five towards our first stop, Jizan. Silhouettes of familiar monuments and the distinctive skyscraper of the National Commercial Bank in the Old Town paraded past us against the orange glow of sunrise. This was the last time I would go down this road.

Jizan is the southernmost city on the west coast of Saudi Arabia. We rode past remembered landmarks on the way, including the disappointing roadside hotel where we stayed for Al Haridhah festival. On this 720-kilometre ride along the flat plain of the Tihama, the southerly winds were blowing again, and sandstorms blasted us for a hundred kilometres. From time to time, we stopped to apply a spray-on coating to protect Maridadi's paint and chrome. Through the thick, ochre-tinted fog, we missed the warning sign for two large speed bumps. Maridadi leapt off the ground and landed hard, just in time to take off again over the second bump. After a slight wobble, we managed to stay upright and keep going.

I saw several road signs warning us we were approaching a "Residential Area". Saudi was the only country I knew of that warned drivers that people *lived* in an area that had houses. Another of the Kingdom's favourite signs read "Inhabited Area". Each one was followed by a derelict settlement where creeping sand had overtaken the buildings. It had blown into the rooms through large openings left by removed doors and windows, building up into dunes where its progress had been stopped by the walls, sometimes almost filling the space. The sole inhabitant of the deserted area might be a Pakistani petrol pump attendant in a surviving fuel station.

Nearer to Jizan, the road ran closer to the sea and the sandstorm cleared. As we rode through the outskirts of the town, I felt like a celebrity arriving. Drivers and passengers in their vehicles gave us an enthusiastic welcome, sometimes leaning out of their car windows to wave both arms at us. Maridadi was probably the first Harley-Davidson or large motorcycle ever seen in the area.

We walked into the Best Western Hotel lobby to find Rashid's contact, Mansour, waiting for us. He spoke little English, but we could communicate enough to confirm our visit to the *ousha attiniya* villages the next morning. I had tried to explain these to Rashid, but he didn't appear to understand what they were. I hoped I wouldn't be disappointed.

The next day, with the four of us in the Linton's Nissan Patrol, we followed Mansour sixty kilometres northwards to Abu Al Gaed, an area we had passed the previous day on our way into Jizan. I remembered it because of the colourful roadside stalls. On one side they sold locally grown fruit: mangos and watermelons. On the other were large displays of multicoloured but crudely made pottery incense burners. Alongside them were terracotta water containers, skilfully crafted with patterns of leaves, palm trees and decorative lines carved into the clay. The stall keepers were friendly Yemenis, and it transpired that the handicrafts were made by their community, the people who lived in the mud hut hamlets. I had expected African immigrants to be living in these settlements.

We got back into our car and followed Mansour. He veered off the main road, taking us along a bumpy track towards a group of huts about a kilometre into the desert. We pulled up near the enclosure and got out. A stout middle-aged man with an orange-hennaed beard and a white turban came to greet us. His dirty white T-shirt covered his ample stomach, and a sky-blue traditional Yemeni wrap was tied askew around his waist. Behind him was a fenced-in area where sheep and goats browsed on scraps of hay and green fodder scattered about on the sand. A few humpback cattle stood under a thatched shelter. After an exchange of pleasantries, he agreed to let me take a few photos of him and for us to wander around. The huts in this part of the settlement appeared to be for the animals. They were made from a dense framework of branches and sticks, topped by ragged thatching patched up with sheets of blue plastic.

In contrast, the two-metre-high walls of the compound and those of the round huts inside were covered with mud plaster. Neat lines of small, vertical zigzag patterns were carved into the mud, decorating the entire surface, yet the straw thatch was as scrappy as that on the stick huts.

Outsiders are often under the illusion that there is no poverty in the oil-rich Kingdom, but these Yemeni communities must have been among the poorest in the country. I felt the care taken to adorn the external walls showed dignity and pride in their surroundings, contradicting their low economic status. The sand between the houses was clean and litter-free. Several basic iron-frame beds without mattresses stood side by side in the large, sandy courtyard. Despite the poverty, I noticed electricity cables trailing along the ground from hut to hut. A long strip light sat above one of the entrances. Through the doorway of one, I saw an electric fan. A naked light bulb hung at the end of a cable dangling from the centre of the coned roof.

An advantage of being female was that Tanya and I were allowed to visit the walled-off women's section. While Tanya played football with a few children, an old, bent woman took my hand and led me away to see her hut. She wanted to show me how she had painted the inside of her roof, a traditional art form peculiar to women in some tribal Saudi communities. This practice was dying out, and I had hoped to see it here, as well as in other areas on our itinerary. The cone-shaped ceiling had been plastered with mud and painted white. Her artwork was naïve, comparable to that done by a ten-year-old child. She had painted an irregular pattern of triangles in royal blue, like upside-down bunting, around the border where the roof met the wall. Above this were two more lines of uneven black chevrons. A little blue aeroplane flew above one line. Further up and on its own was a small painting of mountain and desert scenery, a naïve representation of the Asir mountains and the Tihama plains. Apart from a couple of iron beds against the wall, the room was empty and clean.

I continued my tour of the compound alone, peering inside several other huts, a nosey tourist. The meagre possessions these Yemenis owned were stacked against the wall or stored under the beds in colourfully painted tin trunks. Wooden bed frames, with woven rope bases, had cushions and mattresses folded on top of them. Some garments and a prayer rug were draped over strands of string tied between the wooden roof supports. Plastic bags full of hidden things hung on hooks on the wall. Tin plates, decorated with bright-red flowers, were tucked behind wooden poles supporting the roof thatch. One hut had a two-ring gas cooker on the floor, with a bright orange gas cylinder beside it.

They were all spotless. There was no running water, but I had spotted several aluminium water storage tanks clustered together in a corner of the compound.

Prying into their homes, taking photos of their private spaces, I felt like an intruder. How would I respond if a total stranger wandered around my compound, doing what I was doing? These people were tolerant and accepting. Although the elderly woman wouldn't let me take her photo, a young man and another elderly one resting on their rope woven beds agreed. I treasure my pictures of this community, which was unlike any other I had seen in the Kingdom.

What I forgot to ask was, where were the other women? I never did find out.

In the evening, Mansour was back at our hotel to take us to the Jizan Heritage Village. Before leaving, he looked at Tanya and me and said, 'Abaya. Must abaya.'

When clearing out our flat, I had thrown my old tattered one out. Tanya had lent me one of her more stylish ones for our journey, in case I needed it in conservative parts of the country. For the first time in years, I dragged the garment on, zipped it up and looked down at my long, baggy, shapeless attire. This wasn't me, but at least this abaya had a bright turquoise floral lining under sheer black fabric and was a lot nicer than my old one.

Tanya was more gracious about wearing hers. She saw it as a convenient cover-up for whatever she was wearing that day, be it jeans, a miniskirt or shorts.

Once inside the heritage village, we made our way along an arcade of shops displaying bright striped fabrics worn by Yemeni people, plus palm-woven hats, trays, floor mats and baskets. Cheap versions of traditional daggers, attached to tacky plastic belts, hung on the walls.

Towards the end of the row, the air was filled with the smell of huge bundles of herbs piled high on a nearby stall – fresh rosemary, thyme, wild basil and jasmine – and garlands of bright-orange marigold flowers slung around a metal pole. A man from the Qahtani tribe was making flower wreaths for tourists.

'I must have one,' said Tanya. 'You too, Bizzie.'

We watched as the man deftly wove the herbs and marigolds together for us, then placed the circles on our heads.

Our final stop was Al Baitul Jebeli museum, housed in an imposing, three-storey drystone building. White quartz stones decorated the lintels and small windows and ran around the perimeter of the roof like white bunting.

The exhibits represented the culture of thirteen regions of the Jizan Province, including those from the mud hut settlements. Traditional artefacts hung on the mud-plastered walls, ranging from guns, swords and daggers to more domestic items like woven baskets, clay pots and brass coffee pots. Male manikins wearing the striped Yemeni wraparound, and female ones in traditional black dresses with multicoloured embroidery, stood in the mock-up rooms. The displays were impressive but, like all museum facsimiles of people's lives, they weren't like the real-life, lived-in homes. They were the sanitised portrayal.

While I admired the work that had been put into creating the museum, our visit to the *ousha attiniya* had revealed the simplicity and poverty of the real community. If I hadn't seen the unromanticised reality for myself, I would have continued with a picture-perfect, coffee-table book version. Instead, I took away something far more precious: insight.

In the morning, we were catching a ferry to the Farasan Islands, a trip that had been fraught with difficulties. The online booking system for the car ferry excluded foreigners and, because it was a holiday weekend and the Farasan Festival, the hotels were fully booked. Rashid in Jeddah came to our rescue and arranged everything.

25

THE FARASAN ISLANDS

Mansour met us at our hotel at 5.20am the next morning. With the *Fajr* early morning prayer call blaring out from the megaphones on all the minarets, we followed him to the port.

While our men drove the Nissan and Harley onto the ferry, Tanya and I had to join the throng of black-clad women herding through the departure terminal and ID control. They were fully veiled and wore black gloves, an indicator they adhered to the strict Wahhabi codes. Mansour had insisted that once I was off Maridadi I was to wear an abaya again. After our documents had been checked, we trailed after the incognito figures to the ferry.

Our vehicles were the last of a full load on the high-speed catamaran, and skilled deckhands strapped Maridadi into position. With Mansour out of sight, I removed my abaya and bundled it back into our luggage.

Although our departure had been scheduled for 7.25am, the Egyptian crew slipped the ropes of this extra holiday run at 5.55am. Despite the alleged festival and the many women in the queue with Tanya and me, most of the numerous rows of seats in the vast lounge were empty.

There was no "Welcome Aboard" announcement or safety briefing. We bought ourselves tea and coffee at the refreshment counter and settled into some seats for the fifty-kilometre, ninety-minute crossing.

Soon after we had powered out of Jizan, a young Saudi approached us and introduced himself.

'*Assalamu 'alaikum*. My name is Mohammed. I am a tour guide on the Farasan Islands, and I would be honoured to assist you.'

Mohammed had driven overnight from Jeddah and looked exhausted. We arranged to meet him later for an evening cruise around the islands.

On arrival at Farasan, the mass of cloaked, veiled women reappeared to disembark. Tanya and I once again followed this stream of black figures and a few male pedestrian passengers. A couple of Saudi youths turned and saw me taking photos. They gave me cheeky smiles and waved the V-sign, palm facing forward, a gesture of friendship and fun in Saudi Arabia. I snapped a shot and waved back, enjoying their playfulness which ignored the difference in our ages and cultures. We followed the passengers down a long, covered walkway into the Farasan Port building, a huge, modern structure, glass-fronted from the floor to the roof. Our IDs were checked, and we met our men on the other side.

We headed a few kilometres inland towards a beige, box-like building perched on top of the only hill on the otherwise flat island. During the Ottoman rule of southern Arabia (1517–1918), the Turks had built this small fort, about eighteen by ten metres. They had occupied it at the beginning of World War I until the British took over. I faced a long flight of stone steps to get to the fort. As there was no handrail, I held onto Frosty's arm. Slow step after slow step, we eventually reached the top. Where there's a will, there's a way.

We were now seventy-two metres above sea level, the highest point of Farasan. From the derelict fort, we had a commanding 360-degree view up and down the sixty-six-kilometre length of the island and its narrow six-kilometre width. Gun slits had been cut at regular intervals into the thick, external walls, as well as the parapet surrounding the flat roof. While I was taking photos in the bleak main hall, three lively faces appeared in the window at the far end: teenage Arab boys, dressed in jeans and T-shirts, waving and smiling with the same playfulness as the youths on the ferry.

Our next stop was the nearby Al Qusar Heritage Village, the original town of Farasan, built around a palm oasis and recently renovated. The quality of the little café at the entrance became apparent when the Pakistani barista queried how we liked our coffee.

'Would you like milk with your cappuccinos?' he asked in a strong Pakistani accent. No one had taught him how to make cappuccino, despite the espresso and milk frothing machine standing on the counter.

The coffee was horrible, but the chairs were comfortable and the atmosphere welcoming.

Afterwards, we wandered along the lanes between the old houses. Some were drystone structures, built with coral chunks; others had been plastered over with mud. In keeping with traditional privacy, the entrance to each dwelling was approached via a narrow alley leading to a courtyard.

A group of veiled, chattering women came towards Tanya and me and stopped. Seven pairs of eyes smiled at us from the slim gap in their veils. The women were petite, so I guessed they were Yemeni, like many Arabs in this southern part of the country.

'From where?' one of them asked. She had lifted her veil to speak to us, revealing a plump, friendly face. All the others kept theirs in place. It was difficult to gauge her age – her dark skin was unlined, but I guessed she was in her forties.

'Jeddah. And you?' I said.

'Jizan. My daughter *aroos*.' This was the Arabic word for bride, and she took her daughter's left hand and held it towards us. Both sides and up her forearm were covered in intricate floral patterns made by the dye from henna, one of the rituals of an Arab bride preparing for her wedding. A shiny new gold wedding band contrasted with her brown skin. The family had come to Farasan Island to celebrate her marriage. It seemed it was okay for the mother to reveal her face, even with Frosty and Peter nearby, but not her daughters.

Although I didn't like the constrictive rules governing women's lives in the Kingdom, for them it was normal. The imbalance of power I perceived between men and women, dictated by the Saudi interpretation of Islam and their own culture, was all they had ever known. But I still wondered how they viewed it. I doubted they had travelled abroad, or been influenced by their education or by reading books, to believe otherwise. They were chatty and fun, wanted photos taken with us and appeared happy with their lot in life, but I couldn't help wanting to know what their lives were like at home. Would these young women have to marry men they had never met or didn't like? Would they have to put up with their husband taking a second wife, or even a third, or fourth? And put up with the indignity of an e-divorce by text message? How well educated were they, and were they allowed to work? Although I was interacting with them, it was on a shallow level, and there wasn't time to find out more about their lives. None of them questioned that neither Tanya nor I were wearing abayas.

The next family we met, a couple with three sons and two daughters, were equally amiable. The mother's full-face veil had a sheer section over her eyes, but the girls, who I guessed were teenagers, wore thick veils covering their entire faces.

Because everyone was open and easy towards us, wanting to stop and chat, I figured we were more of a tourist attraction to the Saudis than they were for us. We were conspicuous in this area where we hadn't seen any Westerners for three days.

'Where are you from?' I asked them.

'We are Al Zahranis from Al Baha but live in Jeddah,' replied the father in good English.

'We've been there many times on our *dabbab*, our motorbike,' said Frosty. 'You come from a very beautiful area.'

'Please could I take a photo of you with your family?' I asked the father.

Like his sons, the man was good looking, but his wife's and his daughter's looks remained his secret.

Despite the talk of a festival, there were no other people around. On our drive to Coral Farasan Hotel, there was no traffic on the road. No one in the hotel seemed to have heard anything about a festival. A few Saudi guests were milling around, but when we went into the dining room for lunch, we found it empty.

The Egyptians and Pakistanis who ran the hotel didn't seem to give a damn about the place. Litter was scattered about on either side of the pathway through the gardens to our cottages.

'It's weird,' I commented, 'to be at a beach hotel, but there's no one on the sunbeds or on the beach in a swimsuit, or swimming in the sea. No leisure boats out there, or windsurfers, yet it's perfect for sailing.'

Someone had had fun decorating our room. I walked through the door and was greeted by a jungle of patterns. Colours of ochre, black and red created a mad, linear design of diamond shapes and zigzags from floor to ceiling. This was a modern take on the geometric paintings in the traditional houses of the region. I liked it, so different to normal, bland hotel bedrooms.

Later, while we waited outside the hotel for Mohammed to take us on our evening cruise, Tanya threw a small wobbler.

'Look at you two men, dressed in your board shorts and T-shirts while we have to wear these bloody long trousers and long sleeves!'

'Yes,' Peter teased her, 'it's one of the privileges of being a man in Saudi Arabia, we can wear what we want.'

'Shut up, Peter,' she snapped back. 'It's not funny.'

That made him laugh more.

Mohammed drove us in his 4x4 Toyota back to the small port where the *fluka* tourist boats were moored side by side. They were about seven metres long, with a roof over the central area providing shade for the bench seating on either side. A boatman was waiting for us. Once the two seventy-five-horsepower engines had powered us out of sight of people, Tanya stripped off to her swimsuit. The two of us made our way to the triangular front deck and sat back-to-back, leaning against each other with our feet dangling over the side.

We left the primary island of Farasan behind, cutting through the calm water to cruise around some of the coral islands in this protected archipelago. There are some twenty-three smaller islands, and 140 coral islets, home to the Idmi gazelle, numerous migratory birds, a wide variety of reef fish and many other marine species including dugongs, manta rays, turtles, whales and dolphins. We passed colonies of brown booby terns and white-eyed gulls nesting on coral heads.

Suddenly, Mohammed pointed to the water and called out, 'Look! Dolphins.'

For a few minutes, we watched the pod following us, their sleek grey bodies arching in and out of the wake alongside. There was nothing else in sight, no other boats, no tourists.

Mohammed took us to see other islands which were a mass of mangrove swamps. Great white egrets and black-headed herons perched on the branches. Our boat sliced through mirror-smooth channels that reflected the dark-green foliage on either side, with the splash of deep blue sky between them. As the sun sank towards the horizon, a shaft of gold shimmered across the water towards us. Clouds low in the sky turned a soft shade of pink.

'It is time for our *Maghrib* prayer,' said Mohammed. 'There is a beach near here where we can pray, and you can swim if you wish.'

I watched from the boat as he and the boatman went through the symbolic rituals of washing their faces, hands and feet before starting their prayers. Standing side by side on the beach, facing towards Makkah, the holiest city of Islam, the two men followed the sequence of standing, bowing, dropping onto their knees and bending forward to touch their palms and foreheads to the ground. It was like a series of yoga movements and, according to Islamic doctrine, had to be performed five times a day. While they prayed, Frosty and Tanya went for a swim.

Our hour-long trip back to the port was in total darkness, with only the stars and a small lamp at the front of the boat to light our way. We were all quiet, enjoying the serenity of our journey.

For supper that night, we asked Mohammed to stop off at the fish market on the way back to the hotel. A friend had told me we could buy fresh fillets and have them cooked on the spot in one of the nearby stalls. We found ourselves in a large, almost empty courtyard with a Suzuki trail bike parked in the centre.

'Come and look at this,' I said to Frosty. 'This guy has gone to a lot of trouble with the paintwork on his fuel tank and bodywork.'

Crazy cartoon and graffiti-like artwork covered the bike: skulls, eyeballs, other weird images and jagged-shaped words like "shark", "electric" and "skull". The young biker sat with a group of men of mixed ages, the only other people there, playing a loud game of dominoes. With his long hair held back by sunglasses, he looked like the cool dude of the town. Each man would slam his piece on the table when it was his turn to play. They shouted at each other if someone thought a mistake had been made.

No stalls were open to cook our supper, so Mohammed dropped us and our fish fillets off at the hotel. The chef prepared us a delicious platter of grilled fish, chips and salad.

While we sat in the dining room chatting and waiting for our supper, my phone rang. It was Andreas, a friend from Jeddah who was following my blog on Facebook.

'Bizzie,' he said, 'you know that Saudi Arabia has declared war on Yemen?'

'What? Oh no, Andreas, not another war. We haven't seen a newspaper or watched the news for three days, so we have no idea what is going on in the world.'

'The Saudis started bombing Sanaa yesterday. Jizan, Abha and Najran airports are all closed. Are you sure you want to continue?'

'I'll check with the others.'

'Well, be careful and stay in touch.'

I hung up and stared at my phone, wondering if I had imagined the call. Tanya was watching me. I recounted what Andreas had told me.

'What do you think? Should we carry on?' I asked.

There was always a war going on somewhere in the Middle East, and we had all stayed in the Kingdom during the Gulf Wars of 1991 and 2003. But this time around, we were much closer to the action. Jizan was eighty kilometres from the Yemeni border, and we would be travelling even closer on our way to Najran.

'I think we should carry on,' said Peter. 'What do you think, Tanya?'

'Of course we keep going. What about you, Frosty?'

'I agree. We can turn back if we have to. Bizzie?'

From our peaceful islands, I found it difficult to imagine that bombs were dropping 350 kilometres away on the capital of Yemen.

'I've set my heart on doing this trip. Let's keep going.'

I had blind confidence that the conflict wouldn't affect us. There was a far greater chance of my trip being ruined by the police at a checkpoint getting officious about a woman being on the back of a motorcycle.

In the morning, I looked from the picture window of our room across the lawned gardens to where some girls, who looked about ten years old, were playing in the sea with a few boys, perhaps their brothers or cousins. A small group of women, who I guessed were their mothers, kept an eye on them from where they sat on the beach, covered in their abayas and veils. The children were having a great time, jumping about and splashing each other.

In a few years, I thought, *when those girls reach puberty, they won't be allowed to do this. They will have to sit with their mothers, shrouded in black, looking on while the boys have all the fun.*

Later, while Frosty was packing Maridadi, a group of chattering, veiled women and children from Jizan flocked around us. All seven had their mobile phones out to take photos of us and themselves with the Harley.

'Where you go now?' one of them asked, her sparkling eyes looking out from the narrow gap in her veil.

'Abha,' I replied.

'No good!' Her eyes widened as she looked at me. She shook her head and wagged her index finger from side to side. 'Saudi Arabia war Yemen! Abha Najran road close.'

Turning the screen of her mobile phone towards us, she showed us two photos of missiles striking an urban area.

'Abha,' she said, stabbing the screen with a finger.

I wished we could dismiss this war as fake news, but it wasn't. I would be gutted if we had to turn back to Jeddah. There were alternative roads to Abha, but none to Najran.

We were pretty certain Abha would not be a target this early in the conflict. Saudi Arabia had the support of what they called the Decisive Storm Coalition, comprising the UAE, USA and Europe.

26

WHERE THERE'S A WILL THERE'S A WAY: ABHA

After another night in Jizan we set off towards the mountains and Abha, 240 kilometres away. Looking ahead over Frosty's shoulder, I saw a convoy of hefty, sand-coloured military vehicles coming towards us along the road. Low-loader trucks carrying tanks thundered past us. I figured they were heading for the Yemeni border. As usual, my Nikon D800 camera was hanging around my neck with a 28–300mm zoom lens. My journalist instinct took over, and I snapped a few pictures of the ominous beasts. I didn't envy the people of Yemen.

Near the base of the main escarpment road to Abha, I saw several police cars parked on the sand beside the road. Whenever we approached a checkpoint, I hid my camera in my jacket, to be on the safe side so that they wouldn't demand to know what I was doing with it. We had no police escort to protect us this time. The policemen flagged us down and redirected us and the other civilian traffic to the narrow, steep, 2442 route with its numerous hairpin bends, the one we had ridden down with Mike after the Abha rally.

Before we started the climb, we stopped at Rijal Almaa to see the recently restored drystone heritage village. The historic settlement had once been a trading link for incense merchants on their way from Yemen to Makkah and Madinah. It appeared like a surprise as we came around a corner, a cluster of towering buildings, some of them six storeys high. Stacked one behind the other up the hillside, they looked like an ancient equivalent of high-rise buildings. Most of the small windows had the characteristic white quartz decorations above them, as well as being highlighted by a surround of white paint. Each block had its wooden shutters painted a signature bright colour: blue, red, yellow or green. Many houses hadn't yet been restored and stood in their dilapidated state, further back.

We spent two hours working our way around the accessible buildings and interiors. A few rooms had been newly decorated in the traditional style, with multicoloured linear patterns painted halfway up the walls, like elaborate borders on Persian rugs. One room among these towers still had its original intricate paintings, more detailed than the new ones and unspoilt by UV light or damp. A lack of colour in the landscape outside their homes had turned the women into creative artists inside them.

In another room, we all collapsed wearily onto the inviting string benches against the walls.

'Have you noticed that even here, it's expatriates doing all the work,' I said. 'Even painting the new wall designs.'

'Saudis are too lazy to do it,' said Peter.

'But there are dozens of jobs they could be doing. Why do they need Pakistanis at the reception here?'

'I can see why they need Egyptians to operate the ferry though,' said Frosty.

'Why shouldn't Saudis be doing that as well? They have Saudi harbour pilots, so why shouldn't Saudis be driving the ferries?'

Everywhere we went, we found the same thing: expatriates running tourist facilities, hotels, restaurants, cafés, shopping centres, supermarkets, hospitals, driving trucks and taxis, managing and labouring in the construction industry and this restoration work.

'Come on, guys,' said Frosty, 'it's time to go and tackle the road up the mountain.'

The ride up the series of hairpin switchbacks was far more testing than our ride down in 2009. Controlling our fully laden Road King with both of us on board took all Frosty's skill and concentration, especially with the dense stream of diverted two-way traffic, as unpredictable and dangerous as ever. Holding onto the handgrips beside my seat, I looked over his shoulder, tense yet exhilarated by the challenge as we approached each tight corner. If he left a gap to ensure he had enough space to accelerate up and around the tight bends, an impatient driver behind would try to overtake to fill the vital space. As driving is on the right in the Kingdom, the right-hand bends were the worst. The angle on this inside lane was steeper and tighter. Oncoming traffic sometimes careered towards us in our lane. Saudi drivers thought nothing of overtaking on blind bends. As a pillion rider, there wasn't much I could do except have faith in Frosty's ability and ward off encroaching vehicles behind us with assertive hand-pushing gestures at the drivers. We were a team, and I wasn't going to chicken out and go in the Nissan.

One rickety car with an overloaded roof rack got in our way as it crawled around a corner. As we overtook it, I saw there were seven people inside, a black family, I guessed Sudanese. The driver looked at me with a huge smile, recognising the humour provided by his packed car, and waved.

'*Yalla, yalla!*' Hurry up! I shouted at him, smiling back and waving my arm, beckoning him forwards.

With Maridadi in first gear most of the way, we finally reached the viewpoint parking area at the top.

'Well done, Frosty – that was amazing.' I gave him a high five.

After about ten minutes, I heard the rattle of a car and a voice calling out, '*Yalla, yalla!*'

It was the beat-up car, with the driver waving at me.

During the climb, the temperature had dropped from thirty-eight Celsius to a chilly twenty degrees. Road signs had ranged from "Beware Sandstorms" to "Beware of Fog", with "Landslide Area" and "Dangerous Curves" in between.

Within half an hour of our arrival at the Shafa Abha Hotel, a handsome, slim Saudi walked over to where we were sitting in easy chairs in the lobby. His white *ghutra* headscarf accentuated his lean, dark tan face, which was clean-shaven except for a close-trimmed grey moustache. He was wearing a brown, woollen *thobe* – the kind worn by Saudis during the winter months – and a dark Western men's jacket. Tariq was our Abha contact provided by Rashid, and I had already spoken to him several times on the phone. He greeted each of us with a firm handshake. We liked him immediately, and his English was excellent.

'Please join us for some tea, Tariq,' Frosty said.

'Thank you. Welcome to Abha. Have you been here before?'

'Yes, we have – this is our fourth trip,' I said.

'Customs here have changed a lot over the years. You know, the women here never used to wear abayas or niqabs like they do now.'

'Yes, I remember,' I said. 'I took photos of families working on a farm when we were here in 1986.'

Tariq went on to tell us that in the past, the women mingled freely with the men on social occasions, even dancing with them, because they were all of the same tribe. Over the past thirty years, the infrastructure had improved, providing more roads and opening up the Asir region, thereby introducing Saudis of other tribes and more expatriates.

'You know,' he explained, 'the desert people of Riyadh and the Nejd are different to us mountain people. They have imposed their customs on us, and we have been forced to comply with their incompatible set of rules.'

He explained how Islam had been adopted by numerous tribes, not only in Saudi Arabia but all over the Middle East and other countries. They each adapted the religion to fit in with their own customs. As a result, there are multiple interpretations. He felt that religion was a private matter and that no one should tell him how to be with his God.

'We are living caught between tribal rules, religious rules and modernisation, so there is a lot of conflict,' he concluded.

At last, I had an insight into why there were so many interpretations of the same religion. It was refreshing to meet a Saudi who dared to speak candidly about the fact that not everyone was happy with the Wahhabi form of Islam that Riyadh imposed throughout the country.

The following morning, I stepped out onto our balcony which overlooked the main two-way escarpment road coming up to Abha. A startled baboon leapt off the balustrade to another balcony. I looked across at the steady stream of military vehicles moving in both directions. Those coming up were empty; the heavily loaded ones were crawling down the steep road in their lowest gear.

Tariq had given us directions to two traditional mud and stone villages that had become integrated into the growing town of Abha. Our first stop was in Al Nasab district. The old buildings, with their layers of slate to deflect the rainfall, looked out over a fertile valley. Satellite dishes on rooftops, blankets draped over stone walls and laundry on lines strung between posts indicated people were living there, but no one was around. Thin, grey water pipes climbed up the outside to feed rooftop storage tanks, and strands of cable were slung between the houses from high electricity poles. The wiring dangled down the sides of the buildings to the occasional meter box or disappeared into the houses through holes drilled through the walls. With masses of litter scattered about the alleys between the buildings, Al Nasab had no charm.

Al Basta district, with the same style houses, was the opposite. Tanya and I went for a walk along its clean, crazy-paved pathways and came across an old woman sitting outside a doorway.

'*Assalamu 'alaikum*,' we greeted her.

'*Wa'alaikum assalam.*'

'Is this your house?' I asked in my basic Arabic.

'Yes.'

'May we see inside?'

Once again, I was wanting to invade someone's private space. My curiosity to know what lay behind the walls was what drove me to ask if I could see inside. What was the point of only seeing the outside of the buildings? What did they tell me, apart from what the traditional architecture was like? It was people who made life interesting, and I wanted to know something about their lives.

'*Marhaba.*' You are welcome, she said.

Tanya and I had to duck under the low lintel of the doorway into the old woman's tiny home. We found ourselves in a room with glossy white walls with a metre-high band of bright green around the lower section. There were no windows. Her sitting room, no more than two by four metres, doubled up as her bedroom, and everything was in its place. Four large trunks were stacked up in one corner, two of them tin trunks with elaborate mosque domes painted on them. Several heavy padlocks secured the latches. A mattress and blanket were folded up on top of another trunk on the floor beside a small fan. Bulging plastic bags hung from nails on the wall, and cushions sat on the carpeted floor, propped against the wall.

At the far end was another small room – her kitchen – with space for a dresser where she kept large bottles of drinking water. Squeezed in were a tall fridge-freezer, a four-burner gas stove with a gas cylinder and a washing machine. A squat-down loo was hidden in a recessed corner. Several buckets and a hosepipe served as her bathing facilities. Despite having no windows, her house smelt fresh.

Although she allowed me to take photos, she refused when I asked if I could take one of her. After thanking our gentle hostess, we walked out into the warm sunshine. As someone who is fixated on needing windows and my outside space, I was intrigued that anyone could live in this cave-like dwelling. I wondered how many more were like this behind the closed doors we passed.

We spent the rest of the day with Tariq, driving everywhere in his new 4x4 Cadillac.

'Welcome to our village,' a friend of Tariq's greeted us at our first stop. 'It is the home of Al Okas tribe. My name is Mohammed Al Okasi. You know, Saudis usually take their family name from the tribe of the area they come from. I have lived here in Al Okas all my life.'

I had become obsessed with noticing cleanliness and litter, and my first impression of the small hamlet had been the clean roads and no trash anywhere. Derelict drystone houses, some with trees and cactuses growing out the top and around them, had merged with new buildings. We walked along a narrow street where on one side a drystone house stood next to a modern one with mottled cream-coloured walls and an ochre-coloured one opposite. It reminded me of an Italian village – all it needed was a café on the corner.

Mohammed and Tariq opened a creaking wooden door in metre-thick walls, leading into a courtyard where we ducked through the low entrance into a renovated stone house. In this one, the upper part of the walls was white, the lower sections decorated with the traditional patterns.

'Would you mind if we take a group photo here?' I asked Mohammed and Tariq. 'I want to remember you and how you showed us these houses. I find it sad that there are so few of them left. Thank you for showing us.'

'Yes, no problem,' they agreed.

On the bypass road out of Abha, we passed long bumper-to-bumper military convoys of armoured vehicles and low-loaders with hefty tanks on board. We all took surreptitious photos, except for Tariq, who was driving.

Tariq stopped at a Turkish restaurant to buy grilled chicken, saffron-flavoured rice and freshly baked, thick pita bread for our lunch. A little way out of Khamis Mushayt, we pulled off the road and stopped by a grove of spindly acacia trees. Tariq spread a rug out, and we ate our picnic in the mottled shade.

'Where are you from, Tariq?' I asked him.

'I am from Rijal Almaa, of the Bani Ghalim tribe. The name means "one who doesn't care". In our case, it refers to not caring about stealing others' possessions.'

'So apart from stealing other people's possessions, what do you do for a living?' asked Peter.

Tariq laughed. 'I am a writer and poet. I am also a university lecturer and teach in several universities, including the women's university in Jeddah.'

'How come you are involved in tourism as well?' I asked.

'Because I want to show our real culture to the world, to people like you.'

After half an hour, we packed up and continued on the road towards Najran.

'Now we are going to Al Jahama,' Tariq told us. 'It belongs to the Bani Bashir tribe, and a long time ago it was a booming trade and educational centre.'

About 120 kilometres out of Abha, he took a right turn off the main road, heading southwards. As we continued along the bumpy dirt road, we asked about each other's families.

'I lost my eldest son and two-year-old grandson recently,' said Tariq. 'They were killed in a car accident, but his wife survived.'

'Oh, Tariq, we are so sorry,' said Tanya. 'How very sad for your family.'

'Thank you, Tanya. My daughter-in-law is still in hospital, having surgery to repair the damage to her face. Dealing with this tragedy was very difficult for all of us but, in the end, I felt I had the choice to be miserable for the rest of my life or to put the grief in its private place, to move on and to enjoy the rest of my own life. I have other sons and daughters, and they need me.'

Talking about his loss hit a raw nerve. He was deeply upset for a while and lost concentration on which track to take to the village. I wondered if the baby had been sitting on his mother's lap, or even his father's. We often saw this blatant disregard for infant safety in Saudi.

Twenty minutes later, the deserted stone and mud houses of Al Jahama came into view, sitting on the edge of a ridge. The buildings rose out of the landscape almost like natural features, built using the surrounding pink sandstone and soil. Trees and bushes sprouted out of the hard ground in front of the village, a sign that there was water beneath the barren terrain.

'There are wall paintings remaining in one of the houses,' said Tariq, 'but that one is right at the bottom of the hill. I think you will find it difficult to get to, Elizabeth.'

'I'll have a go, Tariq. I really want to see them.'

Tanya, Peter and Frosty helped me to scramble down a steep, rocky slope with loose stones everywhere. Tariq stood at the top, watching our progress. It was slow and difficult for me, but when I set my heart on doing something, determination takes over.

'I am amazed that you are doing this,' Tariq called down.

'Where there's a will, there's a way,' I shouted back.

'What does that mean?'

More shouting as I explained the expression to him. He then repeated the phrase several times over.

'I like it. You must write it down for me. I want to remember it.'

Among the tall ruins of this remote hamlet, we discovered the faded remnants of original wall paintings. Water had leaked through the roof, running down the white walls, leaving muddy streaks. The geometric patterns around the lower section had survived, the colours still bright. Despite the damage, I could imagine what the room must have looked like when occupied.

Like all the mud and stone houses we had seen, the small windows were low, allowing occupants to see out when seated on rugs on the floor. Through one of them, I saw a flock of sheep with an Asian shepherd dressed in dirty, scruffy clothes. He smiled as he returned my wave.

While he was driving us back to Abha, Tariq often chatted on his mobile phone.

'I know it is dangerous,' he said, 'but we all do it.'

When he dropped us off at our hotel after a long day, we felt we had made a new friend.

'Thank you for a fantastic day, Tariq. We have really enjoyed seeing all the houses, and especially your company,' I said.

'Thank you, Elizabeth, I have had a great day with you all too. If there is anything you need while you are on your journey, please feel free to call me at any time,' he said, with the familiar gesture of the right palm against his heart and a slight bow.

The next day was the seventh of our tour. Abdullah, the owner of Al Hamsan Heritage Village, had invited us for lunch in his museum in Khamis Mushayt.

27

THE FOURTH CHECKPOINT

After our many phone conversations, I was disappointed we weren't going to meet Abdullah. He and his family were stuck in Riyadh, unable to fly home because of the airport closures.

Before we left our hotel room, I looked out of the window again at the road winding down the escarpment to Jizan. The convoys of military vehicles were still crawling up and down. As I watched them, I felt sickened at the thought of the damage and trauma that would be inflicted on Yemen. Why couldn't politicians solve issues without going to war? How long would this one last? The civil war in Syria was now in its fifth year.

Abha and Khamis Mushayt used to be two distinct towns, but now we couldn't tell where one ended and the other began. The road system through Khamis Mushayt itself was under reconstruction, with umpteen diversions and one-way systems. None of them featured on our GPS. Peter and Tanya went in one direction, and we got lost in another. Instead of the anticipated half-hour drive, we had been on the road for nearly two hours.

'Frosty, I'm bursting for a pee,' I said, leaning forward so he could hear me. 'It's becoming an emergency. Next time we see a mosque, please could you stop.'

A few minutes later, a big one came into sight. Frosty stopped Maridadi in a parking bay in front of it.

'Let me see where the loo is, then I'll come back and get you.'

He came back and helped me over to the ladies. I had left it too late. Already, I felt a stream of pee trickling down my leg and there was nothing I could do to stop it. Frosty grabbed the handle to open the door.

'Dammit, it's locked. You wait here, I'll see if I can find someone,' he said.

I sat on the step, mortified to find myself sitting in a puddle of my own pee. Frosty returned.

'No luck – I've only got a key for the men's room.'

'I'm sorry, Frosty, I couldn't hold on. I'm going to need a change of clothes.'

'Don't worry. You go in and I'll get your bag.'

The men's washroom was a pleasant surprise, clean, and with a high step by a trough where the men could sit to wash their feet before praying. This was perfect as I had to sit to change. Frosty stood guard at the door while I tidied myself up.

When I had first been caught short after my operation, I hadn't expected him to be so matter-of-fact and understanding about this problem. I thought he'd be disgusted and would show it. He was the opposite. He never said anything to upset or embarrass me and brought whatever I needed to sort myself out. I dreaded these rare occasions when I had "an accident" (as the rehab doctor used to call incontinence episodes) but had to deal with it. I comforted myself with the knowledge that lots of other women, with or without spinal injuries, lived with weak bladders, as did men with prostate problems.

Changed and ready to go, I called the museum to let them know we were running late as we'd lost our way. Luckily, being late in Saudi Arabia was part of the culture and wasn't a problem.

When we finally made it to the right street, the museum was easy to spot: a newly constructed drystone building, complete with standard white quartz decorations. It was packed with artefacts collected from around the villages, some pieces hanging or leaning on the walls, others displayed in glass cabinets. Most of the doors going from room to room were original carved wooden ones, rescued from derelict buildings. A member of staff took us into a room with wall-to-wall enlarged photos of visiting dignitaries.

'Here is Prince Charles,' he said, beaming. 'He visited us a few years ago.'

One enormous room, which they sometimes used for entertaining big groups, also served as a gallery for black-and-white photographs depicting scenes of up to one hundred years ago. Frosty, forever passionate about anything on wheels, was fascinated by images featuring old cars.

We wandered through rooms where old guns hung on the walls and tribal costumes were displayed in reconstructed homes of old Abha. Wall-to-wall patterned carpets covered the floors, with other hand-woven oriental rugs scattered on top.

On the first floor, we arrived in a room that was set up for a meal. In keeping with tradition, this was on the floor, with a sheet of plastic covering a section of a rug. I took a photo of the setting, the plates with elaborate fan-shaped fabric napkins, wine glasses, bottles of water and soft drinks. Assuming it to be part of the presentation, we moved on.

'Wait,' a voice called out. 'This is where you have your lunch.'

I had expected to eat in the museum restaurant, but in typically generous Saudi fashion Abdullah had left instructions to serve us a private meal. A Filipino waiter brought us two platters of salads with hummus, a large plate of saffron rice with grilled chicken garnished with onions and lemon wedges, mashed potatoes, courgettes and beans, meatballs in a tomato sauce and a plate heaped with warm pitta bread. After we'd had our fill of this delicious meal, he served us tea from an enormous, elaborate silver teapot.

When we came to leave, our hosts – both of them Pakistani, only the owner was Saudi – refused any payment.

We left Khamis Mushayt in the mid-afternoon and headed south-east for Najran. The single-lane road we had driven down in 1976, and then again in 2004, was now a dual carriageway. The procession of military vehicles continued unabated. Khamis Mushayt was a major military base and at one point, traffic was held up to let a long convoy of their vehicles exit across our lanes and onto the highway, heading in the opposite direction.

After going safely through three checkpoints, we stopped to refuel. All the other vehicles topping up were military. Soldiers were milling around the station, going in and out of the shops and using the washroom facilities. As usual, these were in the station mosque, but when Tanya and I arrived at the door to the ladies, we found it locked.

'*Mafi mushkila.*' No problem, said one of the soldiers. 'I find key for you.'

Because of his friendly, courteous manner, I later asked him if he and the other soldiers would mind being photographed.

'Okay,' they agreed.

Wearing mottled desert fatigues, the men posed beside their hunky machines, with the minaret of the mosque in the background. War and Islam. So many wars in the world were in the Middle East.

In the next town, Zahran Al Janub, we passed a white saloon car with the window wide open. The smiling young man at the wheel met my eye, waved at me and gave the familiar V-sign. Of course, I took his photo as well.

The sun was low in the sky when we saw a large checkpoint sign for the fourth time on the journey. We pulled up in front of the barrier beside a small, concrete building to our left on the central reservation. Several officers were also checking vehicles going either way.

Kicking the stand into place, Frosty got off Maridadi to hand over our IDs and motorcycle registration documents for inspection.

After a cursory glance over them, the policeman demanded, '*Tasweer! Kamera! Fain?*' Taking pictures! Camera! Where?

Frosty shrugged his shoulders and said, 'What camera?'

My Nikon was out of sight, tucked inside my biking jacket. The policeman wasn't going to give up.

'*Kamera*,' he ordered. 'Give *kamera*.'

Frosty showed him his mobile phone.

The policeman shook his head.

'*La, kamera kabir.*' No, the big camera, he insisted, demonstrating the bigger size with his hands.

Frosty came back to where I was watching him from the back of the bike.

'They want your camera,' he said. 'We'll have to give it to them.'

'Bugger, dammit,' I grumbled to myself as I unzipped my jacket to take out my precious machine. I wanted us to be able to disappear, ride away, crash through the barrier and ignore the problem.

Frosty handed the camera over. The policeman, trim and smart in his beige khaki uniform, was brisk, businesslike. He disappeared into the central kiosk where a few other officers were on duty.

While waiting for him, I watched other vehicles pause at the checkpoint. A man in a dark brown *thobe* was checking them and telling the drivers to get out of their cars. As they approached him in turn and stood beside him, I saw the man move closer to receive small bundles of cash, shoving them into his pocket. The travellers then continued on their way. Without doubt, he was up to a racket, but what? Perhaps facilitating the drug, alcohol or people smuggling trades for which the region, so close to the Yemeni border, was notorious.

After a few minutes, the officer returned, my camera in one hand.

'You come. Follow me,' he said to Frosty.

He drove off in a Nissan Patrol, and we rode after him, with Peter and Tanya behind us. We followed him across the road, dodging the cars and trucks coming from either direction, and up a stony track to a utilitarian collection of single-storey buildings. Masses of cars filled the gravel parking area outside. I wondered if they had been impounded for smuggling.

We entered a crowded office. I looked across the room to where an officer sat behind a desk. A few policemen were grouped around him, while others stood near the wall. Our officer told us to sit on chairs to the right, and he approached the seated officer. Other civilians were also seated, or standing in front of the desk, presumably trying to sort out their own situations.

I glanced around the room. Dull, sand-coloured walls looked as though they hadn't been painted for years. A naked light bulb hung from the ceiling. Sitting quietly, observing the other people in the room, the four of us were wondering what was going on. By now my stomach felt knotted, and a fizzing sensation was creeping up my throat.

'Why did they want your camera?' Peter asked me.

'I don't know.'

Then I remembered that Tariq had said to call him at any time if we needed anything on our journey.

'Frosty,' I whispered, 'I think we need to call Tariq.'

Frosty dialled his number and explained our predicament.

'Let me speak to the man in charge,' said Tariq.

The four of us watched as the policeman spoke to Tariq, his manner and expression not changing. Stern, official, pragmatic. After a brief conversation, he passed the phone back to Frosty, and Tariq briefed him on the problem.

'Someone has reported you for taking photographs of the military convoys. They want to see the pictures and need to ask you some questions. But I think you will be all right. Call me again if you need to. Please let me know how you get on.'

We were conspicuous travellers. Since leaving Jeddah and riding over a thousand kilometres, we hadn't seen any other

Westerners or motorbikes, let alone one with a woman on the pillion seat.

For half an hour we watched the uniformed men discuss things in hostile, staccato voices, but we couldn't tell if they were talking about us or the other people who appeared to have been detained. Although wearing official khaki uniforms, they looked sloppy. Buttons were missing; trousers had become too tight; and worn-out shoes were covered in dust.

In the end, another policeman came over to us.

'You come. Follow me.'

'Where are we going?' Frosty asked him.

'Zahran Al Janub. Big police station.'

By now, it was almost dark.

'What a bummer,' I said to Frosty. 'We should be near Najran by now.'

We followed the flashing red and blue bar on top of the police vehicle through the darkness for fifty kilometres, back in the direction we had just come from, to Zahran Al Janub.

I hoped this arrest was a small part of our adventure, not the end of it. I would be devastated if we were forced to abandon our trip, simply because I couldn't resist taking photos of the military vehicles.

'Dammit,' I muttered to myself. 'Why am I so stupid, stupid, stupid? I should know better.'

As I sat there on Maridadi, with half an hour of thinking time, I was trying to grasp that this turn of events was real and not a weird dream. Part of me felt like a naughty schoolgirl, in trouble with the headmistress again. But this wasn't boarding school – this was Saudi Arabia where the outcome could be serious.

The conflict with Yemen was in reality a proxy war between the two central factions of Islam: Sunni and Shia. In Middle Eastern politics, these sects are represented by the Kingdom of Saudi Arabia with its Wahhabi Sunni Islam and their enemy Iran, which is Shia. According to the Saudis, the war had been triggered by Shia Houthi insurgents, supported by Iran. They deposed the Yemeni Sunni president who escaped to Riyadh. Under Prince Mohammed bin Salman Al Saud, the new Saudi Minister of Defence, the government decided that the Houthis had to be stopped. Prince Mohammed formed a coalition of nine Middle Eastern countries and, within a few days, the Saudi Royal Air Force led the first airstrikes on Yemen.

My reverie ended when we pulled into the police station through huge, iron gates. The sound of our Harley made a group of young men turn to watch us. One of them, who was wearing a grey striped *thobe*, but without the traditional headdress, surprised us with his big smile and warm greeting.

'*Assalamu 'alaikum!*' Peace be upon you. 'You know me, yes? In car, I wave you. You take picture,' he said, inclining his head and holding up his right hand close to his face, showing the V-sign.

'*Wa'alaikum assalam.*' Peace be upon you also. 'Yes, yes, I remember,' I laughed back. Judging by his jovial interaction with the group of uniformed young men, he was one of them. I figured he had either been off duty or operating in a plain-clothes capacity. I hoped that his warm welcome was a good omen.

We followed our policeman with my camera into the building and up a flight of stairs to a large room on the first floor. He handed my camera over to a younger officer. This one looked as though he spent a considerable amount of time working out. His well-developed chest and biceps were stretching the seams of his short-sleeved shirt. As we were ushered to some seats, I saw him switch the camera on and begin to surf through my images.

What a bloody cheek, I thought, glowering at him. *He's only a junior officer, not the senior one whose job it is to censor the pictures.*

After a few minutes a door opened from an inner room. A soldier beckoned us into the general's office, and the bodybuilder followed with my camera. Sitting behind the desk on our left, the general looked up as we entered and appraised us with hard eyes. Frosty walked towards him, proffering a hand.

'*Assalamu 'alaikum*,' he greeted him in Arabic. 'We are very sorry for any trouble we have caused.'

The general glared back, not accepting Frosty's offer to shake hands. He said something in Arabic in a flat, cold voice. An interpreter translated.

'In this instance,' he said, 'sorry is not good enough. This is a very serious matter. You must be punished.'

I stared at the general, then at Frosty.

Oh fuck, I said to myself, the fizz in my stomach turning into a tight knot and my heart thumping. *Dammit*.

28

NEGOTIATING OUR DESTINY

A soldier pointed to a chair for Frosty to the general's right, and Peter, Tanya and me to a sofa and a chair to his left. The interpreter appraised us with dark, hostile eyes. He was a Sudanese doctor and the only person the police knew of who could speak English. My thoughts over and over were, *stay calm. Take a deep breath. Pray. The situation will be resolved.* When I'd been in trouble before for taking photos in Saudi Arabia, things had always worked out in the end.

'I wonder what they'll do with us,' whispered Peter.

'I'm sorry, Peter,' I whispered back, 'but what should I say? I don't know whether to say I'm a journalist, a professional photographer or I was just taking photos for fun.'

While we sat waiting for the general to speak, the face of the young bodybuilder, still holding my camera, broke into a smile, followed by a chuckle as he paused at one of the pictures. He beckoned to a few of the other officers in the room to have a look. They too smiled and made a few comments. I guessed they were looking at the picture of their colleague.

The general directed his first questions at Frosty, sitting opposite me.

'The general wants to know why your wife was taking photos of military vehicles and why you didn't stop her?' said the hostile Sudanese doctor.

All eyes turned to Frosty. He leant forward, elbows resting on his knees, head face down propped on his hands.

I looked at him, wondering what the hell he was going to come up with. We'd had no chance to discuss what either of us would say.

With a heavy sigh, he looked up at the general. 'How am I supposed to know what my wife is doing on the back of my motorbike?' he said, a weary look on his face. He ran his fingers through his silver-fox hair. Rising to his feet, he mimed the stance of sitting on a motorbike, his arms spread out as though holding onto the handlebars and revving the throttle.

'Here I am,' he continued, 'riding the motorbike, concentrating on the traffic and looking at the road. How can I see what she is doing? She's behind me.'

He straightened up and continued speaking, using his hands and arms like an Italian.

'And you know what wives are like. Have you ever tried to tell your wife what to do? Exactly – it's impossible! Even if I had known what she was doing, I wouldn't have been able to stop her.' He looked straight into the general's eyes with man-to-man intent. 'But I am sure she didn't know it is illegal to take photographs of military vehicles.'

He flopped back into his chair and leant back as if exasperated by his wife, which I am sure he was.

All the men in uniform looked baffled by this unexpected performance. The general, also taken by surprise, was looking at Frosty with wide eyes and raised eyebrows. All they had expected – and what Peter, Tanya and I had expected – was a sensible, straight answer. As the doctor interpreted what he had said, I saw some of the young policemen were finding it difficult to suppress their smiles. When he had finished, the general turned his attention back to Frosty.

'Who else took photographs?' he asked.

'No one. He was driving,' he said, pointing at Peter. 'As usual, his wife was on her phone talking to her mother. And me? I was riding my motorbike.' Again, he acted out the motorcycling stance. 'There was only one person who could take photos, and that was my wife sitting behind me.'

More interpreting by the doctor. The general digested the information, then addressed Frosty again, his head tilted to one side, a puzzled frown on his face.

'Hmm. It isn't in our culture to blame our wives.'

He turned to the soldier beside him and took a few minutes instructing him what to write on the report. His next questions were directed at me. Frosty's off-beat answer made me realise I shouldn't say I was a journalist, which might imply that I had access to foreign newspapers.

'Why were you taking photographs of the military convoys?'

'I am a travel photographer, and when we are on the motorbike, I like to take pictures of everything of interest we pass on the way, whether it is cars, or people or landscapes. It tells the story of our journey. We are very interested in Saudi Arabia and are making a long tour before we leave.'

'What about permission? Do you have permission to do this journey?'

'We didn't ask for permission. We haven't needed permission for any of our other trips,' I replied.

Frosty had called Tariq again and asked him to explain to the general that we were on a cultural tour of the country and didn't mean any harm. The two Saudis chatted for a few minutes, then the general handed the phone back.

'If there are any more problems, please call me. I will drive to Zahran Al Janub if necessary,' Tariq reassured Frosty. He also explained that he knew the father of one of the senior officers involved; they were of the same tribe. This coincidence boded well for us – tribal connections and who you know are important in Saudi Arabia.

Tanya had by now started her own theatrics and had burst into tears. Peter had his arm around her and was comforting her.

'We were having such a beautiful day until this happened,' she sobbed to the general.

At this point, his manner softened. He became hospitable and polite, offering us tea and cold drinks. The Sudanese doctor's hostility had evaporated, and in a warmer tone, he interpreted the general's words.

'We have a procedure to go through. The report of your photography went straight to the governor of the Asir region, Prince Faisal bin Khalid Al Saud.'

The bodybuilder showed the general a selection of my photos, and he then instructed one of his staff to go through them with me and remove those depicting military vehicles. The officer stood looking over my shoulder as I scrolled through them. Every time he saw an offending image, he indicated for me to delete it. He seemed to realise that what I had said was true – my photos were of all kinds of other things we had seen during the day. He put his hand on my shoulder and said quietly, '*Halas*.' Enough. That is okay.

Tariq, with extraordinary generosity, had come to our rescue by agreeing to sign an affidavit that they had faxed to him vouching for our behaviour for the rest of the journey.

'You know, you are very lucky,' he explained to Frosty. 'They wanted to send you straight to Riyadh to the British Embassy and have you deported.'

Once the formalities had been completed and we had all signed the statement, the general pointed first at Frosty, then Peter and Tanya.

'You, you and you are free to go,' he said, his tone amicable. He paused, then turned to glare and point at me. 'But you – you go to prison!'

'Good! You can keep her. She will make a very bad prisoner,' quipped Frosty.

Everyone in the room burst out laughing. Even the general couldn't suppress his smile and a chuckle. More tea was offered.

As we sat sipping the sweet, hot drink from tiny glasses, the conversation became chatty.

Observing Peter's shorts, which were frowned upon in public places for men, the general asked him, 'Aren't you cold in your short trousers?'

'Not at all. I am used to playing football in the winter in England.'

The conversation turned to football, the national sport of Saudi Arabia. After a few minutes of this, the general asked me why I needed a walking stick. I gave him a brief outline of my back surgery and its outcome.

'How old are you?' was his next question.

My reply, 'You should never ask a lady her age,' added to his amusement.

'Once Saudi women reach the age of thirty, they behave as though they are old,' he said.

I smiled but said nothing. *No bloody wonder*, I thought, *with you men controlling them. They're not allowed to do anything but sit at home, breed and cook. No fun, no career, no adventure.*

Our tea finished, we stood up. The men shook hands, and we thanked the general for his kindness.

I couldn't resist a parting cheeky quip. 'Could I take a photo of you?'

He smiled and dismissed me with a wave of his hand towards the door and turned his attention to the paperwork on his desk.

As we left the police station and walked towards Maridadi, voices from behind us called out, '*Dabbab quwais*.' Nice motorbike. A group of young officers, including our friend from the white saloon car, were crowded around a large, barred window overlooking Maridadi to see us off.

It was after 9.00pm, and we now had a two-hour night ride to Najran. A police vehicle escorted us back to the checkpoint, and from there we continued alone.

Soon after midnight, we entered a large town that had expanded since our first visit in 1986. It was unrecognisable. In those days, there had been only one hotel. This time we had a choice of several. A local resident who Frosty spoke to at a traffic light led us through the unfamiliar streets to the Hyatt Najran. We were all exhausted and relieved that things had worked out well. I still couldn't believe the police had been so lenient, with the war just across the border.

When we got to our room, I checked my phone to find I had several missed calls from Tariq. I called him back despite it being midnight. He answered straight away.

'You are extremely lucky that everything worked out well,' he said.

'I know we are, Tariq. We can't thank you enough for your help.'

'I helped you because of the wonderful day I spent with you all. I learned so much from you. I am your brother, Elizabeth.'

Tariq's response was as heart-warming as it was unexpected. He could have reprimanded me for taking the photos or advised me to be more careful, but he didn't. I knew that the reaction of the authorities in any Middle Eastern country could be unpredictable, and although I hadn't thought we would be deported, I fully expected that the general would demand we return to Jeddah. From this point, I had to control my journalistic urge to take photos of interesting but dangerous subjects, especially because Tariq had vouched for us for the rest of our trip.

After a much-needed lie-in, I woke with a sense of shock about what we had been through the day before. The police could have been much more thorough, asking to see photos on everyone's smartphones. Tanya and Frosty had also taken pictures of the tanks but Frosty had successfully exonerated them both and dumped the blame on me. Although his crazy antics sometimes bugged me, on this occasion his unconventional response and ability to make people laugh are what had saved the day. Working with Saudis for thirty-one years, spending hours with his Saudi flight crew in the

747 cockpit and on layovers, he respected and got on well with them. He also understood and enjoyed their sense of humour, and to our advantage and my relief, they understood his.

But my indiscretion had cost us a precious morning of sightseeing in Najran.

29

WEATHERING THE STORM

An afternoon was all we had left to explore the Amara Palace and old mud houses in the valley. This extensive oasis sits on the edge of the Empty Quarter desert and, like every large Arabian oasis, Najran has a long history as a trading stopover. All northerly routes from ancient Yemen had to pass through the settlement. From there, traders either continued northwards through the Hejaz to Egypt and the Levant or eastwards to the Arabian Gulf.

Of all the communities in Saudi Arabia, Najran is one of my favourites. This was due to the hospitality that Frosty and I had received on our first visit there in 1986 and because of its impressive traditional architecture – more like that of Yemen – with lofty mud castles with elaborate, crenellated roofs.

In 2013 I went there for the second time, on a weekend visit with our Natural History Society. Our tour guide had surprised me with his outspoken opinions on the marginalisation of the Shia population of the area. This time, Tariq had asked his friend Khalid to show us around. We all piled into his big Chevrolet Tahoe. His equally vehement condemnation of Riyadh and the government surprised me.

'The majority of Najranis are Ismaili Shia Muslims,' he told us, 'and we are not like the Wahhabi Sunnis of Riyadh. They have prevented any Shias from reaching senior positions in the local government. Riyadh sent Sunni civil servants to fill these positions.'

He explained that the Shia population was further discriminated against in education, political representation, the judiciary, religious practice and journalism.

'In 1997, Sunni Yemenis took refuge in Najran,' Khalid told us. 'The government naturalised them to become Saudis, and they settled here. They did this to upset the balance of Shia-Sunni Muslims even more.'

After all these years in Saudi Arabia I had now discovered that, like the mountain people of Abha, the Shias of this southern oasis resented the imposition of Wahhabi Sunni practices on their culture. That Khalid and Tariq – one a Shia and the other a Sunni – were good friends was also interesting in this contentious environment. Perhaps their bond was due to their intellect and mutual disdain for the Wahhabi establishment in Riyadh.

Our first stop was the walled Amara Palace. Built in 1942 for the municipal principality and courthouse, it also served as the residence for the prince and his family. We walked through large, carved wooden doors into the palace courtyard. Around us towered grand mud buildings. Their small windows, and bunting-like crenellations, were highlighted with white paint. We had the palace to ourselves and took our time wandering around the empty rooms, painted crisp white, with relief patterns decorating the walls. Shiraz tribal rugs covered the entire floor – I recognised them because we had several in our own home. Rectangular cushions were propped against the walls. Soft light filtered through the low, small windows.

Khalid knew his history, and he and Frosty spent some time contemplating an exhibition of black-and-white photographs, some taken by the Arabian explorer and diplomat Captain William Shakespear. He had become a close friend of Ibn Saud, who became King Abdul Aziz Ibn Saud in 1932 when he founded Saudi

Arabia. Shakespear was the one who arranged for Ibn Saud to be photographed for the first time.

Our next stop was to the old part of the town, home to smaller versions of the palace buildings. We ended up in Sagheer District which had been deserted many years ago. Local legend had it that an obscure disease swept through the community. Believing it came from the water, everyone left. The disease and its cause remained a mystery, and no one returned to live or farm there. Khalid drove us along dusty roads where derelict mud buildings, a few of them nine storeys high, stood among dying palm trees. We stopped to have a look and walk around these haunting, beautiful symbols of the past, set against a deep-blue sky. The only sounds came from twittering birds, flitting in and out through the windows.

We had a long journey the next day to Al Kharj so headed back to the hotel soon after sunset.

Khalid refused to accept the tourist guide fee we were ready to pay.

'You are my guests,' he said.

Dinner that evening was in the hotel's smart restaurant but, as usual, there were no other guests there. We were in bed early, and before going to sleep, I psyched myself up for the longest leg of our tour, over nine hundred kilometres north-eastwards to Al Kharj.

The following morning, our alarm woke us at 4.15am, and we heard the prayer call soon afterwards. Getting up before dawn for a long ride was easy. A surge of adrenalin at the thought of the journey ahead, cutting right across the Arabian Peninsula, energised my usual laborious movements. Showered, teeth cleaned, bags packed, last-minute pee.

When I arrived beside our Road King, Frosty said, 'Did you say good morning to Maridadi? Isn't she beautiful?'

I patted her tank. 'Morning, Maridadi.'

Peter and Tanya were packed and ready. We rode out of Najran at dawn, the eastern horizon a rosy pink.

I was enjoying the fresh, morning air, taking photos of the orange sun as it rose behind a silhouette of hills, when I heard a barely discernible change in Maridadi's usual sounds. It was followed by a clattering noise and a shudder in the back wheel, right underneath my seat. I recognised it from our breakdown near Damascus. Frosty had noticed it as well and stopped. He had done as much as possible to prepare her for this long journey but, in Harley-Davidson terms, her 1999 vintage made her an old bike.

Peter and Tanya pulled up behind us.

'Something fell off your back wheel and bounced down the road in a shower of sparks,' said Tanya. 'I'll walk back to see if I can find it.'

She found a nut and bolt, too hot to touch. Using a piece of cloth to pick it up, she brought it back to us. Lying on the tarmac by the back wheel, Frosty searched for where it had come from.

'I can't find where it's broken off, but the whole hub is burning hot. What I do know is that the bearings have gone again.'

'Poor Maridadi,' I said, disappointed that our long ride across the desert was over.

We were a thousand kilometres from Jeddah, and the nearest Harley-Davidson dealership was 1,100 kilometres away in Riyadh.

'Okay, let's make a plan,' said Frosty. 'I'll call Dan Prevost and see if he has a truck going from Najran to Riyadh. They should be able to fix her there.'

Dan was the one who had arranged for Maridadi to go to Tabuk on one of his Naqel Company trucks when we went to Jordan. He answered the phone straight away.

'No problem, Frosty,' he said. 'We've got an empty truck leaving Najran at 4.30pm today for Riyadh. You can put the bike on it and travel with them. All you need to do is get the bike to our depot.'

Frosty hung up. 'Now we need a rescue truck to get Maridadi back to Najran.'

Saudi Arabia didn't have a vehicle rescue system like the Automobile Association in the UK, so we had to work this out for ourselves.

'We passed a petrol station a little way back,' I said, 'maybe Peter could drive me back there and they can find us one.'

Once there, I called Amer AlKhaldi in Riyadh.

'Please could you speak to the attendant here and tell him we need a rescue truck?' I asked.

Within fifteen minutes, a rescue truck arrived and followed us back to our stricken motorcycle. We arrived to find a plain-clothes policeman had seen Frosty and stopped to see if he could help. Najranis are renowned for their hospitality, and this jovial man had invited Frosty to sit in his car and share the egg sandwich his wife had prepared for his breakfast.

The most nerve-racking moments of the morning were when Frosty had to ride Maridadi onto the back of the rescue truck. Her engine growled back into life, and he lined her up with the narrow ramp, about thirty centimetres wide. I looked on with clenched teeth and fingernails digging into my palm. If he hesitated halfway up and the motorcycle wobbled, the two of them would go crashing sideways to the ground. Then we really would be in trouble.

I should have had more faith in him because he made the feat look easy.

Once Maridadi was strapped down, the policeman wanted us to come back to his home for a proper breakfast.

'You are very kind,' said Frosty, 'but we must keep going. Thank you for your help.'

'Is your wife going back to Najran with you?' the policeman asked him.

By now, we had decided I would continue with Peter and Tanya.

'No, I will go on to Al Kharj with our friends, and I will meet my husband in Riyadh,' I said.

'Then I will give you a note to say that he has given you permission to travel with your friends while he fixes his motorbike. I will put my name and number there as well, in case you have any problems.'

We said our farewells; Frosty got into the tow truck to head back to Najran; and I got into the Nissan with the Lintons to start our long section to Al Kharj.

'Thank goodness you came with us,' I said to them both. 'I don't know what we would have done without you at this point. It might have been the end of our trip.'

Our journey took us through bleak landscape via Sulayil, on a two-, sometimes three-, lane dual carriageway in excellent condition. With his double fuel tanks, Peter could keep going for around six hundred kilometres. Apart from the occasional pee stop, we kept going, eating snacks on the way, powering through the desert at 155 kilometres per hour. Peter and Tanya were easy travelling companions, and Tanya let me take her place in the front seat for much of the way where I could keep taking photos. Sitting in the back with nothing to do would have been difficult after my pillion rides on Maridadi. After several hundred kilometres, a threatening yellow haze loomed ahead of us.

'Uh-oh,' said Peter, 'that looks like a big sandstorm.'

After a few more kilometres, a thick, yellow haze engulfed us. Grains of sand scampered along the bonnet and windscreen, and a howling wind buffeted the car.

By now, Frosty had called to let me know he and Maridadi were on their way to Riyadh.

'It's an amazing MAN Truck – huge,' he told me, 'the biggest I've ever seen.'

'You're lucky Maridadi is tucked away inside and not here on this road – there's a horrific sandstorm near Al Kharj,' I said. 'Hundreds of kilometres in this would have killed her chrome and paintwork.'

But I still wished I could have been braving the severe weather outside on Maridadi. This was meant to be a motorcycle road trip, not a tour cocooned in a four-wheel drive.

By the time we arrived in Al Kharj, the air was hot and stuffy with sand still swirling. As soon as we got out of the car, I felt its scratchiness in my hair and on my skin. We were all tired and looking forward to the usual welcome we received in Saudi hotels. As there were no hotels listed on the internet in Al Kharj, Peter and I had booked a two-bedroomed serviced apartment in Nozul Al Leqa Apartments. Tanya and I walked into the reception and presented our confirmation form. An obnoxious *Fawlty Towers* type of receptionist confronted us.

'No any booking for you,' the Egyptian said in an unpleasant tone.

'But here is the confirmation of our two-bedroomed apartment,' I persisted.

'No booking. No two-bedroomed apartment.'

Another man joined him. 'No two-bedroom. You take one-bedroom. All sleep there.'

'We don't want a one-bedroom apartment,' snapped Tanya. 'We booked one with two bedrooms. One for me and my husband and one for my friend.'

'Okay, you take one bedroom,' one of the men said to her and then pointed at me. 'And you come with me to other hotel.'

That did it. I refrained from saying "fuck you" and decided instead not to argue anymore.

'Bloody fools,' I muttered to Tanya. 'I'll call the farm and see if we can stay there.'

Al Danah Dairy Farm was around forty kilometres further down the road. Paddy's response was immediate.

'No problem,' he said in his pleasant Irish brogue. 'I'll drive to the main road and wait for you there as you might miss the turning in this sandstorm.'

The Egyptian Basil Fawlty realised his customers were about to leave. He ran after us shouting, 'No problem, no problem! Two-bedroom apartment free. You stay here now!'

He was too late, and we got a kick out of leaving him pleading with us to stay.

As soon as we set off, Peter's car began to overheat. Despite having been on numerous safaris into the desert, Peter wasn't mechanically minded.

'Let's call Frosty – we've had Nissans for years, and he's good at bush mechanics,' I suggested.

He was hundreds of kilometres away, still trundling across the desert in the truck.

'Try putting some coolant into the radiator. That might do the trick,' Frosty advised.

With the radiator topped up we set off again, the sandstorm worse than before. A few kilometres further on, the engine temperature soared again.

'I'll have to switch the air conditioner off,' said Peter. 'It's the only way to keep the engine heat down.'

Air conditioner off and windows closed, we pressed on. There were stretches where the ochre fog almost obscured the road and vehicles in front of us. All we could see was the dim red glow of tail lights. The temperature in the car was suffocating.

Paddy called me at regular intervals to see how we were getting on, and in the gloom, we saw his hazard lights flashing on the side of the road.

We arrived at Al Danah Dairy Farm entrance with Paddy just before 7.00pm. Because of the farm's health precautions, Peter wasn't allowed to drive his Nissan beyond the first security gates. We transferred our luggage and ourselves to Paddy's car, which then had to go through a dip to clean the wheels and a spray for the car.

Why aren't our shoes being dipped? I thought to myself. *They'll be nearly as contaminated as the car tyres.* I guessed their chief concern was foot and mouth disease, a highly contagious and serious viral infection for cattle.

Paddy showed us two comfortable bedsit rooms and invited us to the staff canteen for supper. As we walked across to the canteen, I had to hold Peter's arm for fear of being knocked over by powerful gusts of wind. A Filipino chef served us a welcome hot meal, and we had a chance to chat with Paddy.

'How long have you been here?' I asked him.

'I've lived in Saudi for twenty-nine years, working on various Almarai farms. My wife and four kids returned to Ireland eight years ago, and I visit them every six weeks.'

After supper, he took me to his enormous, but now empty, family house to use his internet and post my day's blog and photos on my Facebook page. The connection was slow and frustrating, and I didn't get to bed until after midnight.

After our thousand-kilometre drive, including five hours' driving through dense, whirling sand, I was exhausted. The wind and sandstorm were still raging on as I made my way back to my room. It had forced Bahrain, Dubai, Dammam and Riyadh airports to close and turned out to be the worst the Gulf area had experienced for sixty years.

By the following morning, the storm had passed, but the air was still yellow from settling sand particles. The farm had garages for maintaining their vehicles, and Paddy offered their services to take a look at Peter's Nissan.

After breakfast in the canteen with several of the young Irish and British farm managers, Peter, Tanya and I went on a tour around the impressive dairy facility. Charlie, the son of a UK Somerset farmer, was our guide for the morning, together with a Saudi colleague.

'Al Danah farm is seven thousand acres,' he told us, 'with around thirty thousand head of black-and-white US Friesian cows and calves.'

'It must be one of the biggest in the world, mustn't it?' I asked.

'Not quite. China has bigger dairy farms than those in Saudi Arabia.'

Our two guides took us to one of the twelve milking parlours, explaining that each one milked three thousand cows at a rate of 730 an hour. Everything was shiny-clean, and the staff were dressed in white overalls, white gumboots, surgical paper hats and masks and heavy plastic aprons. Placid cows, creatures of habit, knew their way around. I had never seen such huge, bulging pink udders. In their leisurely cow amble, low-hanging udders gently swaying, they made their way along their allocated aisles and reversed into their stalls. Automated milking machines were attached to each of their four teats.

'How much milk do you get from each cow?' I asked Charlie.

'Our top ones produce up to twenty litres of milk in one session.'

'Wow. That's massive! How often are they milked?'

'Four times every twenty-four hours.'

We moved on to the maternity wing where a new calf had just been born. Several cows were gathered around the bewildered-looking little creature lying on the ground, sniffing it.

'They look so tender and loving, exactly like us when we go to see a newborn baby,' I said.

'How many are born every day?' asked Tanya.

'About eighty to one hundred,' said Charlie.

We toured the other enclosures, seeing where the new calves were first separated from their mothers, then through the incremental stages of their growth, until the heifers were ready for artificial insemination with semen imported from America. Then the life cycle repeated itself all over again. Shaded areas provided respite from the blazing sun, and an automated mist spray came on at regular intervals to keep the animals cool.

This hi-tech farming was like being on another planet compared to the outdoor Kenyan farms that I knew, where cows were known by names like Buttercup and Daisy, not by the number tags on their ears. It had been set up by Irish farmers, and under Paddy's leadership, most of the young managers were still Irish. Like every other institution and corporation in Saudi Arabia, the rest of the staff and labour were also mainly expatriates, among them Filipino, Nepali and Kenyan.

Work on Peter's Nissan took all day, so I asked Paddy if we could spend another night on the farm. By the time we left, we had shared several meals with the young managers in their canteen. The three of us were amused at how they ate together in silence at tables set out in a U-shape, watching *BBC World* on the large TV hanging on the wall opposite. This didn't stop us from interrupting their routine with a stream of questions and chatter, but apart from Paddy, the men seemed reluctant to engage in any conversation. They'd answer a question, then turn back to their plates and the television. I wondered if they found our disturbance irritating but were too polite to say so.

Meanwhile, Frosty was having his own trials with Maridadi.

30

GOODBYE MARIDADI

After backing her down the narrow track of the rescue vehicle at the Naqel depot, he helped load Maridadi onto a makeshift pallet, then watched her fork-lifted into the cavernous space of the curtain-sided trailer of a MAN Truck.

'The two Filipino drivers looked in their early thirties and took turns at driving over the ten hours through the night,' Frosty told me later. 'They rarely spoke and drove in a very relaxed way, hands resting on the almost horizontal steering wheel. The truck cabin sits on a kind of big rubber balloon, so I hardly felt any bumps. As the truck was empty, the driver overtook most of the traffic on the way.'

For the first few hundred kilometres, Frosty sat in the cabin with the driver while the other slept in the bunk. Halfway to Riyadh, when the drivers swapped, he insisted Frosty take the bunk, letting him sleep while they drove through the same heavy sandstorm we had encountered earlier. They reached the Riyadh depot in the industrial area at 4.00am.

'It was way out of town,' he said. 'Down a bumpy dirt track. The drivers said it was a dodgy area. They went off to their rest cabins, and I had to find a way to get into town. A guy opening a truckers' café told me to wait outside as someone was sure to come along. Although it was still dark, the first car that came by stopped for me. I was lucky – he was going past the Sheraton, so he dropped me off there.'

Later in the day, the Harley-Davidson dealership sent their rescue trailer to collect Maridadi. The mechanics had a good look at her and discovered multiple injuries. Her rear wheel axle had overheated so badly that it had bonded to the swingarm. The dealership had no spare parts for such an old Harley. They declared her unrepairable.

'We've got a truck going to Jeddah tomorrow, so we'll put your bike on it,' the manager told him.

We had been on several biking tours with Marwan AlMutlaq, the owner of the dealership, and he understood how much this trip meant to us both.

'Your bike is too old for long trips like this,' he said. 'I remember ten years ago when we were in Muscat you had problems with it. You will have to buy another Harley to finish your trip. I have a one-year-old Electra Glide Ultra Limited that's been our demo bike. I can let you have it at cost price.'

Frosty knew the Ultra Limited was a top-of-the-range touring bike.

'And this one was manufactured to European specifications,' Marwan continued, 'so you can take it to the UK when you leave. It will be perfect for touring around Europe.'

'You're right,' Frosty responded. He didn't need any further persuasion. 'I'll call Bizzie to see what she thinks.'

I didn't hesitate.

'Go for it, Frosty. We have to finish this trip, and we're not doing it in the Lintons' Nissan or a rented car. We have to do it on a Harley.'

He had been dreaming of owning another touring Harley, especially an Ultra Classic. Many times when we'd visited the Jeddah dealership, I had listened to, 'Wouldn't it be great if we could have...' I'd noticed that most men who owned a Harley yearned for a second one. As he had worked through one of his holidays, earning a bonus lump sum on top of his retirement golden handshake, he felt he could justify this treat. He made the deal and spent the next two days catching up with friends and playing golf.

After our two nights on the farm, Peter, Tanya and I continued to Al Ahsa oasis, renowned for its extensive palm groves and date production. Although it was only three hundred kilometres to Al Hofuf, the capital city of Al Ahsa region, we were up at 4.30am to be there in good time to squeeze in some culture and sightseeing. We stepped outside to see rosy-pink clouds low in the sky and clear blue above. The airborne sand had settled and it was a clear, sunny morning. When we arrived in the canteen, Paddy was already there.

'You're up early,' I commented.

'Well, on the day shift we start work at 5.30am.'

After breakfast, Peter asked him, 'How much do we owe you for our rooms and meals?'

'Nothing – it's been a pleasure having you.'

Tanya and I both hugged him.

'Thank you so much for coming to our rescue, Paddy,' I said.

The farm workshop also refused payment for the work on Peter's car, only charging him for the spare parts. On top of that, they had washed it.

Not wanting a repeat of Al Kharj serviced apartments, we had booked into the sumptuous Intercontinental Hotel in Al Ahsa. When the receptionist saw me with my walking stick, he booked me into the special needs room, although in the Middle East they called us "handicapped". A spacious, executive suite was mine for the night. Two members of staff came in to carry out last-minute dusting because despite the sealed windows, particles from the storm had found a way in, leaving a fine layer of dust over the furniture, carpet and bed.

Always on the lookout for a good cappuccino and croissant, Tanya and I soon headed for the hotel café. We walked across the shiny, white-tiled floor of the grand lobby. Everything about the design and decor reminded me of the maharajas' palaces Frosty and I had seen in India. Two arms of a staircase curved up to a mezzanine floor with a gallery of elaborate arches overlooking the ground floor. The central section of the ceiling was divided into several large panels, each surrounded by an intricate border, with different patterns within each section. Two huge, ornate brass chandeliers hung from the ceiling at either end of the lobby, one of them over the café. Another guest was sitting at a nearby table, a middle-aged Saudi, dressed in a traditional *thobe* and headscarf.

'Welcome to Al Ahsa,' he said. 'Where are you from?'

'We live in Jeddah, but we're British,' I replied. 'My name is Elizabeth, and this is Tanya.'

'My name is Fuad. It means heart. I am from the Tamim tribe. How long have you been in Saudi Arabia?'

'I have been living in Jeddah for thirty-one years,' I said, trying to recall when anyone had last told me the meaning of their name on the first introduction. Like many Saudis, his tribal kinship was an integral part of his identity.

'And I've lived in Saudi Arabia even longer,' added Tanya.

'Mashallah! That is a long time. You are Saudi! How long are you here?'

'Only one night. We are doing a tour of Saudi Arabia, and we have to go to Riyadh tomorrow afternoon.'

'Before you leave, you must get some red rice. This is a speciality of the area and is only grown here in all of Saudi Arabia. I will see if I can get some for you.'

When we came to pay for our cappuccinos and croissants, the waiter told us that Fuad had paid our bill.

I collected a couple of tourist brochures from reception and, after glancing through them, read out to Tanya the grand claims in one of them.

'According to this, "Al Ahsa is one of the best tourist destinations in the Arab World".'

We laughed over that description. The list of the many recommended castles included the Abeed Castle which "...was totally pulled down in 1979".

An Indian hotel driver from Chennai became our guide for the afternoon. Although he did his best, sightseeing in rural Saudi Arabia on a Friday proved frustrating. All the major attractions we drove to, such as the seventh-century Jawatha Mosque, were closed on the Holy Day. We couldn't even catch a glimpse of them as gates to the fenced-off sites were locked.

'They obviously don't know that tourist attractions are meant to be open at weekends,' Tanya commented.

In the afternoon, the same driver took us into Al Hofuf, the urban centre of Al Ahsa. There wasn't a Saudi in sight, just a steady stream of male Indian workers out for an afternoon stroll. Unlike the Pakistanis in Jeddah who wore the shalwar kameez – the traditional tunic and baggy trousers – the Indians wore slacks and shirts, or T-shirts. I got the weird feeling that Al Ahsa had transmogrified into Mumbai.

We stopped by the Ibrahim Palace, built by occupying Turkish forces under Ibrahim Pasha. This large, fort-like mud building had a conical tower on each of its four corners and dominated the heart of Old Kout, the historical area of Al Hofuf. As with the other sites, the fort was closed, so we couldn't see the museum or the 450-year-old mosque inside either. Our driver suggested another idea.

'Must see Shia mosque,' he said. 'Very beautiful, not like Saudi mosque.'

Like the Najranis, the Arabs in this Eastern Province were of the Shia sect.

Despite it being Friday and time for afternoon prayers, there was no one around the mosque. The elaborate wrought-iron gates in the perimeter fence were locked, as were the main entrance doors.

'Don't tell us,' Peter said, 'the mosque is closed as well!'

'Yes, closed,' our driver confirmed. 'Long time now. Too much politics, Shia-Sunni.'

It seemed the undercurrent of unrest between the Shias and the Wahhabi Sunni authorities was even worse here than in Najran. Influenced by the Arab Spring movement, there had been uprisings in the area from time to time since 2011. What made the Shia-Sunni issue more complex was that the Eastern Province sat on most of the Kingdom's extensive oil reserves, but Riyadh and the Sunni royal family were the beneficiaries. Another factor was that Saudi Arabia's enemy, the Shia country of Iran, was just the other side of the Arabian Gulf. The Saudi government wanted to keep these protests under control.

I guessed Iran had funded the mosque as it was decorated with tiles in the Iranian style: multicoloured floral designs on a turquoise background, creating intricate patterns around the tall entrance and all over the dome.

At last, at 3.00pm, our driver took us to an open tourist attraction. This was the covered *Qaisariah Souq*, or market. The complex was first built in 1823, but after being burned out in April 2004, the *souq* had been rebuilt in its original style. As I admired the architecture of the sand-coloured buildings with their long façade of tall, elegant arches, I had that out-of-context feeling again. I felt as though I was in India, not Saudi Arabia.

Inside, we found ourselves walking along a maze of tall, narrow alleys. Stalls with large, wooden doors ran one beside the other on either side. Most of the ones we saw sold men's and women's clothing. Running along the length of the alleys outside the stalls was a concrete ledge, wide enough to sit on, so we stopped a few times to talk to the friendly shopkeepers. Most were either Indian or Yemeni.

I wondered if the *souq* had been run by locals in the past. Since the discovery of oil in 1938, the Kingdom's wealth had made it possible to pay other people to do almost everything for them.

As I walked along the external arcade, I breathed in air suffused with rich aromas from nuts, bay leaves and assorted spices, all in large open sacks sitting outside the shops.

'You know what I'll miss most about Saudi?' I said to Tanya. 'It's these smells. Here, we buy our spices by the spoonful out of huge bowls, not in little packets or boxes in a supermarket.'

'I agree,' she said, 'and look at those!'

She was pointing to stacks of forty-centimetre-long tubes of cinnamon bark, tied into bundles with pink plastic ribbon and piled into neat criss-cross towers.

The one souvenir I couldn't resist was a tin teapot. My father had been a tea planter, and I was raised in the heart of a vast tea-growing district. Morning and afternoon tea were ingrained into my daily routine. These teapots were unique to Saudi Arabia, decorated with a tri-colour jagged design. I chose a white, yellow and blue one, to match the colours of our house in Kenya.

When we checked out of the hotel the next morning, the receptionist handed me a large bag.

'A Saudi man left this for you,' he said.

I opened the heavy bag and found about four kilos of red rice inside.

'Look, Tanya,' I showed her, 'Fuad from the café kept his promise.'

Having seen how expensive red rice was in the bazaar, we were touched by his generous gift. I had spotted him in the café several times since he had paid for our cappuccinos, always in the same seat at the same table. I suspected he was one of the usual secret police patrolling the Saudi hotels.

Before leaving for Riyadh, we visited the local fruit and vegetable market. Long tables set out under canvas shading were loaded with vivid red tomatoes and a selection of green vegetables. Several varieties of fruit were displayed in bright plastic boxes and baskets. A boy sat on an upturned yellow plastic box, selling prepacked dates. Every August, dates were harvested from the three million palms and the market was taken over by the annual date festival.

Al Ahsa sat above the world's largest oil field, the Ghawar Field, but it also hid an even more valuable resource: water. A massive aquifer extended underneath it, hence the palm plantations and enough water to grow such a variety of fruit, vegetables and its unique red rice.

I wandered through the market camera in hand, checking the other stallholders, including a few veiled women. After a while, I sensed hostility from a man in the crowd. I heard him say the words wheelchair and *tasweer* – taking pictures – so I knew he was talking about me. He turned and glared at me. Before I got into trouble again, I put my camera away.

Our last stop was a pottery at Qara, a short drive out of town. Apart from the traditional hubble-bubble pipes and water containers, there were racks of incongruous gaudy, ceramic animals, all about fifteen centimetres high. I picked one up for a closer look and found these rabbits, dogs, cats and frogs, painted either shocking pink, green, blue, yellow or white, were piggy banks. Garden gnomes with furious expressions sat among them, painted in the same crazy colours. They looked so outlandish I now regret not buying one.

After going in circles following diversions at roadworks, we left Al Ahsa behind and set off on the three-hundred-kilometre drive to Riyadh.

31

RIYADH AND MEETING BLACK BEAUTY

Once we hit the desert on Highway 75, we were confronted with more sandstorms. Whatever was wrong with Peter's car hadn't been fixed on the farm. When we had the air conditioning on, it started to overheat again, so Peter had to turn it off. As before, we kept the windows closed to keep the sand out. With nothing to do but gaze out of the window, I noticed a car parked by the side of the road – a couple and their little boy were sitting on the roadside sandbank having a picnic, with the sand swirling around them.

While we had been sightseeing and suffering the stifling heat in the car, Frosty had been bonding with our new Harley-Davidson. We arrived at our hotel after nightfall to find him standing on the forecourt of the entrance beside the shiny black beast, looking pleased with himself. Our new Ultra Classic looked huge.

'How do you like Cilla?' he asked, head cocked to one side, a silly smile on his face. 'Like Cilla Black.' He was referring to the British pop singer of the 1960s.

'Ha ha, very funny!' His little joke was corny, but I couldn't help laughing. 'But Cilla isn't a good name for a big, beefy Harley. This bike just isn't female.'

'Okay, you come up with something.'

When I looked at the gleaming black motorcycle with its leather saddle, it reminded me of a favourite childhood story about a legendary black stallion that also transported people on roads, pulling cabs in Victorian London.

'How about Black Beauty?' I asked.

We settled on Black Beauty, hoping we might come up with a Swahili name later.

Unlike the other hotels we had stayed in thus far, our modest Ibis Hotel in the heart of downtown Riyadh was full of European businessmen. The guests were mostly French, Spanish and South African, all connected with the building of the new urban metro system. While Peter and Tanya went out to meet some of their Riyadh friends, Amer AlKhaldi picked Frosty and me up in his luxurious Audi. We had only seen him in his biking gear: blue jeans, black leather chaps and a Harley T-shirt. In his traditional white *thobe* – but no headscarf – he looked a different man. I was disappointed that he didn't bring his wife, who we had met at the Beirut rally. He took us to the Fairouz Garden, one of the best Lebanese restaurants in town.

'Amer, this may be the last time we ever see you,' I said, 'because we won't be allowed back into Saudi Arabia once we leave.'

'Insh'allah – God willing – you will return one day.'

The following morning was Easter Sunday. Frosty had left early for the Harley-Davidson dealership to finalise Black Beauty's paperwork with Marwan, and Peter had taken his car to the Nissan dealership and was overseeing repairs to his engine. I walked into the dining room for breakfast to find Tanya had decorated our table with fuzzy-knitted Easter bunnies and a box of twelve pastel-painted Easter eggs.

Some Saudis sitting at a nearby table surprised us when one of them said, 'Good morning. We'd like to wish you a Happy Easter.'

Christianity and its related festivals were banned by the government, but it didn't mean that all the population agreed with this. When Saudis acknowledged our festivals, it warmed me to them. One year, directives from the government warned their citizens to ignore Christmas. This had the effect of making many of them rebel against the insult, and more Saudis than usual made a point of wishing us a Happy Christmas that year.

After breakfast, Tanya and I went to explore the Kingdom Centre, the highest building in the country, located across a major highway from our hotel. Tanya helped me negotiate my wheelchair up and down pavements and across the busy road. It was years since I had been in Riyadh, and I was surprised at how the city made Jeddah look like the poor relation. No money had been spared in developing the capital and erecting iconic skyscrapers, while Jeddah lagged further and further behind. Riyadh now looked like a capital city, and it was cleaner than Jeddah.

Until we were inside the Kingdom Centre, I'd had the impression that Jeddah had a selection of smart shopping centres, but this one made ours look shabby. It occupied the first three floors, with an open, central atrium soaring through them giving a wonderful sense of space. Walkways stretched across from one side to the other at the second- and third-storey levels, and natural light filtered through glazed clerestory windows. Neon letters spelt out British high-street store names like Debenhams and Marks & Spencer, whose clothing from this Jewish-originated company were banned when we first came to the Kingdom.

The exotic café on the ground floor was suffused with seductive purple lighting, oozing an ambience that signalled this place was for the wealthy about town – a cappuccino was double the normal rate. We had hoped to go up to the ninety-ninth floor to walk across the glass skybridge linking the two arms of the inverted parabolic arch, but as with Al Ahsa attractions, our luck was out – it was closed for maintenance.

As my journalist colleague, Roger Harrison, had arranged an introduction for us to see the Ad Diriyah restoration of old Riyadh, Peter, Tanya and I took a black London-style cab there in the afternoon. The site was not yet open to the public, so we were privileged to be taken on a tour of this UNESCO World Heritage project. Once again, thanks to the Lintons, I had my wheelchair with me to make this sightseeing possible.

Our guide, Mo Black, was overseeing the information technology installations, including state-of-the-art sound and light equipment. Like all the historic Saudi Arabian towns, the ruined city of Ad Diriyah was an oasis in the heart of the desert. It had been another important crossroads for pilgrims and spice traders from Yemen and southern Arabia, the Levant, Asia and Africa.

'There are two sides of the site,' Mo explained, 'one on each side of Wadi Hanifah. This dry riverbed divided the Wahabbi tribe from the Sauds and was where the roots of Saudi Arabia first took hold.'

We followed him down a wide, wooden walkway across the wadi to the ruined citadel and main section of the ruins, At Turaif. Some of the towering mud walls had been repaired but not completely rebuilt. We passed workmen with wheelbarrows, and a cement mixer blocked one of the roads. Mo led us along narrow alleys typical of Arab towns, with three-metre-high mud walls of houses on either side. At intervals, a decorated wooden door signalled the entrance to an old home. In a few years, the whole place would be crawling with tourists, eager to see inside all these rooms that were to become museums.

'It will apparently be the biggest open-air museum in the world,' Mo told us.

I had reservations about the site being the biggest open-air museum in the world, rather like Al Ahsa being "one of the best tourist destinations in the Arab World". The Saudis tended to want everything to be the biggest or the best. Eventually, on an expanded 7.5-square-kilometre site, it was destined to have twenty five-star hotels and a hundred restaurants, a fifteen-thousand-seat amphitheatre for hosting sporting and cultural events and facilities to hold spectacles like the E-Prix Formula One races.

It wouldn't be the peaceful place we were experiencing now. I couldn't reconcile the curious combination of Formula E-Prix racing and the archaeological site of a quiet oasis once frequented by nomadic tribes and passing traders with their camel caravans.

As we made our way back to the entrance, a large group of dynamic-looking Saudis came striding towards us, all wearing crisp white *thobes* and headscarves. A tall, handsome man leading them came straight over to me and began firing questions. Where were we from? How did we enjoy our visit? What did we think of it? After hearing that we had been in Saudi for so many years and were now on a farewell tour, he said, 'Are you planning to write a book about it?'

'Yes, that is my plan at some point.'

'Good. We want to produce books to promote Saudi Arabian tourism. Yours will be the first one we publish,' he said.

'Let me give you my card,' I said, fishing my cardholder out of my bag. I handed one to him and asked him for his.

After a brief look at my card, he handed it to a man beside him and said, 'Please give this lady a card.'

After he left, Mo Black said, 'You do know who that was, don't you?'

'No. Should I?'

'That was HRH Prince Sultan bin Salman, the son of King Salman, the current king of Saudi Arabia.'

'Oh my god, he must have thought me incredibly rude! Is he the guy who went up in the space shuttle and confirmed to the religious fanatics that the world is round and not flat?'

'Yes, that's him.'

Prince Sultan was a former Saudi Royal Air Force pilot who had become an astronaut and was the first Saudi to go into space in June 1985. When we met him, he was President of the Board of Trustees of the Prince Salman Centre for Disability Research.

He had made a beeline for us when he saw a group of expatriates with one of them in a wheelchair. He was also the President and Chairman of the Board of the Saudi Commission for Tourism and National Heritage (SCTH), a position he'd held since its inception in 2008. As our journey progressed around the country, we were to see his influence on other areas of antiquity. Applications for UNESCO World Heritage status had been submitted to protect those places and preserve the history of his country, something that had been ignored for too long.

Traffic in Riyadh was horrendous at rush hour, so it took a while to get back to our hotel in our London cab. In the evening, Frosty and I went to Al Faisaliah Centre, another of Riyadh's skyscrapers, to go up to the viewing gallery to see Riyadh at night. Because I was in my wheelchair, they waived the US$10 per person lift fee. A few young Saudi men and women were also admiring the views and taking photographs of each other with the night lights and Kingdom Centre in the background. Like many others we had met on our journey, they wanted to have photos taken with us, the Western expatriates, and perhaps with me because I was the woman without the abaya.

A surprise was waiting for me back at the hotel. Four copies of the book *Wings Over Arabia*, a coffee-table book by Roger Harrison about Prince Sultan's glider flight around the Kingdom, had been delivered to us as a gift. I also received an email from the prince's office asking me to answer a list of questions for a press article about our visit to Ad Diriyah, including what it was like for a wheelchair user.

Another day in Riyadh would have given us time to see the Musmak Palace where King Abdul Aziz Ibn Saud, the founding King of Saudi Arabia, first established himself, but we had to move on. Everywhere we went, I always wished we had more time to explore the area. I felt as though I was skimming over the surface of the country in a last frantic dash to see as much as I could.

Maridadi had been boxed up and was already on her way back to Jeddah. Because she was the one that had brought adventure back into my life after my spine operation, and had carried us thousands of kilometres around Saudi Arabia and the Middle East, I was disappointed that we couldn't complete our farewell tour on her. We had often overloaded her with more than the recommended weight, and this long journey had proven too much for her.

Meanwhile, Black Beauty was parked in the garage under the hotel, ready to carry us on the next section of our journey from Riyadh to Haïl.

32

RIYADH TO AL ULA

Our gleaming new Harley was bigger than Maridadi, which I could get onto without any help. Now I needed Frosty to lift my right foot across Black Beauty's higher saddle. Once we got going, I didn't feel the same familiar security as I had on smaller Maridadi. To me, the bike felt too huge for Frosty to handle.

'I know it's heavier, but I find it easier to ride,' he had said before we left.

The seventy-three-year-old Frenchman I had met in Lebanon had said the same thing about his Ultra Classic, and Diamond used to show us how he could cruise on his machine in a straight line without holding the handlebars. 'These machines are really well-balanced; there's no hint of a wobble,' he'd said.

Along with being new and more reliable, Black Beauty had a fuel range of 300 kilometres compared to Maridadi's 250 kilometres, plus a cruise control button. Frosty also liked the car-like dashboard showing the fuel gauge, speedometer and rev counter, plus a digital read-out of the number of kilometres left to go and GPS navigation. I missed Maridadi's little clock, which we had added, and her air temperature gauge.

From Riyadh, we took Highways 505 and 65, riding north-west towards Haïl in the central Nejd region. When we stopped to refuel, I noticed another shift in the Asian diaspora. In western Saudi

Arabia the workers were mostly from Pakistan and Bangladesh. Here, they were Afghans, recognisable by their beards, the way they wore their turbans and shalwar kameez tunic and baggy trousers. Unlike the cheerful Indians in Al Hofuf, these men had disconcerting surly stares.

Black Beauty cruised effortlessly at 140 kilometres per hour, but I had to keep my full visor down because breathing in the high-speed air was painful if I didn't. Even when going this fast, he was quieter than Maridadi but didn't have the signature Harley rumble and lovely massaging vibration. The pillion seat was fine until we went over a bump; then I felt the punishment of harder suspension than I was used to.

'How can such an expensive bike have such rubbish suspension?' I yelled at Frosty's helmet after a small ridge in the otherwise good tarmac highway had sent a shock-jolt up my spine.

'I'll try to adjust it when we get to Haïl,' he yelled back.

We travelled under an overcast sky, in the unusual aura of a gloomy winter's day. Further into the desert, high clouds had turned an eerie yellow from the sandstorms, and near Buraydah we rode through the only rainstorm of the tour.

As Black Beauty carried us through this changing weather, with landscapes metamorphosing from flat desert into sensuous, undulating dunes, I sent Marwan a telepathic thank-you for finding us a Harley to complete our trip. After the hundreds of kilometres I had done with Peter and Tanya in their Nissan, I felt the kick of adrenaline coursing through me now that I was back on a motorcycle.

When we stopped at the mosque loos at the Sanabia petrol station, the caretaker produced a mobile camping-style loo stand that turned the squat-down toilet into a sit-on one. I could have hugged him. I had tried to buy this accessory for the trip but hadn't been able to find one. The mosque even provided handwashing facilities and tissues to dry our hands.

By the time we had covered the 658 kilometres to Haïl, with fewer stops than we would have had on Maridadi, my bum was suffering. I eased myself off the saddle and gave it a good rub with both hands.

'I'm glad we've got Black Beauty, but I miss Maridadi,' I said to Frosty. 'I never used to get such a sore bum on her.'

'I agree – we'll plan more frequent stops tomorrow.'

When we went to check in at the Raoum Hotel in Haïl, the Egyptian receptionist was the opposite of the obnoxious one in Al Kharj. When I showed him our booking confirmation, he said, 'Are you Elizabeth?'

'Yes, I am, and this is Richard, my husband, and our friends Peter and Tanya.'

'Welcome! My name is Zeezu. We are very pleased to see you,' he said with a beaming smile that suited his effervescent name, a nickname derived from Abdul Aziz.

He showed us to our two-bedroomed apartment with its tiny bathroom and a small sitting room with a TV. Zeezu organised room service for our supper, bringing us burgers and chips from a local restaurant. He refused to let us pay for them.

In the morning, day fifteen of our tour, we caught up with the CNN news. None of it was good. The Saudi bombing of the Houthi Shia insurgents who were trying to take over Yemen continued. As always, war created trauma for the civilian population, leading to refugees trying to escape. Some were going across the narrow Bab el-Mandeb Strait to Djibouti, a tiny state between Eritrea and Somaliland in the Horn of Africa.

Kenya was also reeling in shock from an attack by Al Shabab Islamist terrorists on the Garissa University. Gunmen rounded up seven hundred students, released the Muslims and shot all the Christians.

It was a relief to turn the TV off and return to a few days' respite from the troubles of the world.

Frosty enlisted the help of one of the hotel employees to polish Black Beauty, whose fairing was covered in sand. My husband was obsessive about keeping his vehicles clean, and I often teased him about it. We set off with our machine looking shiny and new but had to stop shortly afterwards in a fuel station to spray on more anti-sandblasting solution – the air was once again loaded with gritty particles.

Our 360-kilometre ride that day took us across the Nafud Desert, known for its red sand and unique horseshoe-shaped dunes. Frosty and I had driven through the heart of it in January 1993 when there hadn't been a road in sight, only a few random tracks in the soft sand. We had been on an expedition with three other couples, two of whom were in the British Army. They had brought a Bedouin guide from the Saudi army to lead the way. When we'd camped for a night somewhere in the middle, the temperature had dropped to zero Celsius.

This three-lane dual carriageway, with camel fences on either side, as well as down the centre, now carved the desert in half. A high bank to our right carried the new Saudi Railway Company North-South track while on the left, electricity pylons marched alongside the camel fence. Although obvious how the new infrastructure helped transportation, as well as local and national industry, I still felt sad that man-made structures were scarring another area of wilderness.

We stopped halfway across the desert to take photos and look for the Peaks of Aalem. These two black, conical hills stood side by side in the depths of the Nafud, the larger one called the Sheikh of the Nafud, the smaller known as his son. We had stopped beside them in 1993 and had climbed to the top of the higher one. Although Highway 65 followed almost the same course we had taken, there was no sign of our hills. When Frosty used to fly over the Nafud in a Boeing 747 at thirty-six thousand feet, he would say to his incredulous Saudi first officers, 'You see those black dots down there in the desert? They are the Peaks of Aalem. I have climbed to the top of one of them.'

The ruins of Marid Castle at Dumat Al Jandal, with its mosque and ancient minaret of Omar ibn Al Khattab, were our destination today. When we had seen them in 1993, these mud and stone ruins had stood apart, surrounded by the desert and palm groves, as they had been for centuries. Now, the town encroached up to the old wall. The few Saudi tourists who were there greeted us with a friendly *Assalamu 'alaikum*. Then a car full of veiled young women drove in. They wound down their windows and, eyes bright with laughter, blew kisses at us.

That's something else that has changed since 1993, I thought. *We didn't see any women then, let alone ones bold enough to blow us kisses!*

Dumat Al Jandal dated back to the third century BCE, from Nabataean to Roman times. As the largest oasis on the northern end of the Nafud Desert, it was another important settlement on both the north-south and the east-west trading routes. We had followed these oases trade stops all the way from Najran, nearly two thousand kilometres away.

Setting my mind to where-there's-a-will-there's-a-way mode, I started my hike up the rough and uneven stone steps leading to the top level of the circular castle with its four conical watchtowers. There was no handrail, and Frosty and Tanya helped me up sections that had no wall on one side. When I saw the panoramic view from the top, it was worth the struggle.

We looked out over the ruins of the stone and mud Al Der village. Beyond them were extensive palm groves, orchards and the town. Immediately below us was the mosque with its pyramidal-shaped minaret, said to be one of the oldest in Islam. Two young Saudi men sat on chairs in a small courtyard next to the mosque, having tea and pita bread. This was the new castle café. They looked up, saw us and waved.

As we rode away through the town, with Peter and Tanya following, a 4x4 with three Saudis on board chased after us. A bearded man was sitting in the front passenger seat, wearing a red and white headscarf without the black *igal*, the sign of a religious *mutawa*.

'Have you seen who's after us?' I shouted to Frosty.

In Saudi Arabia we always assumed we were in trouble when someone like that pursued us. But their smiling faces and enthusiastic waving told us they were just having fun. They signalled for us to stop and told us they were from Riyadh. I guessed they were in their forties, but they were behaving like overexcited schoolboys. Two of them got out of the car – they wanted to check out the bike, have a chat and take a photo with us. I figured no one had ever seen a Harley-Davidson here before, with or without a female passenger.

By the time we left Dumat Al Jandal it was almost dark, and we still had a sixty-kilometre ride to Sakaka. Once we reached our serviced apartment, the Yemeni receptionist, Safwan, couldn't have been more helpful. He ordered a takeaway supper for us and refused to let us pay for it. When we had finished eating there was a knock on our door. It was Safwan again.

'*Dabbab* not safe outside,' he said. 'Must bring inside.'

'But where?' asked Frosty. 'You have a garage?'

'No, no, you bring in reception.'

He insisted that Frosty park Black Beauty inside the smart lobby, right near the reception counter. The black and chrome decor was a perfect match for our Harley.

In the morning an Egyptian receptionist again refused to let us pay for our breakfast.

'You are our guests,' he said. 'We cannot let you pay.'

As we posed for a photo with Black Beauty in the reception before leaving, I said to Frosty, 'You'd better savour this moment. I don't think anyone will ever invite us to park our Harley inside a hotel reception again.'

The Egyptian helped Frosty reverse Black Beauty out onto the pavement, and we were ready for day sixteen of our tour. The days were slipping by too fast.

Perfect conditions accompanied us on the eight-hundred-kilometre stretch to Al Ula and Mada'in Saleh. The first fuel station we stopped at looked like an installation in an art gallery. I looked up at a life-size, blue, stretched limousine sitting on top of two high pillars, providing shade for three petrol pumps. An identical pink one provided shade for two additional pumps. Frosty had to check on Black Beauty's tyre pressures, which turned out to be a struggle. Harley-Davidson designers hadn't tried doing this themselves or they wouldn't have angled the nozzle the way they had. While Frosty lay on the ground alongside the repairman, trying to pump up the back tyre, I sat and watched their arduous progress from the comfort of one of two armchairs outside the workshop.

As our journey progressed, we came to a series of diversions where the road was being widened. Saudis didn't use traditional traffic signs to warn motorists of roadworks. Instead, we passed a series of characterful scarecrows in overalls, complete with hard hats and reflective safety jackets. Stiff arms stretched out on either side, an orange flag fixed to one of them to point where we had to go. My favourite sight of the day was when we caught up with a large pickup truck, fully loaded with seated white camels, with two little ones. They stared out at us – haughty, bemused and curious – as we rode past them.

When we got nearer to Al Ula, I spotted a sign pointing to the town via a smaller two-way road that wasn't on the GPS.

'Why don't we take the next turning on the right,' I shouted over Frosty's shoulder. 'It goes to Al Ula, and it'll take us off the highway. I think it'll be more interesting.'

Here, there was no traffic, no electricity pylons or anything else man-made to detract from the familiar desert of giant monolithic rock formations. We were now on our third ride through this dramatic landscape of north-western Saudi Arabia. With their surfaces sculpted into intricate patterns by wind erosion, the rocks looked as though a delicate lace blanket had been draped over them. It was an idyllic evening, with the setting sun bathing the bizarre shapes in a golden light. We shouldn't have stopped because it was getting late, but I couldn't resist taking a few photos. After all, we might never be here again, and certainly not in this perfect light.

While Peter was taking a few photos of us with Black Beauty, Tanya wandered off towards one of the inselbergs. She stopped and started to shuffle sand away with her foot, then bent to pick something up.

'What did you find?' I asked when she came back.

'Look,' she opened her hand to show me, 'if you dig around in the sand, you can find them.'

In her palm was a cream-coloured stone, about five centimetres across. Years under the shifting, abrasive grains had created a smooth, rounded pebble.

Our mellow evening ride continued through the fading light. Huge rocks loomed out of the gloom until massive ones on either side of the road created a kind of gateway to Al Ula. In the clear sky above us, I saw Orion and the Seven Sisters, the constellations I had monitored as we sped across the Central Arabian Desert nine years ago on our first ride to Muscat.

Darkness had fallen as we approached a dual carriageway ring road around Al Ula. Once again, Peter had to pull over as his car was still overheating. Even the Nissan dealership hadn't fixed the problem. In the end, with Peter and Tanya shining torches over the engine, Frosty diagnosed the cause.

'There's an airlock in the cooling system,' he said.

With the water pipe gurgling a protest, he bled it out, topped it up with more coolant, and we continued on our way.

A few minutes later, we were at the ring-road junction. We had to turn right, then make a U-turn at the gap in the central reservation to get to the other side of the highway. In the dim glow of a few street lights, Frosty checked both ways, then began the U-turn, heading for the centre lane. I took a quick safety-check glance to my right. Out of the darkness, a vehicle with no lights was hurtling toward us.

'*Get to the right fast!*' I screamed at Frosty. He didn't hesitate. He accelerated and by a split second we were out of the way of the Toyota pickup. It flew past without slowing down. If the car had hit us, it might have killed us both. One big motorcycling accident in my life was enough, and this episode brought the fear rushing back into my gut. Frosty pulled up on the side of the road, and I could feel my heart pounding against my chest.

'Shit, that was close,' I said to him. 'Stupid bastard had no lights on.'

'Thank God you saw him.'

It was 9.00pm by the time we parked Black Beauty outside Al Urac Hotel. I walked into the lobby on legs that felt shaky from depleted adrenalin. After supper in the large courtyard garden, I was up until 1.30am writing and posting my blog. Then I couldn't get to sleep for a long time. I lay staring into the darkness, drenched in memories of my previous accident and reliving the recent terrifying moments over and over again.

We still had over 700 kilometres to go before we arrived back in Jeddah, and I dreaded the final two legs of our trip being ruined by an accident.

33

PILGRIMS' REST AND MADA'IN SALEH

In the morning, I could appreciate the setting of the hotel. The single-storey rectangle of rooms, each with a small veranda, enclosed us in a large, lawned courtyard dotted with palm trees. A four-metre-high sculpture of a Mada'in Saleh façade stood at one end. We'd had our supper the night before at one of the few tables and chairs set out among the trees. A luxurious garden like this was a rarity in Saudi Arabia, but because Al Ula was an oasis, water sprinklers could be used every day. Barren hills loomed high outside the low buildings, emphasising the charm of this tranquil, green haven.

Soon after breakfast, our guide, Rahman, arrived. He drove a new Toyota Land Cruiser and looked immaculate in his cream-coloured *thobe*, with a white *ghutra* headscarf held in place by a black *igal*. He was a slim, good-looking man with a goatee beard, I guessed in his early thirties.

'Welcome to Al Ula,' he said. 'Why don't we all go in my car? I think that will be easiest. We will go to the Old Town of Al Ula first and then to Mada'in Saleh.'

The mud and sandstone brick settlement of Al Ula's Old Town dated back to the seventh century BCE. With its plentiful water supply, it was part of an ancient trading network, like the other major oases we had seen. We had now followed them for almost four thousand kilometres, from Najran to Al Ahsa, on to Ad Diriyah and Dumat Al Jandal and now Al Ula. After the arrival of the Prophet Muhammad and the introduction of Islam, it became a rest stop for Muslim pilgrims making their way to Makkah. Over the centuries it had been rebuilt many times. In its heyday, there were 1,032 dwellings, all constructed adjacent to one another, creating a wall around the town.

'The town used to have fourteen gates,' Rahman told us. 'They opened at dawn and closed at sunset, to monitor access to it.'

The rows of terraced houses were two storeys high and created a labyrinth of narrow alleyways, similar to those we had seen in Ad Diriyah in Riyadh and Dumat Al Jandal. Until the late 1970s, these mud dwellings were still occupied. Again, it was Prince Sultan bin Salman who had initiated their recent restoration work.

'All these houses were built on higher ground away from the valley to protect them from any floods,' Rahman told us, 'and you can see that some of these lanes have a roof over them. This was to give more floor space for the upper levels.'

As we walked through the partially covered narrow lanes with Rahman, Frosty lagged behind and then disappeared. When he reappeared, he was carrying two huge plastic bags in one hand and an old box and a broken lamp in the other.

'What are you doing?' asked Rahman. His astonished expression silently said, *picking up rubbish is something Bangladeshis do, not Western expatriates.*

'No one seems to notice rubbish in this country,' said Frosty, 'I have picked all this up on our walk around here, including the plastic bags. You need to encourage the people who work here to do the same or provide somewhere for people to throw their litter.'

'You are right,' said Rahman. 'I will try to do something about it. Why don't you let me help you?'

He took the two plastic bags, leaving Frosty with a free hand to collect more litter.

I had one more where-there's-a-will-there's-a-way mission and that was to climb the 190 steps winding up the outside wall of the ancient stone fortress of Umm Nasir, which towered above the ruins of the Old Town.

'Come on, Bizzie, you can do it!' said Tanya. Ever since my back operation, Tanya had encouraged me in my recovery. When most people around me had seemed stuck on what I couldn't do, Tanya got me involved in things I could do or at least could try to do. About two years on from my rehab, it was she who motivated me to join a fitness group with her and Peter. Participating with them and the others in these classes had been a turning point for me, a transfer from medical physiotherapy to normal, fun exercise with other people. Her attitude to what I was capable of doing had inspired my own.

My struggle with the 190 steps was worth the effort. Until 2009 it wasn't possible to get to the top of the fortress, but the steps had been renovated with solid, pink sandstone blocks. Although they were big steps, they were easier to climb than the uneven ones at Marid Castle. From the top, we had a commanding 360-degree view over the entire old and new town. Date palm groves disappeared up the valley into the distance in either direction. I now saw that the Old Town extended much further than I had imagined, on two sides of the fort. The restored section represented a small portion of the entire site. All that remained of the rest was the ragged walls, as the roofs had caved in.

Having now seen Ad Diriyah, Dumat Al Jandal and Al Ula, I recognised the similarity in the structure and architecture of these early Islamic trading settlements. I paused to read a plaque on the wall which told of what the traveller Ibn Battuta had to say about Al Ula in the fourteenth century.

'Al Ula is a large and fine village with orchards, date palms and water. The pilgrim caravan stays there for four days to resupply and wash. Pilgrims leave any excess belongings they might have with them with the townspeople, who are known for their trustworthiness and only take with them what they need for the journey.'

Another plaque described how the pilgrims collected their belongings on their return journey and how Syrian merchants would travel as far as Al Ula to sell them supplies.

Once we were back at ground level, Rahman said, 'Before we go to Mada'in Saleh, I would like to take you to see my racing camel and my museum.'

Fifteen minutes later, we arrived at his farm in the desert. He ducked under the barbed wire fencing to fetch a large, white bull camel wearing a rope headcollar.

'This is Hami,' he said, 'which means he is strong. He races at the track in Tabuk.'

'Do they use robot jockeys there?' Frosty asked.

'No, we still use child jockeys.'

This news shocked me as the use of child jockeys at camel races in the Middle East was controversial and generally banned. Children as young as four years old used to be purchased from poor families in countries like Sudan and brought to Saudi Arabia. Once they were too heavy to be jockeys anymore, they were often turned out into the street where they led vagrant lives. Over the years, we had been to many camel races in Taïf. I knew from our last visit that young men had replaced the child jockeys. In the UAE, robots had replaced all jockeys.

'How do you prepare your camel for racing?' I asked.

'We feed him on dates,' said Rahman, 'and to keep him fit, we tie him to our pickup and then drive at forty kilometres per hour.'

Racing camels can maintain this speed for up to an hour. After admiring the large beast, we went into a shelter made from wooden poles and palm fronds. Deep-red patterned rugs covered the floor, with cushions up against the walls. Shelves displayed a few local artefacts as well as canned, fizzy drinks on offer. Once we were settled on the floor, an Indian man with a beard came in, carrying a tray with a red- and yellow-painted metal teapot with matching small cups and small, clear glasses. He was a very small man, reaching no higher than my shoulder. On his head, he wore a beige baseball cap backwards. His long-sleeved shirt had black, olive and white horizontal stripes, and his baggy trousers were purple. His feet were bare. Until this point, I had quite liked Rahman, but he spat orders at this submissive Indian servant as though he was a street dog. Yet the Indian's face showed no malice or anger, just acceptance that this was his station in life.

While we sipped our hot, sweet tea, Rahman excused himself to pray. It was this hypocrisy between praying five times a day like a good, pious Muslim and then coming away from prayers and mistreating humble people that I found distasteful about many Saudis.

After our tea, we had a look around the little museum, housed partially in a Bedouin-style tent and a mud-walled house beside it. A variety of traditional items hung on the walls or lay on the floor: old muskets, brass coffee pots, long-handled pans for roasting coffee beans over an open fire, grinding stones, wooden well wheels, a wooden camel saddle, ceramic water containers and more.

On our way to Mada'in Saleh, Rahman said to us, 'Do you have a permit to go to Mada'in Saleh?'

'No,' said Frosty. 'We didn't know we needed one.'

'Ah, well, we could have a problem, because now you need a permit to visit the site. But we will still go there, and I will try to persuade them to let us in.'

'I won't believe it if we've come all this way and we can't see Mada'in Saleh,' I said.

I had set my heart on seeing these Nabataean tombs once again. On our previous two visits, we had needed permission from the

Department of Antiquities, but it hadn't crossed my mind to apply for it on this occasion. In those good old days, we had driven up from Jeddah using a combination of hand-drawn maps and a few written instructions from previous campers and had been allowed to camp close to the tombs under a cluster of acacia trees. A ragged barbed-wire fence had separated us from the area with the tombs.

We now pulled up at a large, official gate. As Rahman chatted to the man in the kiosk by the car, we listened in with furrowed brows. Then he turned to us with a big smile.

'Ha! I was joking. You don't need permission. Of course we can go in.'

Like the men at Wadi Rum teasing us about scorpions for dinner, he had enjoyed winding us up.

In 2008 this southernmost Nabataean site, along with the Hejaz Railway Museum, had become Saudi Arabia's first UNESCO World Heritage Site. The 1,621-hectare site, with its 111 tombs, was now fenced off from the rest of Al Ula and the surrounding desert. The Hejaz Railway Museum had undergone extensive refurbishment and now displayed a complete train, dating back to 1908, with restored carriages painted in black, green and red livery, like the one we'd seen at Wadi Rum station in Jordan. An old steam engine housed inside the original workshop had also had its dull black replaced with this new colour scheme.

A new network of sandy roads led us to the various tombs with their magnificent, sculpted façades carved into the scattered sandstone inselbergs. Mada'in Saleh, meaning the Cities of Saleh, dates back to the first century BCE and was the second-largest Nabataean settlement after the capital of Petra in Jordan. There were no other tourists in sight, just as we remembered from our visits in 1988 and 1996. Few Saudis came to Mada'in Saleh as they believed it was a cursed place. The legend recounted in the Quran describes how, in pre-Islamic times, God sent the Prophet Saleh to warn the Thamudi inhabitants against idol worship. They were told to look after Saleh's she-camel and her calf, but they killed her. According to the legend, the calf haunts Mada'in Saleh. As a punishment from God, the Thamudis were destroyed by earthquakes and lightning strikes.

Our first stop was the *siq*, a narrow passage between two towering inselbergs. Unlike the 1,200-metre one at Petra, this one was only a forty-metre walk. At the entrance, a large *diwan*, or sitting room, was cut into the rock face. As with Petra, water channels ran along the length of the wall of the *siq*. The people of this ancient civilisation were hydrologists with a unique knowledge of how to harvest and store water and how to use it for farming as well as desert survival.

We moved on to the Qasr Al Bint, the Palace of the Daughter, a gigantic loaf-like hunk of sandstone. Inside the tombs, which would have been reserved for wealthy families, a pattern of rough chisel marks had been left on walls hewn thousands of years ago. Rectangular, coffin-like shelves of differing lengths were cut into the walls, once resting places for the deceased. Outside, we admired the fifteen-metre-high façades, modelled in the Greek Hellenistic style. Eagles sculpted into the high capitals had had their heads knocked off, the work of religious zealots who believed only God can create a living creature. Conversely, I discovered from a book on Mada'in Saleh that the Nabataeans were a peaceful community of idol-worshipers but tolerant of other faiths such as Judaism.

After seeing how Tanya had found her pebble, I tried searching in the loose sand surrounding these tombs, hoping that I too would find one. I was lucky and found my pebble, a rustic memento of Mada'in Saleh: a smooth, almost flat, oval stone, an opaque sandy-pink colour.

Our final stop was to see the Qasr Al Farid tomb, the Lonely Castle, carved into a massive, isolated outcrop. In the late afternoon sun, the sandstone took on a deep-orange hue, set against a darkening indigo sky. We took our time admiring the scene, walking around the magnificent tomb and taking photographs.

When the time came to leave, the ancestors' spirits must have laughed as they watched us all pushing Rahman's 4x4 Toyota out of the soft sand, hoping to get it out before darkness fell.

On the way back to the hotel Rahman stopped again, a conspicuous move to demonstrate his piety as he performed his *Maghrib* sunset prayer, the penultimate one of the day.

That night, I drifted off to sleep with happy thoughts of seeing so much of Saudi Arabia before we left but sad that we had only two more days' riding left.

34

MA'ASSALAMA: YANBU AND HOME TO JEDDAH

Breakfast the following morning was in the dining room, with its picture windows overlooking the garden. Slanting early morning sunshine and a blue sky showed it at its best.

After our near miss two nights before, I was again jittery about being on a motorbike. Visions of something dreadful happening to spoil our farewell to the Kingdom interrupted my thoughts like splats of mud on a windscreen. *Please God, don't let anything go wrong*, I repeated like a mantra to myself. I didn't want my nervy concerns to transfer to Frosty.

I made my way to where he was polishing Black Beauty, parked in a sheltered car space. A young African from Kenya was helping him and was delighted to see fellow citizens and to speak Swahili again.

When we left the hotel grounds, we found a highway patrol escort vehicle waiting for us. In February 2007, four French expatriates were attacked not far from Mada'in Saleh. Three were killed and the fourth wounded. Since then, the authorities were taking no chances with other Western expatriates travelling in the area.

'Do you realise, Frosty,' I said, 'we've ridden four thousand kilometres without a police escort. That's the furthest we've ever been without one. It's a bit of a shame to have one now.'

With all our previous escorts, including our solo ride back from Damascus, the relays had been seamless and carried out with supreme efficiency. This time around, the rules were different, and paperwork was involved with each handover. Every change took at least twenty minutes, and we had to wait under the sweltering, unshaded sun. The officers were polite, offering us water and tea at the various stops. At the midday stop, they invited us into the air-conditioned reception of their police station where we waited an hour for them to say their prayers.

Although we had left Al Ula on a clear, sunny morning, as the journey progressed, we battled against strong winds and a swirling haze of sand, so thick in places we were reduced to a crawl. Having our escort ahead of us helped, thanks to the flashing lights on their vehicle roof. Whenever they came to unmarked speed bumps or camels crossing the road, they turned on their hazard lights.

I looked out at the arid, inhospitable scenery, intrigued as always by what I saw. It was like riding through miles of outdoor installation art. I spotted Bedouin settlements and a well, in the middle of nowhere. I snapped shots of more bright-red signs with white writing that warned, "Reduce Speed", "Inhabited Area Ahead". We passed desolate roadside buildings, perhaps shops or fuel stations. I couldn't tell if they were half-derelict or half-built. A small, square box of a building, white with a green door, sat alone in a vast expanse of desert. Attached to the roof was a crescent moon, indicating that it was a mosque. Black graffiti was scrawled along one wall. Similar ugly little houses of worship followed. Stunted palm trees that had dried up and died stood by the roadside, their straw-coloured fronds drooping around the brown trunks like bad hairdos. Two scruffy petrol pumps – one yellow, one white – stood under a narrow, white awning. The posts had been pushed sideways, making it look drunk. Another petrol station, again set alone in a desert landscape, was painted candyfloss-pink with a soft, peppermint-green roof awning. We passed two playgrounds, which appeared through the sandy haze in the empty landscape. Their brightly coloured plastic slides, climbing frames, swings and carousels were incongruous with their setting. Electricity had been diverted to set up several street lights around them. Remnants of the past were evident in the numerous ruins of old mud and drystone villages.

In the early afternoon, we wound down through the mountains to the coastal plains. The temperature soared to thirty-eight Celsius, and we were engulfed by heat loaded with sand.

As we neared Yanbu, a saloon police car took over from the highway patrol. On the outskirts of the city, we sped past a graveyard for crashed cars. Despite their staved-in roofs, bonnets or rear ends and doors falling off, the sand-covered relics were parked in neat rows.

The journey of four hundred kilometres that we had expected to take around five hours had taken seven and a half. It was a tough, hot ride on a single-lane, two-way road. Our escort led us through Yanbu to the Movenpick Hotel. Sliding steel gates opened for the police car, and we followed it along a palm-tree-lined avenue to the entrance. Brian Hawley, a friend we had known from his Jeddah days, had arranged to meet us there. What a relief it was to pull off my helmet, go into a clean, stylish washroom, scratch my head – it always itched after hours sweating in a crash helmet – and brush my hair.

Brian, now manager of the exclusive seaside compound, The Cove, had offered to host us for our final night stop. After a cappuccino in the cool, sparkling-clean lobby of the Movenpick, we set off behind Brian. In May 2004, five Western expatriates and several Asians had been killed in Yanbu, so this town was also super-cautious about security. Our police escort followed us to the first set of steel security gates, which slid open to let us enter the interim space before the next gates.

'*Marhaba*, hello and welcome,' said the Saudi security officer, dressed in a white *thobe*. 'Have you got any guns or bombs?'

From the tone of his voice and look in his eye, we knew he was joking. It wasn't Western expatriates who carried the guns and bombs; it was the locals. We gave a straight reply.

'No, we haven't.'

The next set of massive gates slid open, and we were in The Cove. Brian showed us to the guest villas, approached via a path alongside a manicured lawn. Our bedroom overlooked the swimming pool and vast, man-made lagoon that the compound was built around. Several kilometres of wide, paved promenade ran in front of a chain of luxury villas, curving in either direction around the beach and seafront. Palm trees, green lawns, low hedges and pots with colourful bougainvilleas framed the curve.

This upmarket compound was still new, with very few of the homes occupied. Potential clientele were the expatriates working in Yanbu's oil refineries and the industrial city. It was a secure but surreal world within a world, isolated from the local community which had constricting dress codes for women.

I woke in the morning feeling emotional, almost tearful, with the realisation that this was day nineteen, the last one of our farewell tour. It was Saturday, 11 April, and in eleven days, we would leave Saudi Arabia for good. We lingered over breakfast by the pool with Brian, and our 8.00am departure crept forward three hours.

'Biz, I think we need to leave – we've still got 350 kilometres to go,' Frosty said.

'But before you go, Frosty,' interjected Tanya, 'you promised me a ride on Black Beauty.'

He knew she had been dying for an opportunity to have a ride on our new Harley.

'Okay, let's go, but I'm afraid it won't be very far.'

He took her for a short spin, and when I saw the delight on her face, I thought, *maybe I should have offered her a ride on one of the sectors between petrol stations.* But I couldn't give up my pillion seat on any of this final journey, even if being on a Harley sometimes scared the hell out of me.

And then it was time to say goodbye. Tanya and Peter were staying on for another night with Brian, so that was the end of our days together on the road. We all hugged each other and said those farewell words that had seemed ages away when we set off.

'I can't believe it's over,' said Tanya. 'It's been fantastic.'

'I am so, so pleased you asked to join us,' I replied. 'I don't know what we would have done without you.'

'See you back in Jeddah before you go,' said Peter. 'It's my birthday on the sixteenth – you'll have to come over for that.'

'It's a date, Peter. And Brian, thank you for a great final evening of our trip,' Frosty added.

'Ride carefully, and let us know when you get home,' Brian replied.

After more hugs, thank-yous and goodbyes, we pulled on our jackets and helmets for the final stretch home, Yanbu to Jeddah.

Frosty edged Black Beauty out of the solid, metal gates at 11.30am. Our police patrol was waiting for us to continue our journey.

The blue sky and clear morning in Yanbu didn't follow us home. Once we got onto Highway 55, the weather changed. Saudi Arabia wasn't letting us leave without one final sandblasting. At our second escort handover, by a checkpoint, we had to wait for half an hour. I was bursting for a pee, so the police car drove me over to the nearby mosque. As I couldn't brace myself against the fierce wind, three separate officers took turns to help me battle my way through it and the stinging granules, up the steps to the washrooms and then back to the car. I must be one of the few expatriate women who has held hands with three Saudi policemen.

We rode on towards Jeddah through the ferocious sandstorm and wind for another two hundred kilometres. I could feel sand and small stones pelting my legs through the dense fabric of my jeans. Thick bands of sand zigzagged one after the other across the road ahead of us. At one point we came across a car that had been rear-ended by another going too fast in the gloom and shoved into the camel fence in the central reservation. From then on, our escort vehicle followed behind to prevent it from happening to us.

Whenever we rode through bad weather – rain or a sandstorm – I loved the sensation of being cocooned in my biking gear and full-face helmet, protected from the elements yet still out there.

As we got closer to the city, the sandstorm cleared, but the powerful wind meant that Frosty had to ride Black Beauty leaning at an angle.

Soon after we passed the sign to Rabigh, our escort flashed his lights and pulled over, leaving us to ride the last 150 kilometres alone.

We had not been forgotten, though. On the outskirts of Jeddah, we spotted a roof bar of red and orange lights flashing ahead of us. A VIP Mercedes saloon security vehicle, with blue and grey stripes, was waiting for us on the hard shoulder of the fast Madinah Road dual carriageway. As we approached, he pulled into the lane in front of us. If anyone encroached into our space, he activated the siren and the loud squawk of the police vehicle horn.

I had to hold back tears as we rode into our home city for the last time. Did the Saudi authorities know this was the end of our 6,400-kilometre farewell tour of their Kingdom? Whatever their instructions, they were making sure we arrived home safely. After the near-miss in Al Ula, their presence was reassuring. I still carried the fear in my gut that even at the last minute, everything could go wrong. The hectic evening traffic was swept out of our way; we sped through red traffic lights; and I savoured every moment of this escorted ride home. We had left the sandstorm behind, and now it was a beautiful, clear evening.

To my relief, Jeddah didn't look as much like Riyadh's poor relation as I had imagined, and of course, we had a tingling sense of homecoming. Our police escort led us to the British Consulate, stopped his car and got out. He walked over to us and shook Frosty's hand.

'*Ma'assalama*.' Peace be with you. Goodbye.

'*Ma'assalama*,' Frosty replied. 'Thank you for looking after us.'

We had a few more kilometres left to get home, a final ride along roads we had used hundreds of times since 1984: the hectic King Abdul Aziz Road, then a U-turn to ride back past the Prince Sultan Aviation Academy where Frosty had done his annual simulator training; soon after, a right turn up Prince Saud Al Faisal, with its continuous line of red and white concrete barriers creating a protective space for our compound against car or truck bombs; onwards past the green glass headquarters of Saudia.

As we made the right turn into our Saudia City entrance, a skinny, Bedouin military guard, complete with his metal helmet, stepped into the middle of the road behind the barrier. He spread his arms wide and with bright, humorous eyes and a big smile shouted, '*Welcome!*'

It was the first time in thirty-one years that any security or military guard had ever said "welcome" to us when we entered our compound. It was as though even he knew we'd achieved something special. The barrier lifted, and we shouted '*Shukran!*' as we rode in. Thank you.

Frosty parked our sand-covered Black Beauty in the carport for the first and last time. We eased our stiff bodies off the saddle and removed our helmets.

'I can't believe we did it!' I said as we gave each other a big hug. Relief flooded through me now that we were safely home. 'Well done, Frosty. What a great ride.'

'Well done to you too, Biz – you planned a fantastic trip.'

'Do you realise we didn't see any other motorbikes the whole way?'

'You're right – not even in Riyadh.'

I could not have asked for a finer conclusion to our years in Saudi Arabia. Now that I had given the Kingdom one final metaphorical embrace, I was emotionally ready to leave the country that had been my home for half my life. All the boxes had been ticked. With our 6,443km tour over, there was nothing more I wanted to do.

Over the next few days, Frosty was tied up with detailed paperwork for our final departure, especially for exporting Maridadi and Black Beauty to the UK. I had the sorting of our UK shipment to organise and didn't leave the flat for five days. Poor Maridadi was in a sorry state, and the Jeddah dealership didn't have any of the required spare parts either. After spending a few hours surfing the internet, I discovered Harley-Davidson no longer made spare swing arms for 1999 Road Kings. By persevering, I sourced one on eBay, but it was a used one. The owner was in the US, so we paid for it to be couriered to London.

Our beloved Road King had not only injected adventure into my lame life, and boosted my self-confidence, but had also enriched our lives together, as well as our last ten years in Saudi Arabia. Without Maridadi, I don't know how I would have survived them. At a time when I didn't think a motorbike was the answer to an activity we could share, she had stolen my heart. If we weren't off on some exploit around the country on her, she was still there to take us for an evening ride along the Corniche or a Friday morning run to meet with other Harley friends at the Atallah Mall cafés. The usual depression I felt when I returned to Jeddah after time abroad had been cut short since we bought Maridadi. She had been the inspiration for my newspaper column, "Café Cruising". If I wanted Frosty to take me to a new venue to review, all I had to say was, 'Let's go on Maridadi!', and he wouldn't hesitate. Our long farewell tour had been too much for her, but she had broken down in a convenient spot twenty-five kilometres outside Najran, not halfway across the desert on the nine-hundred-kilometre ride to Al Kharj. Black Beauty had carried us the rest of the way but hadn't yet developed a personality or found his way into my affections.

Home safely from this final adventure, I had an inkling I might not have any urge to keep going with our motorcycle touring. I felt I'd achieved everything I wanted to. There were no better rides I dreamed of going on, nothing I had wanted to do as much as that final trip, one that no one else had ever done on a motorcycle. I wasn't sure I wanted to push my luck and the risks of being on two wheels anymore.

Time would tell, but our Road King could now only be used for short day rides in the UK. Our long-distance travels with Maridadi were over.

ARABIC GLOSSARY

Abaya — The full-length black cloak worn by Saudi, and some other Arab, women. More recently, the women are wearing different coloured and beautifully decorated abayas.

Ahlan — Welcome.

Ardha — Saudi Sword Dance. It originated as a celebration of military achievements and victory in battle.

Assalamu 'alaikum — The Arabic greeting, literally meaning "Peace be upon you". The response is "Wa'alaikum assalam! Peace be upon you also".

Bedouin, Bedu — The term Bedouin is derived from the Arabic Bedawiyin and refers to people who live, or who are descended from tribes who lived, nomadic lives outside the cities, raising camels, sheep and/or goats. Bedu is the plural of Bedouin, but in English, the term "Bedouins" is often used. They traditionally believe that they are descended from Shem, the son of Noah (see the Old Testament book of Genesis, Chapter 5).

Eid ul Fitr — The holiday following Ramadan.

Ghutra — White square head scarf, sometimes with embroidery, worn by Saudi men.

Haram — Forbidden.

Hejaz Mountains — Part of the Sarawat Mountains which run down the western side of Saudi Arabia from Jordan, all the way down to Yemen. The Yemeni section is known as Sarat al Yemen; the southern section in Saudi as the Sarat 'Asir; and mid section all the way to the Jordanian border as the Sarat Al Hejaz.

Hijab	The scarf that Muslim women wear over their hair. It can be any colour, but Saudi women usually wear black, often with decorative trim to match their abayas.
Hookah	The local name for a "hubbly bubbly" or water pipe.
Iftar	Literally means "break fast". It is the first meal Muslims eat at the end of the fasting day, just after sunset.
Igal	Two coils of thick, black cord which sits on a man's head over the ghutra or shammagh to keep it in place. If one isn't worn, it is the sign of a religious scholar, or a religious policeman. For ceremonial occasions, the igal can be gold with three or four coils. Supposedly, the Bedu used to use the igal to hobble their camels and then carried it on their head when not in use.
Iqama	The work permit and identity card required by all expatriates in Saudi Arabia. In the 1980s and 90s, a married woman was on her husband's iqama, and then around 2005, the authorities decided they should have their own.
ISIS, ISIL, IS	The acronym for Islamic State of Iraq and Al-Sham, ISIL for Islamic State in Iraq and the Levant, but both were abbreviated to IS, Islamic State. Al-Sham and Levant refer to the modern states of Syria, Lebanon, Palestine, Israel and Jordan. It is also known as Da'ish. The organisation was formed following the fall of Saddam Hussein in December 2003. It has members of different ages and ethnicities and is a Salafi (an ultra-conservative form of Sunni Islam) militant organisation in Syria and Iraq. Their goal is to establish an Islamic caliphate. Its roots can be traced to former members of Al-Qaeda and Baathist followers of Saddam Hussein.

Kabsa	A traditional Saudi dish of mutton served with rice flavoured with onions, cardamon, saffron and sultanas. The food is served on a large, round metal dish, with the sheep's head sometimes placed on top of the dish. Everyone sits around and helps themselves, eating with their right hand (the left is used for cleaning oneself in the toilet).
La. Kamera kabir	No. The big camera.
Ma'assalama	The Arabic term to say "goodbye". Literally, "Peace be with you".
Mafi mushkila	No problem.
Maghrib	The sunset prayer.
Maneesh	A Middle Eastern type of flat bread that is often topped with zatar, a mix of thyme, sesame seeds, and sumac. There are variations which include cream cheese and tomatoes.
Marhaba	Welcome or hello.
Mezze	A selection of small plates of dips and food that are shared by everyone at the table. The word stems from the Turkish "meze" meaning "snack" or "flavour". Mezze is common in all the countries previously within the Ottoman Empire, as well as Iran.
Mezze dishes	These include humous, muhammarah, baba ganoush, labneh, tabouleh, fetoush, stuffed courgettes, falafel, kibbeh, chicken kebabs.
Mutawa	The mutawa/mutaween are the religious police, the body of men who worked for the Committee for the Promotion of Virtue and Prevention of Vice.

Niqab The black face veil worn by some Muslim women. Sometimes it completely covers the face; at others it reveals the eyes. Unlike the tarha/hijab, it is not a requirement in Islam; it is the personal choice of a woman, or her family. In Afghanistan, they call it the "burqa" and it is an integrated part of the entire abaya.

Prayer times There are five set prayer times in Islam, namely: Fajr – the dawn prayer; Dhuhr – the noon prayer; Asr – the afternoon prayer; Maghrib – the sunset prayer; Isha'a – the night prayer.

Ramadan kareem Have a generous Ramadan. A general greeting during Ramadan.

Shalwa kameez A style of clothing from Pakistan and Afghanistan, worn by men and women, with loose trousers worn with a long-sleeved tunic reaching below the knees. It can be very casual in cotton, or formalised with expensive types of fabric – often silk inter-woven with elaborate embroidery. Women often wear a matching long scarf, either loosely around the hair, or simply around the neck, and draping softly over the tunic.

Shammagh A red and white square piece of cotton cloth, sometimes with tassels, worn as a headscarf by Saudi men. Folded in half to make a triangle, it is worn over a skull cap and held in place by the "igal". An alternative to the ghutra. It comes in other colours, like the Palestinians are known for their black and white one, Kuwaitis for their green and white. Westerners who live, or have lived, in the Arab world often use them as scarves.

Shia Muslims	They look upon the Prophet Muhammad's son-in-law, Ali ibn Abi Talib, as his rightful successor. Basically, their belief is based on the Quran, and the Hadith, but there are many different sects of Shia Islam, such as the Ismailis. They are marginalised in Saudi Arabia.
Sunni Muslims	They are the largest denomination of Muslims. They believe that Muhammad's father-in-law, Abu Bakr, was his true successor, and they follow the Sunnahs, as well as the Holy Quran.
Tasweer	Taking pictures.
Thobe	An ankle-length cotton shirt, with long sleeves, worn by Saudi men. It is usually white, but in winter months, they favour darker colours, especially brown or black, usually made from wool instead of cotton. They sometimes wear a European/Western-style jacket over it.
Wadi	Dry river bed.
Wa'alaikum assalam	The response to the greeting "Assalamu 'alaikum", and it means "Peace be upon you also".